D1094927

The Priceless Gift

The Priceless Gift

The Love Letters of
Woodrow Wilson and Ellen Axson Wilson

EDITED BY ELEANOR WILSON McADOO
WITH A FOREWORD BY RAYMOND B. FOSDICK

McGraw-Hill Book Company, Inc.   New York   Toronto   London

THE PRICELESS GIFT

Contents

Book I   *Courtship*

Book II   *Marriage*

Illustrations

following page 156

Preface

Douglas Freeman, in his valiant attempt to decipher the character of George Washington, was forced to this admission: "The tradition that Mrs. Washington destroyed all her husband's letters to her must be accepted as correct, though the time and circumstances of this lamentable disservice to history are unknown." Consequently in spite of Freeman's far-flung research and his great gifts as an interpreter, the inner life and character of Washington still remain obscured. What an asset it would be to our understanding of the man and his times if the many letters which we know he wrote to his wife during the Revolution were now available! —letters like the one, fortunately preserved, in which he described his emotions on being appointed to command the Continental forces.

Mrs. Washington's probable reasons for destroying the letters are not difficult to understand and even appreciate. The letters were doubtless intimate and they were intimately hers. Why should she share what was personal and private to herself either with her contemporaries or with the fortunes of an uncertain future?

What, of course, Mrs. Washington did not appreciate was the overriding claim of history to the inspiration and recuperative values of the past—the past with all its triumphs and heart-breaks, its courage and evasions, its personal greatnesses and weaknesses. It is the vision of the past that makes the present livable, and no generation should be denied access to its secrets.

This is a point of view which is now becoming increasingly accepted, and the growing collections of personal letters and papers in the Library of Congress and elsewhere are an eloquent testimonial to a new attitude toward privacy. With the passage of years, privacy becomes at best a relative term. There is a kind of statute of limitations which after a reasonable period allows us to unlock the secrets and intimacies of a given generation without embarrassment or lack of taste. The richness of the past is not denied us because of a modesty or sense of inappropriateness which, however valid at the time, has outlived its relevance and meaning.

For this reason, it seems to me, Mrs. McAdoo's decision to publish the intimate letters of her father and mother, Woodrow Wilson and Ellen Axson Wilson, is to be applauded. That they are extraordinary letters and that they reveal an aspect of Wilson's character which neither the outside world nor his close friends had suspected, is at once apparent to anyone who reads them. With the possible exception of the love letters of the Brownings I doubt if any such outstanding collection is available in the English language, and they are bound to take a prominent place among the classics of this category.

In editing the letters, Mrs. McAdoo has performed her work faithfully and with a high degree of judgment and competence. While she naturally looks at her parents through the eyes of loyalty and affection, the narrative by which she binds the letters together in a coherent unity is as objective as the circumstances permit. Very wisely she lets the letters speak for themselves, with all their ardent intensities and utter lack of self-consciousness.

To read the original letters is a rare treat. Those of Woodrow Wilson are inscribed in a careful, meticulous handwriting, almost copperplate in its legibility. In the latter part of the period, particularly when he was in the White House, he typed his letters to her on his own typewriter, writing with the same ease and articulateness with which he used a pen. His last letter, typed on White House stationery, and dated October 12, 1913, contains these sentences: "I have been desperately lonely.... I can now tell you of the deep longing that has filled the summer, the longing for you ... There will be a happy man in this old house on next Friday ... My exile is over."

Ellen Axson's handwriting is not always easy to decipher, although she had a gift of expression almost equal to her husband's. She apparently wrote rapidly, and the handwriting sometimes did not seem able to keep pace with the surging flow of ideas and emotions. Occasionally, she would cross-hatch the final page, writing in checkerboard fashion up and down the sheet. But she was as ardent in her expression as her husband, and the last line of her last extant letter to him, dated October 8, 1913, reiterates the central theme of nearly thirty years of correspondence: "My heart is overflowing with love of you."

Well over half a century ago I was a student of Woodrow Wilson's at Princeton. A small group of us occasionally met in the evening at his home on the campus—"Prospect"—to hear him or his brother-in-law, Stockton Axson, read Browning or Tennyson or Wordsworth, or any of the other favorite Victorian poets. While I do not now recall the reading of the particular poem, I have no doubt that among those we heard in that room was Browning's "One Word More." Wilson quoted three lines from it in one of the letters he wrote Ellen Axson during the period of their engagement, and it seems to me that it symbolizes not only the deep, inner compulsions of the man, but the nature and spirit of the entire correspondence:

> "God be thanked, the meanest of his creatures
> Boasts two soul-sides, one to face the world with,
> One to show a woman when he loves her!"

Raymond B. Fosdick

Foreword

During the two years of their engagement and the almost thirty years of their marriage Ellen and Woodrow Wilson were never separated for more than a day or two without writing to each other.

Separations after their marriage were infrequent. Yet after my father's death over fourteen hundred letters were found in his house on S. Street in Washington and, since I am the only living member of his immediate family, they came finally into my possession.

My decision to publish them was not an easy one. To invade my parents' privacy, which they had always treasured, seemed almost like a breach of confidence. They had written these letters, never imagining that anyone would read them, except perhaps their daughters. Yet Woodrow Wilson, in spite of the millions of words written about him, has never been entirely understood by anyone except my mother. And, since his impact upon his time—and the future—is historically important, I decided that these letters, which reveal his inmost self, should not be withheld.

Ray Stannard Baker, who was given permission to read all of this correspondence, wrote in the introduction to his eight-volume biography, *Woodrow Wilson, Life and Letters:* "Here in these intimate writings was the soul of the man with all his burning intensities, his aspirations, his doubts. Better far than any self-conscious diary could have been; better than any half remembered memoir. Here, in vivid language, with no premeditation, no sense of audience, speaking to the woman he loved devotedly and trusted utterly, he poured out the deepest things of his life.''

My mother's letters are, in my opinion, of equal importance, for they reveal not only the deepest things of her life but also how profoundly she influenced Woodrow Wilson and his career. She was a quiet, gentle, unassuming woman who avoided the limelight so successfully that she has been almost forgotten. Yet without her selfless love, wise advice and constant encouragement, my father might never have attained the place which he occupied in his generation.

Needless to say, fourteen hundred letters cannot all be included in one book. I have, therefore, had to omit some of them entirely and use only excerpts from many others. The omissions can be put in three broad categories:

1. Unimportant family matters, such as minor sickness, children's activities, household problems, etc.

2. Visits with friends and relatives, people met in passing, small incidents on journeys, descriptions of scenery.

3. Repetitions of love passages. (Even Woodrow Wilson, with his unusually large vocabulary, sometimes ran out of different ways to say, I love you!)

I have used the narrative form, rather than voluminous footnotes, to tell the story of my parents' life together, where it is not revealed in their letters, because I think it makes easier reading and relieves the monotony of uninterrupted letters. But there is no imaginative writing in my narrative. My sisters and I, even when we were children, often questioned our parents about their lives before we were born. My mother especially loved to talk about it. My father sometimes teased us. (He had asked all the girls in the world, he told us once, to stand in a row, and he had looked at them all and had chosen our mother.) There were also several close relatives who had been "eye-witnesses" and told us what they knew. Everything in the narrative comes from these sources, or was known or heard by me.

Although, to my certain knowledge, my father and mother kept every letter they received, some are missing here and there throughout the collection.

I am greatly indebted to Dr. Raymond B. Fosdick, not only for reading all the letters at my request, and for his preface, but also for his invaluable advice and encouragement during my two years of work on this book.

Eleanor Wilson McAdoo

The Priceless Gift

Book I
Courtship

(From Woodrow Wilson's last letter to
Ellen before their marriage—June 21, 1885)

I feel as if this last love message were in some sort
sacred.... I would have you catch a glimpse of my
purpose for the future and of the joy which that future
holds for me, of the gratitude I feel for your priceless
gift of love, and of the infinite love and tenderness
which is the gift of my whole heart to you.

Part 1
The Engagement

There is a city in Georgia called Rome because it is built on seven hills. In 1883 it was a very small city. Gardens enclosed its stately old houses, tall trees sheltered the streets and no one was ever in a hurry.

On an April Sunday the hills were bright with new grass and the apple orchards in the valleys were in full bloom. It was a warm day, made for picnics or for lazy talk on cool verandahs, but it never occurred to young Thomas Woodrow Wilson to do anything of the sort. All his life, wherever he was, or whatever the weather, he went to church on Sunday.

His father, Dr. Joseph Ruggles Wilson, a Presbyterian minister, and his mother, daughter of Dr. Thomas Woodrow, who had been pastor of the Carlisle Congregational Church in England, had taught their children that good Christians always attended services on Sunday unless they were seriously ill. And their elder son had never rebelled because he enjoyed it. When he was so small that his feet barely touched the floor and too young to understand the sermon, Tommy was so fascinated by his father's beautiful voice and resounding phrases that he was only occasionally conscious of his thin frame growing numb on the uncushioned pew. There were also the hymns—the fine, stern Presbyterian hymns. He knew them all by heart, and he had a good ear for music and raised his voice lustily with the rest of the congregation. As he grew older he learned to relish a good, strong sermon, especially his father's. The Reverend Dr. Wilson never spared the sinners, nor failed to assure them that repentance would surely bring forgiveness. The God of the Wilson family was stern but very kind. They worshipped Him joyfully.

Thomas Woodrow Wilson was practicing law in Atlanta in 1883 and had gone to Rome to consult his uncle, James Bones, about a legal matter. He was twenty-six—a tall thin young man with large gray eyes, brown hair, side-whiskers and a stubborn chin; a determined young man, with a goal in life. He intended to have a distinguished career. In politics? In the literary world? That remained to be seen. In the meantime, he had discarded his first name. Short, alliterative and unusual, Woodrow Wilson would be a name not easily forgotten.

Mr. and Mrs. James Bones and their married daughter, Jessie

Brower, took Woodrow to their own church, the First Presbyterian, that
morning, and his usual Sunday mood of contentment was increased by
the fact that his father's friend, Mr. Axson, was the minister of the
church and a fine Christian gentleman. He was also, Woodrow found
when Mr. Axson began his sermon, a very good preacher. Then a girl in
a pew near the pulpit turned her head to whisper to the small boy beside her and Woodrow's attention wandered. Her profile, silhouetted
against the black veil draped over her hat, was delightful. A tip-tilted
little nose, a perfect complexion, a sweetly curved mouth and hair like
burnished copper. Woodrow stared shamelessly until the girl looked
again at the preacher and only the black veil was visible. He realized,
then, that she was in mourning. She must be a widow, he thought, and
the boy was her son. And why, he wondered, did he feel sorry for himself as well as for her? A fine thing to be jealous of a man he had never
seen, because of a girl he had never met! He forced his eyes and his
mind back to Mr. Axson and the sermon. But when the service was over
he asked his aunt who the pretty girl in mourning was.

"Why, that's Ellie Lou Axson," she told him.

Miss Axson! Not a widow. The boy must be her brother, he thought,
remembering what Aunt Marion and Jessie had told him about her.
Ellen Louise, the pastor's daughter, was a "talented artist" and had
read "all the classics." She was "one of the rarest and most beautiful
girls that ever lived in Rome," and everyone loved and admired her.
Her mother had died in childbirth and Ellie Lou kept house for her
father and "took care" of her two young brothers. An aunt in Gainesville, Georgia was "mothering" the baby.

Woodrow decided then and there that it was his duty to call on his
father's friend, Mr. Axson, as soon as possible.

Six months later, in a letter to Ellen Louise Axson, he wrote,

146 N. Charles St.

Baltimore, Md., Oct. 11th, 1883

... The first time I saw your face to note it was in church one morning
during the first of my last spring's visits to Rome—in April, wasn't
it? You wore a heavy crepe veil and I remember thinking, "What a
bright pretty face! what splendid laughing eyes!... And when, after
the service, you spoke to Mrs. Bones, I took another good look at you
and concluded that it would be a very clever plan to inquire your name
and seek an introduction. When I learned that this was Miss "Ellie Lou"
Axson, of whom I had heard so often, quite a flood of light was let in
on my understanding and I was conscious of having formed a small

resolution. I took an early opportunity of calling on the Reverend Mr. Edward Axson. That dear gentleman received me with unsuspecting cordiality and sat down to entertain me under the impression that I had come to see him. I *had* gone to see him, for I love and respect him, and would have gone to see him with alacrity if he had never had a daughter; but I had not gone to see him *alone*. I had not forgotten that face, and I wanted very much to see it again: so I asked rather pointedly after his daughter's health and he, in some apparent surprise, summoned you to the parlour. Do you remember?—and do you remember the topic of conversation? how your father made me "tackle" that question that was much too big for me. "Why have night congregations grown so small?" What did you think of me *then,* my darling?

But though I was still delighted with that face, I still at the end of that call could regard it with dispassionate criticism. But that dispassionate state of mind did not last very long. It was not very long after that that I walked home with you from Jessie's ... and I remember leaving you that afternoon with a feeling that I had found a new and altogether delightful sort of companion. Passion was beginning to enter into the criticism, and had pretty nearly gotten the better of it by the time we had climbed to the top of the hill. ...

Jessie Brower was responsible for that second meeting. She had match-making tendencies and had noticed the gleam in her cousin's eye when he had asked about Ellie Lou. Woodrow had called at the parsonage on Monday. On Wednesday Jessie asked Ellie Lou to come to the Brower house for a cup of tea, not mentioning that Woodrow would be there, too. And when, after tea, he asked Miss Axson if he could escort her home, Jessie watched them go with a pleasant sense of accomplishment.

Woodrow did not know until months later that the girl walking demurely beside him was remembering when she had first seen him. Two days before he discovered her in church she had been calling on her friend Agnes Tedcastle. They were on a front verandah when Woodrow strolled by, too absorbed in his own reflections to notice them. Ellen had asked who the fine-looking young man was and Mrs. Tedcastle was surprised. Ellen had told her often that she wasn't interested in men.

"I don't know whether to tell you or not, you man-hater," she said. "That's Tommy Wilson, Jessie Brower's cousin."

The day after Jessie's tea party Woodrow went back, reluctantly, to the frustrating practice of law in Atlanta. He and his partner, Edward

Renick, had been students together at the University of Virginia law school and had opened their law office in the fall of 1882. The office consisted of one small room on the second floor, back, at 48 Marietta Street, but it was in the center of town, and at an intersection. Their shingle in the window would be seen, they hoped, by passers-by on two streets. It read:

E. I. Renick   *Woodrow Wilson*

RENICK & WILSON
ATTORNEYS AT LAW

48 Marietta Street   *Atlanta, Ga.*
Room 10

Renick and Wilson, waiting optimistically for clients, had been proud of their office and their equipment—one desk, two chairs, a book case, contributed by the junior partner's * parents, an elocution chart, one calligraph, ancestor of the modern typewriter, and their keen young minds. They were sure of success, not realizing that a host of lawyers had already flocked to the only city in the South which had recovered from the ravages of the "War Between the States." There was one attorney for every two hundred and seventy citizens, including Negroes and children, in Atlanta in 1883.

"The potentially great firm of Renick and Wilson," Woodrow wrote to a friend after six discouraging months, "is doing *very* little but hoping very *much*. In the course of about one year we hope to be making expenses after some sort; but at present we are not doing so by a very large majority." †

But before the year was out he was hoping very little. When he met Ellen in April he had only two clients—and one was his mother.

Now, back in Atlanta, with no sign of more clients, he came to the conclusion that he had chosen the wrong profession. Aside from his failure to meet expenses, he did not like the practice of law. It had very little to do with justice, the young idealist decided. And what about his plans for the future? It had appeared from his perusal of American history that a lawyer had a better chance to enter politics than anyone else. But one must be a successful lawyer and this, it seemed, was beyond his reach. He had time and to spare for writing, but not the right environment. The libraries in Atlanta were inadequate, and he had found no intellectual companions. He wrote, finally, to his most valued confidant and friend, his father, and asked for advice. Joseph Wilson sug-

* Wilson was the junior partner.
† W.W. to Heath Dabney, Jan. 11, 1883.

gested that he give up his law practice and take a post-graduate course at Johns Hopkins University. After that he could easily earn a living as a professor and a writer. There was, Joseph wrote, enough money in the family savings account to pay Woodrow's expenses.

A few weeks before, Woodrow would have readily agreed to this plan, but ever since he had left Rome, he had been haunted by a pair of luminous brown eyes and tormented by the thought that he had not made a good impression on Miss Ellie Lou Axson. He knew now that he was in love with her, and he was afraid that if he went to Johns Hopkins he would lose her. It would take at least a year to finish the course and he could not ask her to marry him until he was able to support her. He knew one thing for certain. He must see her again—soon—and try to find the courage to tell her that he loved her. If she returned his love, he would try to overcome his distaste of the law and make a success of it. In June, like an answer to prayer, Uncle James Bones asked him to come again to Rome for further consultation.

Woodrow planned his campaign on the train. He must be very careful, he decided. Miss Ellie Lou was shy and might be shocked by too impetuous an approach. And in those days young men, especially sons of clergymen, were trained to "court" with formality. The next morning, at his cousin's house in Rome, he wrote a note to the Reverend Mr. Axson's daughter, asking if he might call, sent the Browers' small son, Lefoy, to the parsonage to deliver it, and waited impatiently for an answer. When it came, he read it with mixed emotions.

Mr. Wilson,

I am sincerely sorry that a previous engagement will deprive me of the pleasure of your company this evening. I would have been glad of the opportunity to welcome you back to Rome.

Sincerely your friend

Thursday   *Ellen Axson*

Her extreme formality did not worry him. Well-brought-up girls were not supposed to write "My dear" when addressing a young man. He was disappointed because she could not see him, but there was one straw to grasp. She had signed herself "your friend," not merely "sincerely yours." Yet it was not until four days later that he found the courage to try again. He could make little progress, he decided, in the solemn atmosphere of the parsonage, so he hired a horse and buggy for the afternoon and sent another note by Lefoy with an invitation.

Ellen replied,

Mr. Wilson,

I have no engagement this afternoon and it will afford me pleasure to take the drive. I will be ready at the appointed hour.

Very sincerely,

Monday   *Ellen L. Axson*

"It will afford me pleasure!" It would certainly afford him pleasure, Woodrow thought, but it would scare him, too. Here was his chance to make a good impression, and he would probably make a fool of himself.

They drove through the apple orchards, sitting stiffly side by side. Ellen was very shy, Woodrow painfully self-conscious. She had very little to say. He talked too much. But after he had left her at the parsonage, he comforted himself with the thought that she had listened closely to everything he said, and agreed with most of it.

Uncle James Bones, briefed by his daughter on the budding romance, deliberately prolonged his consultations with his nephew. So Woodrow stayed on for a week or more and saw Ellen as often as possible. He called on her, escorted her to prayer meeting, took her to a concert and monopolized her at picnics arranged by Jessie Brower. Again and again he tried to tell her that he loved her, but kept putting it off, waiting for some sign that she cared for him. Then, one day, there was a sign. Jessie had planned another picnic and once more her long-suffering son delivered a note at the parsonage. Ellen wrote,

Mr. Woodrow,

Very unwillingly and with the firm conviction that I am the most unfortunate of mortals, I write to tell Jessie that I won't be able to go on the picnic, either. I, last evening, made an ill-timed engagement to take a boat-ride on that afternoon and, like Sterne's starling, "I can't get out of it." Excuse my keeping Lefoy so long, but all this time I have been trying to devise ways and means of escape.

There is no reason, not even—strange to say—any *disinclination,* to prevent my saying most truthfully that I will be happy to walk with you this afternoon. With love to Jessie, I remain,

Your sincere friend,

Monday morning   *Ellen L. Axson*

He read it again. For a very reserved young lady it was a breath-taking note. And she had called him "Mr. Woodrow!" The probability that this was due to absent-mindedness was significant. He was Woodrow now in her secret thoughts. He decided that, during their walk, it would be safe to at least hint that he was in love with her. He wrote later concerning that walk:

146 N. Charles St.,

Balto., Oct. 23rd, 1883

... I have observed that no diplomacy is very profound; all diplomats are very soon found out; and you no doubt saw through my devices long before I suspected; but I did not dare to throw them off, although they were so very burdensome and so very clumsy. How cheap and awkward a poor fellow feels when he is trying to find out something about which he dare not ask a direct question! I remember walking one afternoon in the early summer with a certain sweet friend of mine. We had chosen the railroad bed because it led along the bank of the river and would lead us to where we would find a seat near the water on a big jutting rock which stood with its feet in the river commanding a view of one of the prettiest bends of the stream. Not an incident of that walk have I forgotten ... I was quite conscious that I was very much in love with my companion and I was desperately intent upon finding out what my chances were of winning her. I adopted a plan which was doubtless very indiscreet, but which was the best I could devise upon the moment. I made her my confidante concerning a very foolish love affair of mine, some time before exploded, and with that preface, proceeded to discourse somewhat at length upon my needs and embarrassments as regarded her sex. I told her what sort of life I should probably lead as a teacher, pointed out the uncertainty of my prospects and the narrowness of my means and then, as an indirect invitation of her opinion, avowed the disinclination I felt to ask any such woman as I could love to make the sacrifice of marrying me. All this I could say in perfect earnestness and good faith, of course; but I said it with diplomatic purpose in order to ascertain whether *she* was inclined to regard such an alliance as a very dreary and uninviting prospect. I don't know yet whether or not she suspected my purpose, but her comment was very brief and non-committal, tho' not altogether uncomforting. She thought that such a marriage might, like Mrs. Carlyle's, be less burdensome than the common fate of marriageable damsels who might expect to keep house for some humdrum tradesman, or at best, for some plodding village doctor. I was left to suppose that it was a question in no way concerning herself, but that, in her disinterested judgment, I was maybe wasting my pity on professors' wives. That was one of my many diplomatic failures. . . .

Ellen, of course, more than "suspected his purpose." She had known that he was in love with her before he knew it himself. She was twenty-three and had had beaux ever since she was sixteen. Love symptoms were an old story to Miss Ellie Lou Axson and easy to detect, especially now that she too was in love—for the first time. But there was a decorous Southern convention which the Reverend Mr. Axson's daughter could not defy. It was considered most unladylike to show the least sign of interest until a young man proposed, and in this respect, Woodrow told her later, Ellen was "a consummate little dissembler." *

Yet there was a chink in her armor. She blushed easily, and in another letter, written afterwards, Woodrow told her about the time this weakness had almost betrayed her.

146 N. Charles St.,
Baltimore, Oct. 16th, 1883

. . . You knew that I loved you before I told you, didn't you, love? Why, I had told you often enough by plain enough signs, and even by pretty plain words. Do you remember the verses I gave you as we rode home from a picnic? I remember the charming blush with which you read them, but did not dare interpret it as I wished I might. Did you imagine that I had copied all those lines to give you just because I thought them pretty and hoped they would interest you from a literary point of view? Had you not noticed my manner as I asked you to correspond with me during that delightful talk in the hammock? And did you not remember what I told you then about how I regarded you?—how near I had come to telling you *then* that I loved you? I would have done so if I had dared—what would you have said? . . .

To Ellen's great disappointment, he went back to Atlanta still not daring. Try as he would, he could not convince himself that he could earn a living as a lawyer. He had nothing to offer her, he told himself —no money, no prospects and, in his opinion, a plain face and a difficult nature. He was also desperately afraid that if she rejected his love, he could never see her again. Their next meeting was not planned. Ellen

* Letter of Dec. 4, 1883.

and Woodrow were always sure that it was arranged by the kind Providence in which they both believed.

When the firm of Renick and Wilson finally gave up the struggle to make ends meet, Woodrow went home to spend the summer with his family in Wilmington, North Carolina. And there his immediate future had been settled. He agreed to go to Johns Hopkins for one year, although he was not happy about the financial sacrifice his parents would have to make. But Joseph's wish was still law to his elder son. If Woodrow wanted to be a great writer and teacher—and Joseph was sure that he could be—then he must have the best available training.

On his way to Baltimore, in September, he stopped over in Asheville, North Carolina, at his father's request, to take care of some matters connected with Dr. Wilson's work as Stated Clerk of the Southern Presbyterian Assembly. And there, standing at the window of his hotel room, he saw Miss Ellie Lou Axson, walking down the street. He had not known that she was in Asheville and he might have failed to recognize her if it had not been for one small detail. A month later he wrote:

> *146 N. Charles St.,*
> *Balto. Md., Oct. 30th, 1883*

... I need not be ashamed of being dominated by circumstances, for they are big things. Consider the arrangement of a lady's hair, for instance: her habit in the matter is a trivial enough circumstance; but if a certain little lady who is very dear to me had departed once from her usual way of coiling her hair about the back of her shapely head, it is more than probable that I should not have recognized her vanishing figure at the window of a certain hotel in Asheville—and what then?

Woodrow Wilson got to the street in a matter of seconds, caught up with Ellen, found out where the friends she was visiting lived, and begged her to see him very soon.

There followed three enchanted days. On the last afternoon, too desperately in love to remember his uncertain future, Woodrow proposed, and Ellen, immediately and joyfully, said "yes."

He could hardly believe it. Weeks later he wrote,

> *146 N. Charles St.,*
> *Balto., Md., Nov. 18th, 1883*

My precious Ellie,

Sometimes when I think of our engagement I wonder if I have not been dreaming the last two months. When I recall my first feelings for you; how passionate love grew rapidly upon me; how all my thoughts used to centre in plans to win you; what castles my hopes used to build and how I used to sicken at the prospect of hope deferred; and then how, much sooner than I had dared to hope, how by a seeming accident, we met and you gave your heart to me, it all seems so like a sweet dream that I am afraid to credit my memory. The impression is perhaps heightened by the fact that I left you before I had time to realize that you had pledged yourself to me. Although you had spoken the words which will always live in my memory, "I will do anything to make you happy"; although I had taken that sweet sealing kiss; and had been permitted to hold you in my arms, I remember calling you "Miss Ellie" to the last and being utterly unable to speak any part of the love and joy that were in my heart. . . .

Sitting dazed and incredulous in the train after he had left her, Woodrow Wilson thought that, if she had really accepted him, no success that he might achieve would ever compare with such a victory. He was to believe this all his life. Yet his elation was tempered by a sort of desperation when he faced the fact that he could not ask her to marry him for at least a year—a year at Johns Hopkins, and after that the search for a professorship with sufficient income to support them. Baltimore seemed a bleak and dreary place when he arrived, and the college buildings looked more like a prison than a famous university when he went to sign up for his courses.

Part 2
The Graduate Student

The first days were difficult. He spent most of them looking for an inexpensive place to live, writing to Ellen, and haunting the post office in the hope of finding a letter from her. No letter came. His parents were vacationing at Arden Park, not far from Asheville. He had asked Ellen to call on them before she went back to Rome. Had something gone wrong there? Had she changed her mind about marrying him? He was frantic.

Balto., Md., Sept. 25th, 1883

My own darling,

I am sick at heart from not hearing from you. It is now a week since you must have reached home and not a line have I had from you. I am filled with apprehensions. I have been dreaming of sickness keeping you in that horrid, yet blessed little Asheville, of mishaps in Knoxville, of accidents by the way; I have imagined you ill; I have scared myself with all sorts of images of misfortune that might account for your silence that has seemed to me so long. I know that there must be some reason, but what can it be? ...

The past week has seemed like a month—I am astonished to find that it is still September—so full the time has been of searchings in all quarters of this great town for a boarding place, of meetings with strangers, of joy and hope, of weariness, and, latterly, of apprehension. See what a foolish, doting swain I am—and how much in need of your sweet, sunny disposition to look always on the bright side of things! ...

I found a ring today that suits me and shall send it to you at once ... I know that you will think it pretty. I have had nothing engraved in it. I preferred having that done after conferring with you and ascertaining your taste and preference in the matter. I want you to wear the ring as it is until I can come to you. Then we can have what you please

put in it and I can put it on your hand with appropriate ceremonies
of our own invention, and of which I should like to have the direction!

With a heart brimful of love
Your own
Woodrow

Two days later Ellen's first letter came explaining why she had not
written sooner. She had returned from Asheville to find her father quite
ill and her younger brother, Edward, with a fever. Helpless without her,
they now needed all of her time and love to cure them. When the crisis
was over Ellen had a fever too. Woodrow wrote at once,

Balto., Md.,
Sept. 27th, 1883

My own darling,

Your letter reached me this morning, together with the enclosed lines
from your father. I was very grateful for those lines of his: they were
so kind and so cordial and bore such a reassuring and gratifying message
that I actually found my eyes filling with tears when I read them. Your
own letter, my love, I read with mixed feelings—with overflowing joy
at your sweet confessions of love, with pain and apprehension at the
news of your sickness as well as your father's and Eddie's ill health. . . .

So I was wise after all in putting off opening my heart to you until
I was about to come away! That declaration was on my lips many times
during those three days in Asheville, but it was kept back by my inability
to read your heart before you had opened it. I realized that a refusal
would send me at once away from you, and, wishing, under any conditions, to be with you as long as possible, I delayed the revelation, in order
that, if the worst came, my heart might be preserved from breaking by
being plunged at once into the distractions of travel, of a new life in a
strange city, and of hard study. That study would have been a poor,
half-hearted thing without your love to illuminate it and your promise
to animate it; but it *might* have saved me from despair. Since you loved
me, my darling, it would have been cruel to send me away without a
promise and a kiss; and I am profoundly thankful for the joy of a
sudden meeting and the pain of an imminent parting which prevented
you from making the great mistake of with-holding your hand where
you had given your heart. I cannot describe to you my delight at the

receipt of your letter. I had come away from the post-office with a heavy heart so often that the revulsion of feeling was tremendous when I took your letter from the envelope and I was almost frightened at the way my heart beat. It was the sweetest letter ever written—and it seems to have been written with great rhetorical art for it observed the laws of climax, beginning "My dear Friend" (as if I were nothing more!) and ending with confessions of love which are the sweetest, as well as the most modest that ever a maiden made. May God bless "my own Ellie."

What are the things, my love, which you would like to ask, and hear, and say, but which you cannot gain the courage to write? It need not require much courage to say to me anything you please. I do not know of anything that I would not tell you without reserve; and I cannot imagine anything in any way concerning yourself that I should not delight to hear. It is the greatest privilege of our present relation to one another that we can open our minds to each other absolutely without reserve, and I shall esteem it the best earnest of your love if you will write to me as freely as you commune with yourself. . . .

Ellen's next letter was written before she received his, and again "observed the laws of climax."

Rome, September 25th, 1833

My dear Friend:

As I find myself today at the most comfortable stage of convalescence, doomed to do nothing at all but enjoy myself, it occurs to me that there is no reason why I should not write a few lines to you, notwithstanding my long scrawl of yesterday. Ah, that was a white day; it brought two letters from you! They both came to-gether which constitutes excuse enough for writing again today.

This is a perfect autumn day and I have been spending it in the most luxuriously lazy fashion, swinging in the hammock and reading Shakspere and those letters by turns (I vow to you, my love, the last were the finer of the two). . . .

I am glad that you have found such pleasant friends in Baltimore, am especially glad that you have found them at the first, when you needed them most, and when being at leisure you have most time to show yourself friendly. . . .

I thank you very much for sending your dear mother's note and *with all my heart* I thank her and your father for their kind words. I think they must like me because they had made up their minds beforehand that they would and were determined not to be thwarted. I am not really "likeable," at least not to well regulated minds, under the best of circumstances, and I must have been most emphatically the reverse on that day at Arden if, as I know was the case, I looked and acted half as "queerly" as I felt. In truth, I was frightened beyond measure— no, not frightened exactly; yet that word must answer for lack of a better. I can usually exercise a fair amount of self-control, provided always I am not taken unaware, but have given me time to "screw my courage to the sticking point." But as we drove through Arden Park, I certainly felt it oozing out of the tips of my fingers; as I took off my hat I could see for myself that I was positively *pale* with fright—or whatever it was and I couldn't for the world have told them why or wherefore.

By the way I don't know why you should abuse your letter to Father. I am sure I heard it very much praised. I was too confused myself to give a clear report but have a vague recollection of hearing the words "manly," "earnest," "the right ring," etc. with an assortment of other complimentary adjectives.

. . . I am going to East Rome on Friday. On that day we all scatter for a time. Father and my grandparents to Gainsville, *Stockton* * to school at Fort Mill while Eddie and I go to sojourn with Agnes. Papa seems quite himself again now but I am determined he shall get away for awhile. . . .

I was taken ill very soon, and before that I was so desperately busy with the effort to evolve order out of the confusion which one's absence is sure to engender and with the nursing—the latter beginning before I had taken off my hat, indeed I hadn't time to take it off for half an hour or so.

. . . I have scarcely left myself light or space to say once again that *I love you.* Ah, my darling, I have no words—will never find them— to tell you how much; nor how very happy it makes me to hear you say —and repeat it—that you love me. Whenever I read it in your letters,

---

* Stockton Axson—elder of Ellen's two brothers.

were it several times on one page, it gives me a new and distinct thrill
of delight. Good night, dear love.

> *Yours with all my heart*
> *Ellie*

Woodrow's boarding house on North Charles Street was, he had
written, "in one of the pleasantest portions of the town, within one
square of the monument and within three of the University. I am just
across from the Peabody Institute, in whose splendid library I shall do
most of my reading this winter, and my room is bright and comfortable." *

Now that he was settled and happy in the sure knowledge of Ellen's
love, he was able to concentrate on his work. Every day, except Sunday,
was taken up with classes, and long hours of study, yet he never failed
to write to Ellen two or three times a week and to read her letters over
and over. It was difficult for her, brought up to conduct herself with
extreme reserve and modesty, to write a love letter. Woodrow was also
reserved, to a fault, but he had no inhibitions where his beloved was concerned. He opened his mind and soul to her, as well as his heart, and,
pleading, teasing and praising by turns, tried to persuade her to follow
his example: "What a timid little girl you are in your love making!"
he wrote. "You seem almost half afraid of your own words." † And
again,

> *146 N. Charles St.,*
> *Balto., Md., Sept. 29th, 1883*

... Your sweet letters ... fill me with indescribable delight: all the more
because I know that such confessions cost you a little struggle with your
natural shyness in such matters. I love you with all my heart, my
darling, and it makes me unspeakably grateful to know that I have
won your *first* love and won it so completely by I know not what attrac-
tions. I am really, then, the only man you ever met that you thought
you *could* love? ...

Are you thinking, my love, as you read this, that you were *not*
the first to win *my* love? And did I guess right when I guessed that what
you were hesitating to ask was about a certain un-named lady of whom
I told you once as we walked by the railroad? Well, to make the asking

* To Ellen, September 22, 1883.
† Dec. 2, 1883.

easy (if you want to ask) I'll volunteer one piece of information, which
is that I never knew what love was until I knew you, and that, if it was
love that I felt for the character which I supposed that lady to possess,
it was a very contemptible dwarf beside the strong passion that is now
at large in my heart and which leaps with such tremendous throbs of
joy at thought of your love. You need not shrink from hearing me speak
of what I have hitherto taken for love: for no woman, my darling, ever
had more entire love given her than I have given you. . . .

Slowly, and with frequent relapses, Ellen's courage grew. She never
again called Woodrow her "Dear Friend." And, when her own words
embarrassed her, she let the great poets she knew so well speak for her.

East Rome, Oct. 2, 1883

My darling

This morning brought me at once your two letters—of the 27th & 29th—
and therefore this day has been, like the day on which I last wrote,
"high holiday." "All its moments lightly shaken sow themselves on
golden sands."

I wonder if you would laugh, or what you would say, if you knew
how perfectly daft your letters make me! But no-one could be expected
to receive such letters and keep very cool. . . .

Ah me, what would I not give to be everything that is good and lovely
for your sake! Surely it is true that one may grow better and wiser
when one wills it so strongly. Yet how can I deceive myself into believing
that I will become, for your sake, what in all these years I have not
become for my Savior's sake whom I love still more.

The ring also came this afternoon. It is a *perfect beauty* in every
respect. . . . I can't tell you, my darling, how much I prize it. You
are very, very good—but are you not also very extravagant? Please excuse my impertinence, but really I was startled and amazed at the unexpected apparition of a *diamond*. You know it is not absolutely necessary to wear that particular sort of ring in order to "feel engaged."

Yes, perhaps I do feel more engaged with this outward symbol of
it on my hand. . . . I seem already to look back at my former self, the
girl who had never loved, as at a stranger, and I recall with wonder
and amusement some of the thoughts and opinions she entertained. Yet

my "theories" have been by no means overturned.... I was writing to Beth * the other night—about *you*.... I could honestly say that I had found my—yes, I must say it—my "ideal," though I am a little out of humour with that much abused word. Now I know you will laugh at me, but it is so! Why even those lines which Beth and I selected together, years ago, as best expressing our ideal were written for you! I never saw so perfect a description of anyone. A "jersey" jacket couldn't fit more closely! You may remember the words, for with calm audacity I once quoted them to you myself, knowing that you could not read my thoughts as I did so.

> "A mouth for mastery and manful work,
>   A certain brooding sweetness in the eyes,
>   A brow the harbour of grave thought."

She wore the ring on her right hand because they had agreed to keep their engagement a secret from everyone except their families and intimate friends.

Woodrow had never been able to talk to anyone about himself, but now, because he was afraid that Ellen would be disappointed if she did not know in advance exactly what sort of man he was, he wrote the first of many letters of self-revelation.

146 N. Charles St.,
Baltimore, Oct. 2nd, 1883

My own darling,

This is a dark and stormy day and I am lonely and homesick. With all the hardening experience of eight years absence from home, I have never grown altogether reconciled to being away from those I love. I suppose there never was a man more dependent than I on love and sympathy, more devoted to home and home life; and, my darling, my heart is overflowing with gratitude and gladness because of the assurance that it now has a new love to lean upon—a love which will some day be the centre of a new home and the joy of a new home life. I shall not begin to live a complete life, my love, until you are my wife. Who is more affected by the character of his home than a student, and who has sweeter opportunities for unselfish ministrations than a student's wife? She may be all in all to him.... Unless, indeed, he be a bear who repels

* School friend. Later Mrs. Erwin (maiden name not known to ed.).

her love and receives sympathy with ungracious surliness. I don't think, my precious one, that I shall prove a bear. I think that I can promise you that you will have no reason to regret having married me; that is, if love and tenderness can keep regret away.

I dreamed about you all last night, my darling.... That was a joyous dream ... I woke up laughing. I had been doing in the dream what I have never done in reality; had been showing you a side of my disposition that you have never seen. I dreamt of the jolliest frolic that we had to-gether ... and so it was that I awoke in glee. You don't know what a goose I can make of myself upon occasion, when I am with people of whose esteem I am sure and who will think no less of me for my nonsense. Can you love me in every humour? or would you prefer to think of me as always dignified? I am afraid it would kill me to be always thoughtful and sensible, dignified and decorous. But I'm not apprehensive as to what you may think! If you love the uninteresting man that is in me—for "I am not really likeable, at least not to well-regulated minds"—I have no fears as to what you will think of the boy that is constantly cropping out when I'm not under the constraint of "company manners"....

Ellen's letter of October second did not, for some reason, arrive for a week. In the meanwhile he tortured himself again with fear for her health and a slight case of jealousy.

146 N. Charles St.,
Baltimore, Oct. 4th, 1883

... Have you written yet to that poor fellow in Florida? I pity him from the bottom of my heart. He has lost what it has *made* me to win, the sweetest treasure in the world, the love of a peerless woman.... But he is not the only one—is he?—whose hopes have been dashed. In spite of all your shy avoidance of society, I know that you have not been able to hide yourself from men's eyes, and I have some recollection of a certain persistent widower who made me furious one night at prayer-meeting by presuming to join you in your own pew; and of a certain young jeweller of whose attentions Jessie warned me (for Jessie's shrewdness guessed my secret long ago) and for whom I was at one time inclined to feel the utmost antipathy....

When Ellen's letter came at last, he wrote,

My own darling,

I *did* laugh at the idea of being your "ideal" (because I am such very gross stuff out of which to construct an ideal!) but my amusement was mixed with another feeling which was the predominant one—with keen delight at the assurance that your love for me is great enough to over-look my faults and weaknesses and enthrone me in your gentle heart. God grant, my precious Ellie, that you may never have cause to regret my kingship there!... I promise to remain (?) humble, in spite of the triumphant pleasure of being loved and admired by the lov[e]liest of women. ...

Do you know, dearest that I am sometimes very much embarrassed when writing to you? I don't mean that I am ever embarrassed in the ordinary sense, but that I am at a loss to know how to express myself. Here's the difficulty: my inclination is to be "making love" in every sentence. ... No term of endearment could run beyond the reality of my feelings: *but one can't convey vocal tones to the written sheet,* and I have as great an aversion from "sweet talk" as from set and formal expressions of affection. ... There are no words which can express the sentiment of a kiss. A kiss is one of the gestures of that unspoken language which is often so much more eloquent of the deeper and subtler feelings than are any spoken words. And so it is that, when I write to you, I don't know *how* to write. My heart is so full of yearning tenderness for you, is so dominated by feeling, that every attempt I make to express myself seems to me at best only stiff and artificial. ... I would tell you all my thoughts, my darling: for will it not be our joy to be wedded in mind and in heart as well as in legal form?—but I cannot with this pen. ...

Ellen's next letter dealt briefly and definitely with Woodrow's lapse into jealousy and countered with searching questions about the "unnamed lady" he had loved.

East Rome, Oct. 6, 1883

... Your charming letter of the second full of dreams and other good omens was received yesterday. You dear, delightful boy! I don't

think I am dreadfully shocked at any of the revelations it contains and
I faithfully promise to love you in your every humour....

...Now...I will play jealous and ply you with questions. So you
will inform me, Sir, if you please, who the girl was and when and where
and how and why and wherefore—the beginning and the end! Was the
wound entirely healed before last summer and did it leave a very deep
scar? Are you sure there isn't the *least* little rankling pain remaining?...

As for the things I would—and would not like to "say," there is
no need to concern yourself about *them,* my love. It is very evident that
I *do* find the necessary courage and *am* saying them with a vengeance.
True, I always want to *unsay* them again immediately.... This very
letter has had several narrow escapes from burning....

When in my calmer moments I suddenly strike, after my fashion,
the spectator attitude, I cannot but laugh at the pendulum regularity
with which I am continually passing from one conflicting mood to another. But, if my darling *likes* to hear whatever comes into my head,
or rather whatever comes out of my heart, so it will, although it makes
my cheeks burn....

But are you very sure that you are not haunted like myself by the
dark suspicion that I am a desperately brazen sort of creature?

...By the way I don't know what could possibly have suggested
that jeweller story. I solemnly assure you that never in my life have I
had even a "bowing acquaintance" with *any* jeweller. As for the little
widower, why should we waste time over him when there are so many more
interesting subjects to talk about?

A full account of Woodrow's first love reached her promptly. He
told her the girl's name and that she was a cousin. He confessed that,
when he had met her in Staunton, Virginia, in 1880, he had been "hungry for a sweetheart." This, he claimed, was only natural after four
years at Princeton "spent away from all society, but the society of
men."

146 N. Charles St.,
Baltimore, Md., Oct. 11th/83

...I went to Virginia...with a definite determination to find a lady-
love, if possible.... No young man lives a complete life who is not lifted
out of himself by love for some woman who stands to him for a type

of what is pure and lovely. If he has no such love a great motive power is lacking in him. Even you, my darling, don't know yet how intensely I can love (though you shall know it some day); and at the time I speak of I did not know you, who were to claim the utmost gifts of my love. I felt then that I had a great unexpended store of affection which someone ought to appropriate; and it was with that feeling that I met, at Auntie's house, the girl I came to think entitled to that store of affection.... I had not seen her since we were both children; but I had received occasional letters from her, and I had formed a very extravagant idea of her character.... I had about made up my mind beforehand to fall in love with her, and afterwards it seemed an easy enough thing to do. During the next winter (for she was then at home in Ohio) we corresponded regularly and quite voluminously, and, in the summer of 1881 Jessie * and I went out to Ohio to make her a visit; and it was during that visit that I completed the little drama by proposing to her and being refused....

Before last summer came all traces of the wound she had given me were gone. No scar remained anywhere but on my *pride*, which winced a little at the memory of the huge mistake I had made with such wilful blindness....

Most of Ellen's letters to Woodrow while he was at Johns Hopkins have not been found. His frequent references to them, however, make the story of their relationship almost complete.

> *146 N. Charles St.,*
> *Baltimore, Oct. 16th, 1883*

... You say that "memories of Rome will always be interwoven with the fairest passages of your life." I am glad, unspeakably glad, my darling, that you are so happy and that the memories of our first meetings are so sweet to you; but I have a small remark to make concerning that confident assertion of yours, which is that I hope it won't prove true, since I intend to do all in my power to make your *married* life the fairest part of your mundane experience. It is a delight to me to think of those first days of our acquaintance (though I remember being very much concerned about the *impression* I was making) but there is a much keener delight in looking forward to that blessed time when you shall be mine,

* Jessie Bones (Brower) was living then in Staunton.

always with me, sharing my joys and sorrows, the beloved mistress of my
home. . . . It is odd, isn't it, that almost at the very time that I was writing
to you, begging you to tell me the secret of the inner history of those
first meetings of ours, you should have been in a measure complying. I
want to know *all* if my precious one will tell me. What did you think of
me that night we went to the concert together? I remember that, when
we started out, I was in ordinary spirits; but before the entertainment
was over some evil spirit seemed to have gotten hold of me—a dumb
spirit. On the way home I was conscious of being insufferably dull, and
after leaving you I was down in the very depths, being convinced that
I had proved myself in your eyes an empty-headed, stupid fellow! Were
you not really very much bored?

. . . How I wish that I could write you tonight such a letter as I
should like to write; but it seems as if my love for you were *literally*
unspeakable. . . . Thoughts of you fill my life. You seem to be in everything I read, in everything I do. I can't enjoy myself without wishing
that you might share the enjoyment; I can't read anything that is
stimulating or eloquent or instructive without wishing that I might
share it with you. I involuntarily smile in sympathy with anyone who
seems happy, because I am happy; I pity everyone who seems downcast,
because I imagine that they are not loved by those whom they love. I
am fast losing all semblance of a reputation for dignity because of the
way I frolic and joke and rejoice in the manufacture of light-hearted
nonsense when I am with my friends. I feel as if I should like very much
to repeat poetry all the time—if I knew any to repeat. I am in a fair
way to be run away with by this love that has taken possession of me.
If you continue to love me and write me such elating letters I don't
know what will become of this hitherto respectable person!

I am feeling very much encouraged tonight, about my work at "the
Hopkins." I had been somewhat downcast at finding that there was
no line of study pursued here that could quite legitimately admit under
it such studies as have been my chief amusement and delight during
leisure hours for the past five or six years, namely, studies in comparative politics. I have looked into the administrative machinery of England
and our own country enough to get a pretty good insight into them, and
it was my strong desire to make a similar study of the national govern-

ments (as perhaps also of the local governmental machinery) of France and Germany. When I got within range of the professors here, however, I found that they wanted to set everybody under their authority on what they called "institutional history," that is, into the dusty records of old settlements and colonial cities, to rehabilitating in authentic form the stories now almost mythical, of the struggles, the ups and downs of the first colonists here there and everywhere on this interesting continent —and other rummaging work of a like dry kind, which seemed very tiresome in comparison with the grand excursions amongst imperial policies which I had planned for myself. But this evening I went to see Dr. Adams, my chief, and made a clean breast of it, told him that I had a hobby which I had been riding for some years with great entertainment and from which I was loath to dismount. He received my confidences with sympathy, readily freed me from his "institutional" work and bade me go on with my "constitutional" studies, promising me all the aid and encouragement he could give me and saying that the work I proposed was just such as he wanted to see done! Do you wonder that I feel elated and encouraged?

You see, my sweet Ellie, I want to give you a share in all my thoughts and aspirations. If I loved study as much as I love you, I could soon make the world ring with admiring plaudits of my scholarship. I want to give you, in these small doses of my plans, some warning of the way I intend to inflict you some of these days when I shall have you in my power and shall make you listen to all sorts of political and historical disquisitions. . . .

A cloud appeared on the horizon. Ellen was hurt by Woodrow's story of his first love. She was probably jealous, too, although she would not admit it. She had "played jealous" when she questioned him, but she had not known then that he had asked the girl to marry him, and she thought that he must have been blindly in love to propose to a first cousin. She wrote what must have been a rather stern letter, because, judging by his reply, it frightened Woodrow. For once he did not confine himself to "love-making." He tried, instead, to convince her that he needed her to make his life complete, and in the process described with remarkable perception the ideal intellectual relationship between a scholar and his wife.

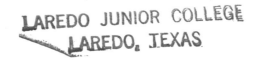

146 Charles St.,
Baltimore, Oct. 18th, 1883

... My dear sensitive girl seems to have been a good deal shocked by some of the revelations drawn out by her questions. ... Was it because she was not prepared to receive conclusive evidence that her "ideal" was, after all, a very weak, foolish fellow?

Did you think that I had invited your questions as I did because it would be pleasant to answer them. Very far from it. I invited them because I wanted to have no secrets to keep from you. It would break my heart, my precious Ellie, to lose your love—I could not now live without it—but it would break it quite as surely to have you imagine me wiser and better than I am and afterwards discover that you had been mistaken. Not that I thought that there was anything discreditable in what I had to tell: ever since long before Chaucer and Dryden did so, all mankind has been prone to fall in love with its cousins (as someone has said); but then one would like to have people think him *less* of a fool than his fellows. ... It *was* weak and silly in me to do so "unfortunate" a thing ... but I may say, by way of excuse, that even I should not have done so if she had been, before I met her in Staunton, *like* a cousin to me, if she had not been ... as much a stranger to me as if there had been no kinship between us.

But, happily, all that is now passed by, and as if it had never happened. I am not a boy any longer. It was left for you to teach me the vast, the immeasurable difference between a youth's fancy and a man's over-mastering love. Why, my darling, I am sometimes absolutely frightened at the intensity of my love for you. It makes me tremble to think what might become of me if my present confidence that you will one day be altogether mine should be blotted out, if anything should come between us, if any turn of Providence should take you from me. Do you remember what I said to you as we sat in the hammock at the picnic? How I declared that you were the only woman I had ever met to whom I felt that I could open all my thoughts? I meant much more than I dared say; I meant that I had begun to realize that you had an irresistible *claim* upon *all* that I had to give of the treasures of my heart as well as of the stores of my mind. I had never dreamed before of meeting any woman who should with no effort on her part make herself mistress of all the forces of my nature, in the exercise of a sort of right of dominion which I could not explain but had to recognize.

I am proud and wilful beyond all measure, my darling; and I used to think, like other young men I suppose, that I should never pay any but entirely voluntary homage to any woman. With an absurd pride of intellect, like Lydgate's,* I thought it might be possible to get along with a wife as a leisure-moment companion, dispensing with intellectual sympathy. Not that I did not want such sympathy—I knew that there would be a dreary side to life without it—nor because I thought women, as a rule, incapable of giving it; but principally, I believe because I thought it would be unreasonable to expect my wife to go with me, even in spirit, into all the so-esteemed dry paths into which my studies were naturally leading me? See, therefore, how valuable to me, my precious Ellie, was that conversation about the characters in "Middlemarch" as we were returning once from a certain walk up a hill. I had not read "Middlemarch" then, but I had the delight of hearing you expound the significance of its plot; and from that exposition I made a discovery that thrilled me: that you knew what sort of wife I needed—though you were not applying the moral to my case, and did not know how directly the story came home to my experience. I don't mean to compare myself with Lydgate. I have not yet proved myself possessed of any extraordinary talents; and I cannot claim the possession until I have put away certain discursive habits and brought all the powers I have into the line of some concentrated effort.

But there is a very distinct parallel between Lydgate's aspirations and my own and between the conditions of home-life necessary to my ultimate success and those which might have ensured his. No man who has a heart cast for the domestic relation, no man who isn't *merely* a student, simply a thinking machine, could wish to marry a woman such as John Stuart Mill married—and doted on—who expels sentiment from life, knows as much as her husband of the matters of his special study, and furnishes him with opinion, ministering not to his love but to his logical faculty. . . . But, on the other hand, a man with any of the keen sensibilities of the student must be miserable if he have a study into which his wife cannot come as a close companion. I don't expect or wish my darling to go back with me into those prehistoric times in which govern-

* Character in *Middlemarch*, by George Eliot.

ment originated ... but I know that she will not frown at my abstraction in such matters. As we came down from that hill I had found a girl who *could* give me all the intellectual sympathy I might desire, if I could but make her love me. And I *did* make her love me! how I don't know, but of the blissful fact I am sure. ...

I was surprised beyond measure, my darling, to hear that your father's thinking seriously of leaving Rome; and I am grieved at the news not only because of the reason assigned, but also on the church's account, and because I know that to leave your long-time home will be a sore trial to you whom I love and whose griefs are henceforth my griefs. Don't fail, dearest, to keep me informed of his plans. I hope he will have reasons for changing his mind. Guard your own health, I beg you, my love. ...

Ellen's father was seriously ill. A gentle, over-sensitive man, Edward Axson had never recovered from the shock of his wife's death. His grief was so intense that it injured his health. There had been terrifying nights when Ellen had heard him knocking his head against the wall of his bedroom and moaning pitifully. She had tried to comfort him, sometimes walking with him hour after hour back and forth across the room. Her patient understanding had gradually pulled him through the crisis, and, at the time she met Woodrow, Mr. Axson had apparently recovered. Then in September he began to fail rapidly and, in October, relapsed into long periods of melancholy.

A week passed without a letter from Ellen and Woodrow was miserable. She was "cruel," he wrote, and begged her to "have pity on a poor lonely mortal." * When she finally wrote, he was ashamed of himself.

146 N. Charles St.,
Baltimore, Oct. 25th, 1883

... I take back what I said about your being cruel in not writing to me oftener. It is I who am unreasonable, not you who are unkind. I knew, without being told by the note that came this morning that there was some good reason for your not writing and I was afraid, too, that the reason was just what I now know it to have been, your dear father's need of your care. I cannot tell you how distressed I was to hear of the continuance of his nervous troubles, or how startled I was at learning

---

* October 23, 1883.

that his resignation of his pastorate was already an accomplished fact and that the breaking up of your home in Rome is now an immediate prospect. . . . What are *your* plans? Are you going to Savannah? . . .

Hoping to comfort her a little, he told her how much his own family loved and admired her. His father and mother "already thought of her as their daughter," Marion and Annie, his married sisters, longed to meet her, his brother, young Joseph, always spoke of her in his letters as "sister Ellie." Then to distract her mind, he sent her the sort of letter she had often asked for. Ellen wanted to know more about his work and why he had undertaken it. So he told her, covering twenty closely written pages with his fine neat script; revealing not only his character, but the unchanging purpose of his life. One has only to read this letter to understand a great deal about Woodrow Wilson.

> *146 N. Charles St.*
> *Balto., Md., Oct. 30th/83*

My own darling,

Being quite sensible of the tendency of a certain very alluring topic to engross all the spaces of my letters, if I once allow myself to enter upon it, I purpose *beginning* this one with the fulfillment of a long-standing promise. I am going to tell you something about the ways and means of "the Hopkins," as far as those ways and means concern me. And I am going to do this, not because I think the subject intrinsically a very interesting one, but because I have, heretofore, been showing you only what was in my heart, and nothing of all the schemes that are in my head. I want to share everything with you, my darling; I want your sympathy in everything.

You know I am naturally extremely reserved. It would be a sheer impossibility for me to confide anything concerning only myself—especially any secret of my intellect—to anyone of whose sympathy I could not be absolutely sure beforehand; but there can be no greater delight in my life, my love, than making you the keeper of *all* my secrets, the sharer of all my hopes, *because I am sure of your love.* I used to *try* to tell you of the objects of my ambition when I was sure only of my love for you; but I could not do it because I did not know of your love for me.

Then, too, there is something else that urges me to tell you all about myself, and that is the desire that your love should be founded upon knowledge. Of course I don't believe that a woman can love a man for anything but qualities of heart and traits of character. She can't *love* his *intellectual* qualities. But it is nevertheless true that those qualities enter largely into the make-up of his character. They cannot all be acquired. Some of them must be in the essential fibre, current in his blood and native to his constitution. I know that you love me altogether and that you are quite willing to take me on trust:—if I were not convinced of that, I should be miserable indeed; but in giving myself I don't want to give by halves. I want you to know just what sort of fellow you are getting.

I think that it is only very recently that I have known myself— indeed I am not altogether certain that the acquaintance is complete yet. Like everybody else I have learned chiefly by means of big mistakes. I've had to earn my own experience. It took me all my college days to learn that it was necessary and profitable to study. Having made that tardy discovery, I left college on the wrong tack. I had then, as I have still, a very earnest political creed and very pronounced political ambitions. I remember forming with Charlie Talcott (a class-mate and very intimate friend of mine) a solemn covenant that we would school all our powers and passions for the work of establishing the principles we held in common; that we would acquire knowledge that we might have power; and that we would drill ourselves in all the arts of persuasion, but especially in oratory (for he was a born orator if any man ever was), that we might have facility in leading others into our ways of thinking and enlisting them in our purposes. And we didn't do this in merely boyish enthusiasm, though we were blinded by a very boyish assurance with regard to the future and our ability to mould the world as our hands might please. It was not so long ago but that I can still feel the glow and the pulsations of the hopes and the purposes of that moment—nay, it was not so long ago but that I still retain some of the faith that then prompted me. But a man has to know the world before he can work in it to any purpose. He has to know the forces with which he must cooperate and those with which he must contend; must know how and where he can make himself felt, not reckoning according to the conditions and possibilities of past times but according to a full knowledge of the conditions of the present and the possibilities of the immediate future. He must know the times into which he has been born: and this I did *not* know when I left college and chose my profession, as I proved by my choice.

The profession I chose was politics; the profession I entered was the law. I entered the one because I thought it would lead to the other. It was once the sure road; and Congress is still full of lawyers. But this is the time of leisured classes—or, at least, that time is very near at hand —and the time of crowded professions. It is plain to see why lawyers used to be the only politicians. In a new country, in communities where every man had his bread to earn, they were the only men (except the minister and the physician) who stopped amidst the general hurry of life to get learning; and they were the only men, without exception, who were skilled in those arts of forensic contest that were calculated to fit men for entering the lists at political tilts, or for holding their own in legislative debate. They could hope, too, when a turn of parties might have come, or their own popularity might have waned, to return to their places at the bar to find a place still open for them, to find themselves not altogether and hopelessly crowded out; they could even, like Webster and Jeremiah Mason and many others of less genius, make law and state-craft live and thrive together, pleading causes in the courts even while holding seats in the Senate or leading parties in the House.

But those times are passing away. A man who has to earn a liveli-hood cannot nowadays turn aside from his trade for intervals of office-holding and political activity. He cannot even do two things at once. He is constrained by a minute division of labour to bend all his energies to the one thing that is nearest at hand. Even in the law men are be-coming specialists. The whole field of legal knowledge, which former generations of American lawyers have superficially worked, is too big for any one man now, and practitioners are contenting themselves with cultivating small corners of it, digging deep and getting large crops out of small areas. And of course these small tenant farmers have to work much more diligently than did the great proprietors of former times. The law is more than ever before a jealous mistress. Whoever thinks, as I thought, that he can practice law successfully and study history and politics at the same time is wofully [*sic*] mistaken. If he is to make a living at the bar he must be a lawyer *and nothing else*. Of course he can compass a certain sort of double-calling success by dint of dishonesty. He can obtain, and betray, clients by pretending a knowledge of the law which he does not possess; and he can often gain political office by the arts of the demagogue. But he cannot be both a learned lawyer and a profound and public-spirited statesman, if he must plunge into practice and make the law a means of support.

In a word, my ambition could not be fulfilled at the bar; the studies for which I was best fitted, both by nature and by acquired habit, were not legitimate in a law office, and I was compelled in very justice to myself to seek some profession in which they would be legitimate. Evidently, however there was small latitude of choice. A professorship was the only feasible place for me, the only place that would afford leisure for reading and for original work, the only strictly literary berth with an income attached. True, professorships were scarce and hard to get, and professors could not participate actively in public affairs; but even a professorship might be gotten as soon as a competence at the bar, and the occupancy of office had never been an essential part of my political programme. Indeed I knew very well that a man without independent fortune must in any event content himself with becoming an *outside* force in politics, and I was well enough satisfied with the prospect of having whatever influence I might be able to exercise make itself felt through literary and non-partisan agencies: for my predilections, ever since I had any that were definite, have always turned very strongly towards a literary life, notwithstanding my decided taste for oratory, which is supposed to be the peculiar province of public men.

With manhood came to me an unquenchable desire to excel in two distinct and almost opposite kinds of writing: political and *imaginative*. I want to contribute to our literature what no American has ever contributed, studies in the philosophy of our institutions, not the abstract and occult, but the practical and suggestive, philosophy which is at the core of our governmental methods; their use, their meaning, "the spirit that makes them workable." I want to divest them of the theory that obscures them and present their weakness and their strength without disguise, and with such skill and such plenitude of proof that it shall be seen that I have succeeded and that I have added something to the resources of knowledge upon which statecraft must depend. But the *imaginative* writing? I don't mean that I want to write poetry. I am quite aware that at my birth no poet was born; but the imagination has other spheres besides the creations of a poetic fancy and can freshen and beautify the world without the aid of the musical cadences of verse. I believe that there's entirely too much moping and morbid thought amongst jaded human beings, that there's a great deal of joy and fun in the world that people miss for lack of time to look around; and I believe that there are inexhaustible sources of cheer, just as there are endless combinations of music, in our *language*. Now isn't it a legitimate ambition to wish to write something (!) that will freshen the energies of tired people and make the sad laugh and take heart again : some comedy full of pure humour and peopled with characters whose livers are in order, who live up to the moral that life, even with the pleasures of vice left out, is worth living : lay sermons full of laughter and a loving God : a fiction that may be suffered to live, if only because it has real people in it and no sham enthusiasm ? I could wish to be the favoured correspondent of children, as well as a counsellor of the powers of the earth.

But where does oratory come in ? It does not generally come into the lectures of college professors ; but it should. Oratory is not declamation, not swelling tones and an excited delivery, but the art of persuasion, the art of putting things so as to appeal irresistibly to an audience. And how can a teacher stimulate young men to study, how can he fill them with great ideas and worthy purposes, how can he draw them out of themselves and make them to become forces in the world without oratory ? Perfunctory lecturing is of no service in the world. It's a nuisance. "The mind is not a prolix gut to be stuffed," as father used to tell his students, "but a delicate organism to be stimulated and directed."

And so I'm brought back, by association of ideas, to the point from which I set out, the University. Its chief charm for advanced students, as well as its chief *danger* perhaps, is its freedom of method. The professors act rather as guides and counsellors than as instructors. Their lectures are intended to direct our work, to point out sources of information and suggest points of view. Each man is allowed to follow his own methods of study, which he can safely and profitably do if he have matured purposes, but which allows him full opportunity to fritter away his time if he have no fixed habits of study. The temptation in my own case is to confine myself to those paths of constitutional study which have become familiar, and therefore most attractive, to me. I have a

distinct dread (partly instinctive and partly instilled by my home training) of too much reading, and I am, consequently, so much averse from
scattering my forces that I possibly limit them to too narrow a sphere.

The sessions of the *Seminary* are occupied in the reading of papers
(generally by students of longest standing in the University) upon
special subjects political and social, such as the Spanish settlements in
Florida and the constitution and history of such socialistic communities
as Brooke farm and others more obscure; and the preparation of these
papers illustrates one of the best features of the University work, its
cooperative feature. Instead of requiring all to go over the whole field
in any given branch, each man is assigned a limited topic for special
study upon which he is expected to make a report in class; and his
knowledge of the other topics involved is gained from the papers read
by his classmates.

But I must really draw this huge letter to a close. Its bulk is already
alarming, and I have a dim suspicion that, after all my writing, I have
told you very little that you did not know before. What I have wished
to emphasize is the *object* for which I came to the University: to get a
special training in historical research and an insight into the most modern
literary and political thoughts and methods, in order that my ambition
to become an invigorating and enlightening power in the world of political thought and a master in some of the less serious branches of
literary art may be the more easy of accomplishment. To charge me with
egotism and presumption in entertaining such an ambition would, I freely
admit, be a just commentary on my plans; but I am conscious in my
most secret heart of making not the least pretension to *genius* and of
relying altogether on hard work and a capacity for being taught. I am
by no means confident of reaching the heights to which I aspire, but I
am sure of being able to climb *some* distance; and I shall never be
embittered by finding myself unable to get to the top. It will be invigorating to breast the hill anyway—much more invigorating than easy
walking on level ground—and all my energies are eager for the exercise.
One thing at least shall not retard my influence, if I can help it, and
that is a lame *style* in writing. Style is not much studied here; *ideas*
are supposed to be everything—their vehicle comparatively nothing. But
you and I know that there can be no greater mistake; that, both in its

amount and in its length of life, an author's influence depends upon the power and the beauty of his style, upon the flawless perfection of the mirror he holds up to nature; upon his facility in catching and holding, because he pleases, the attention: and style shall be, as, under my father's guidance, it has been, one of my chief studies. A writer must be artful as well as strong.

You will doubtless smile at the character of this profuse epistle, as I have done; but its composition has done me lots of good. I've worked off any amount of stored-up steam in writing it!...

He had been writing to Ellen twice a week. Now, while she struggled through the long, depressing task of packing and getting the parsonage ready for its new occupants, he sent her a love letter every other day.

> *146 N. Charles St.*
> *Balto., Nov. 4th, 1883*

... How I long for your presence, my darling, on these Sabbath afternoons when my work lulls and I can stop and think about myself—about my privileges and my duties, about my relations to my fellow men and about my relation to God. It would be *such* a comfort and such pure delight to sit in sweet communion with you at such times; to talk of the future, of how we shall sustain each other in love, of how we shall work together to do good, to make a bright spot around us in this world, to construct a perfect Christian home from which pure influences shall go out to those around us....

> *146 N. Charles*
> *Balto., Nov. 6th, 1883*

... You must have wrought a sort of revolution in me, my love, for I have hitherto had the reputation for being undemonstrative! Don't be incredulous; it's so, though I admit that *you* would be justified in disbelieving it. You have a great deal to answer for. How can a fellow in Baltimore write a lecture on Adam Smith when he's forever thinking of a girl in Georgia?...

146 N. Charles St.
Balto., Md., Nov. 11th, 1883

My darling Ellie,

I sometimes wonder nowadays how I ever got along without you. Thoughts of you, purposes and plans of which you are the centre, constitute so large a part of my life that I look back upon last winter as full of a very blank existence. There is one view of my past life which may not have struck you during my late confessions. Just as I was entering upon my preparation for the bar, I met and fell in love with my cousin, thus at the same time choosing a profession for which I was not suited, and which I was eventually to leave in disappointment, and being led away by an infatuation which was to issue in nothing but distress; but as soon as I had determined to leave the law and had set my face toward the right intellectual goal, *I found you*, my darling, the woman whose love was to make my life complete. These things were not accidental. Everything goes wrong with a man until he gets on the right road. Of course, there are trials in store for me—for *us*—on *this* road, but they will be as tests of strength, not like burdens of chains; and for my part, they can't hurt me as long as they come in the course of duty and I am sustained by your love.

. . . The only news that I have to impart is that I have been elected a member of the "University Glee Club" and shall warble with them every Monday evening. My "pipes" are somewhat out of singing order, but I know I can sing with a lot of fellows: it's the best fun of its kind that I know of, provided the other fellows can avoid strong-voiced discord. . . .

Fun was as necessary to this ambitious and indefatigable student as to less serious young men, and the Glee Club was not his only source of amusement. He liked to go to parties, if they were informal, for he was, then and always, bored by elaborate dinner parties and more than a little contemptuous of what he called "soulless society talk." He wrote to Ellen the day after a very informal party:

146 N. Charles St., Balt., Md.,
Nov. 13th, 1883

. . . We had a very jolly time, and I am afraid that I was not as dignified as I might have been. The company consisted of the young lady aforesaid, her two sisters, a young damsel from Philadelphia, Miss Woods and two of her brothers, and one or two other men besides myself. We compounded the caramels in the dining-room, boiled them in the kitchen, and ate them in the parlour; but before these numerous stages had passed I had had numerous frolics with the young lady aforesaid and had been three times locked up in the pantry, each time gaining my freedom by making demonstrations toward demolishing the larder, and once having one of the young ladies as a fellow-prisoner. I don't always misbehave so when I go out in company; but candy making is scarcely an occupation requiring much dignity. . . .

146 N. Charles St., Balto., Md., Nov. 20th, 1883

. . . (I) re-found in Burke, the other day, a passage from which I must often unconsciously have been quoting. Here's the pith of it: ''Public duty demands and requires that what is right should not only be made known, but made prevalent; that what is evil should not only be detected, but defeated.'' That it seems to me, is no bad motto.

It delights me to know that my letters give you comfort and relief from sorrow, my darling; and I need not tell you how much I wish that my love could take the place of all love that is lost, even though that love were a mother's. Ellie, *my* Ellie, my *darling!* Oh that I could show you my heart that you might see how much you are loved and how that heart is torn by the thought that there is *any* love or sympathy that you lack. Even my love, I know, cannot take the place of your sweet mother's love; perhaps a man's love can never replace a woman's sympathy. . . . I know not what subtile quality a woman's sympathy possesses, but this I do know, that my Ellie will never open her heart to me in vain and that I *would* be all in all to her.

God has indeed been merciful to us in giving us each-other's perfect love. Indeed God has never had anything but blessings for *me*. It makes me almost tremble to think of the uniform good fortune that has followed me all my life. . . . Love has brightened all my life, *your* love crowning the wonderful dispensation. As if to fortify and prepare me against the coming sorrows I have never tasted, the loss of dear relatives, which cannot be long delayed, I have, it would seem, been given your love to be my stay and solace. I don't know why I should think of these things. Possibly it is because my dear mother . . . has had malarial fever. . . .

On the twenty-second of November the Axson family left Rome to live with Edward's father and mother in Savannah. It was a sad day. The parsonage had been home too long to be left without grief. Ellen, calm on the surface, was so miserable and so worried about her father's condition that for a while after she arrived in Savannah she could not even write to Woodrow.

Her grandfather, Dr. Isaac Stockton Keith Axson, was a man of strong religious belief and a famous preacher. He was pastor of Savannah's Independent Presbyterian Church and known in church circles as "the great Axson." His wife, although rigid in her conceptions of morality and conduct, was warm-hearted and very fond of her granddaughter. Ellen, able to rest and share her anxieties for the first time in years, finally recovered her spirits. Woodrow's, as usual when he did not hear from her, were at a low ebb.

> *146 N. Charles St.*
> *Balto., Md., Nov. 22nd, 1883*

... My heart is nearly starved for want of a letter from you and I know not what desperate strait it may be in, if one doesn't come very soon. ...

When her letters finally arrived, he thought they were wonderful.

> *Dec. 4th, 1883*

I am quite sure that if you were to write me twenty pages a day I should think each day's epistle too short and finish it with impatience at the fact that next day's mail was too far distant. ...

> *146 N. Charles St.*
> *Balto., Md., Dec. 11th, 1883*

I haven't your art of making love the pervading colour rather than the predominant figure of the picture. Of course it is not given to everyone to paint this way, but can't you give me a few leading rules or guiding hints? You are under a sort of obligation to undertake my instruction because you have encouraged me in the opposite method, allowing me to take literally your declaration that I couldn't tell you of my love for you too often. ... I'll tell you what I'm going to do: I'm going to continue this inartistic, self-indulgent practice of saying the same thing over and over again until you cry "enough!" So you see you have the remedy in your own hands . . . you have but to say the word and I'll fill my letters with the most wonderful lot of stuff about professors and students and studies; about city folk and city ways and city entertainments you ever conceived of. . . .

The Christmas holidays that year were very dreary for a man who loved his family and had now to be separated, not only from them, but from his sweetheart too. But his funds were meagre and he had to stay in Baltimore with only his books to keep him company and his correspondence with Ellen to comfort him.

> *Balto., Md., Dec. 18th, 1883*
> *146 N. Charles St.*

. . . During my daily walk, my "constitutional," . . . I was attracted by a card which announced from behind the generous pane of a broad window, that a collection of Mr. Whistler's etchings and "dry points" was an exhibition within. In I went, of course, and after being constrained by a handsome young woman to buy a catalogue which I did not want, I set myself to as critical an examination of Mr. Whistler's productions as my ignorance of artistic canons would allow. Well, I must confess that, in my unenlightened soul, I was disgusted and more than ever indifferent to the possession of the catalogue except that *it* was much more interesting as a curiosity than the etchings are as pictures. Some of Mr. Whistler's critics object that his later productions, of which those I saw are specimens, are mere *suggestions;* I think they would have been nearer the truth in some cases if they had said that they suggest *nothing* —a few lines, a possible face, a conjectural group, a hazy beginning of something—one cannot tell what the picture might have been, had it been completed; though here and there one does find a sketch suggestive of life and beauty. As compared with these unsatisfactory dashes of helter-skelter lines and irresponsible patches of shade, recommend me to the staring *chromo* with its honest ugliness! . . .

What would I not give to spend the holidays in Savannah! I'll hardly realize the passage of the Christmas season here because I expect to have to study all through it; and I am rather glad of the necessity; for only imperative work can save me from the blues that would be sure to master me if I had time to think of those delights which I am compelled to forego. But let's change the subject! I can't trust myself yet awhile to speak about being with you. I am so grateful for the assurance of your love that I am ashamed to rebel against being denied those sweet joys which we might derive from eachother's presence now that we know eachother's hearts....

"Bluntschli Library"
J. H. University, Balto., Dec. 21, 1883

... There will come Christmas seasons which I *may* spend with you, when you will be mine, my precious wife, the joy and light of my life; when, in a home of our own—a home made happier than all others by the constant interchange of the little services of love, which make up the great whole of life for those who are wedded in love, and rendered as holy as any love by love for God and diligence in the work He gives us to do. This I know, that, if love can make you happy, your life shall be full of joy and sunlight: I have given you my whole heart without reserve...

Bluntschli Library, J. H. University, Balto., Dec. 22, 1883

My precious Ellie,

I confess that this is sheer self indulgence, this daily letter writing, but it's Christmas time and why shouldn't I indulge myself?... The biggest part of my preparation for examinations is done.... I still have plenty to keep me busy, but not to drive me at the top of my pace; and it has always been my habit to study by brief spurts rather than with steady and persistent speed. I like to read *much,* but not *many things,*— at least not many things at once.... I *can't* "cram": I must eat slowly and assimilate during intervals at rest and diversion. My chief ground of indictment against my professors here is that they give a man infinitely more than he can digest. If I were not discreet enough to refuse many of the things set before me my mental digestion would be utterly ruined....

His Christmas present to Ellen was a photograph of a painting called "Checkmate," by "some modern 'master' with an unpronounceable name." He chose it, not for its artistic value—there was none—but because the girl in the picture was so like Ellen that it made his "heart

quicken its beat tumultuously.'' * It became one of their most valued possessions and always hung in a prominent place in every house in which
they lived. Ellen sent him a knitted band for his hat. He wrote:

Baltimore, Md.,
Christmas Eve, 1883

... It was the truest of instincts that told you that I would value most
as a gift from you something you made with your own hands. ... This
hatband is exquisitely beautiful—prettier than any other I ever saw—so
that it has a double value. You would have had a good laugh at me if
you could have seen me struggling with thread and needle with fingers
that were stiffer, bigger thumbs than usual to fasten it on my hat.

On his birthday, December 28, she delighted him still more by
sending him a portrait of a child, by Ellen L. Axson.

Bluntschli Library,
Balto., Dec. 28th, 1883

... It is more than beautiful, my darling, because it contains in speaking
counterfeit, a face upon which it does one good to look long and often.
There's real education and a very pure pleasure in dwelling on its lovely,
wide-eyed childish innocence, its thoughtful, unconscious wondering
gaze. ... You must have known how I delight to study a beautiful child's
face. I seem to be able to get an inspiration of innocence and of purity
of thought, to recover such a child-likeness as is a preparation for the
kingdom of heaven. ...

This is a pretty serious business, this thing of growing older; isn't
it? To think that this is my twenty-seventh birthday! It's well it's no
worse. The season of preparation has been long, and will yet last a while;
but there's still time, God willing, to do some good, honest, hard work
in which the accumulated momentum of the time past may be made to
tell. I am sometimes a little startled and out of countenance when I think
how small a proportion my achievements bear to my years, but that's
a very idle and unprofitable way of looking at the facts. ... Steady resolution, slow and sure of its resources, is worth all the regrets that were
ever wasted; and, if I, with sound mind, strong health, backed by the

* W.W.'s letter, Dec. 18, 1883.

devoted love and confidence of my family, *and promised a wedding with you,* were to suffer regrets to drive out hopeful determination, I'd deserve to be kicked and deserted!...

Baltimore, Md., Dec. 29th, 1883

... When my birthdays are crowned with the supreme happiness your presence will bring "we'll live and pray and sing and tell old tales." That's not a bad programme, if the "old tales" be made to stand for unpedantic learning, the living for its *full* meaning, the praying for a true trust in God, and the singing for hope and light-hearted courage. It will be worth while to live that way. ...

In his senior year at Princeton Woodrow had written an article called "Cabinet Government in the United States." It was published in the *International Review* for August, 1879, and he had intended ever since to develop the theme. Now, on the first of January, 1884, he finally got around to it, not realizing that the result would be the beginning of his fame as a writer—his first book, *Congressional Government.*

146 N. Charles St.
Baltimore, Md.
New Years Day, 1884

My own darling,

If you should, in the course of this letter, notice any marked degeneracy in the hand-writing, pray attribute it, not to carelessness, but to the fact that I have been writing all day long and that my hand threatens to rebel against hard usage. I've opened the New Year by a day of diligent work on my favorite constitutional studies. I've planned a set of four or five essays on "The Government of the Union" in which it is my purpose to show, as well as I can, our constitutional system as it looks in operation. My desire and ambition are to treat the American Constitution as Mr. Bagehot * (do you remember Mr. Bagehot about whom I talked to you one night on the veranda at Asheville?) has treated the English Constitution. His book has inspired my whole study of our government. He brings to his work a fresh and original method which

* Walter Bagehot—English journalist, economist & author of *The English Constitution,* etc., 1826–1877.

has made the British system much more intelligible to ordinary men, and which, if it could be successfully applied to the exposition of our federal constitution, would result in something like a revelation to those who are still reading the Federalist as an authoritative constitutional manual. An immense literature has already accumulated on this subject but I venture to think that the greater part of it is either irrelevant or already antiquated. "An observer who looks at the living reality will wonder at the contrast to the paper description. He will see in the life much which is not in the books; and he will not find in the rough practice many refinements of the literary theory." (B)

Of course I am not vain enough to expect to produce anything as brilliant or as valuable as Bagehot's book; but by following him afar off, I hope to write something that will be at least worth reading, if I should ever publish it, and which will, in any event, serve as material for college lectures, which will put old topics in a somewhat novel light. Does this big programme make you wonder what I've been writing today? Something very ordinary. Only an historical sketch of the modifications which have been wrought in the federal system and which have resulted in making Congress the omnipotent power in the government, to the overthrow of the checks and balances to be found in the "literary theory." This is to serve as an introduction to essays upon Congress itself, in which I wish to examine at length the relations of Congress to the Executive, and that legislative machinery which contains all the springs of federal action— But what sort of New Year's letter is this I am writing! I've been so absorbed in my pet subject all day that I forget myself. . . .

I have never been inclined to regard the opening of a new year with any special reverence. Of course the passage of time is a solemn thing, and it does a man good to reckon with his past and by its results plan his future. But that's a rather silly spasmodic sort of virtue which indulges in "good resolutions" at this special season. Such resolutions, to be satisfactory to the resolver, must have such a definite shape that they are for that very reason unserviceable. It may be an excellent plan to read a scene from Shakspere every day, for instance, or to refrain from all harsh speech, and yet it is easy to imagine circumstances unnumbered under which very harsh words and total abstinence from Shakspere might very properly and virtuously be permitted. . . .

I need not tell you, my darling, how often I have thought of you in connection with this opening year. All my future is to be linked with yours; and the happiest office of my life is to make your life bright and full of love. May God bless you, my peerless little sweetheart.

Bluntschli Library,
J.H. University,
Balto., Jan'y 4, 1884

... I am beginning to think that I made a mistake in working all through the vacation without allowing myself any respite at all. I kept to my books almost all the time and did not go near any of my friends. I am, as you have no doubt found out for yourself, an excessively proud and sensitive creature (or ''wretch'' as you would say of yourself) and, since I look upon the Xmas season as one especially sacred to family reunions and festivities, I did not choose to call upon any of the families of my acquaintance lest I might interfere in some way with the freedom of their holiday arrangements. So, in order to escape intolerable loneliness, I went in self-defense to my studies. As a natural consequence I overdid the business—a discovery which I made on Near Year's day, after the hardest day's work I ever did. I was both exhausted and intensely nervous and I am just now beginning to feel like my old self again. The last day or two I have been restlessly wandering about trying to bridge over a sort of enforced idleness, the most interesting results of my half-crazy condition having been three successive all-night dreams of you. The first visions were delightful, but in the last from which I awoke only a few hours ago and which still haunts me, *I dreamt that you were dead*—you, without whom I would not care to live, nay, whose loss would make me wish to die. But why should I distress you by telling you of all this. I am ashamed of my weakness. It need not distress you, for it's all past now. I am not often subjected to the dominion of my nerves, and it requires only a very little prudence to enable me to maintain that mastery over myself and that free spirit of courageous, light-hearted work in which I pride myself.

Interpreted by the accepted canons of superstition, even that terrible dream of last night brings a delightful prophecy of marriage, which ought to remove one of my chief causes of anxiety—indeed the *only* thing that stands in the way of my complete happiness—namely the uncertainty of my prospects. When nobody else's future depended on my own, I used to be wonderfully free from this particular sort of anxiety. I always felt a sort of calm, uncalculating assurance of my ability to make successful shift to support myself; but now that the time for the realization of my sweetest hopes depends upon my securing a good position, I begin to feel very keenly the uncertainty of the prospect. I know what you would say, my darling; I have a perfect assurance of your love and of your willingness to abide the chances of my fortune; but I am none the less eager to make our engagement as short as possible....

Woodrow's eyes as well as his nerves suffered from this self-imposed overwork. He had used glasses for reading since his early youth; now he had to wear them all the time, but this did not distress him. He was, he believed, so homely that glasses increased this misfortune only a little; and he was amused, as well as puzzled, when in his later years a friend, looking at his clear-eyed, intensely alive, firm-jawed face, remarked, "God made you a homely man, but you've made yourself a handsome man."

When Ellen wrote that she was terribly discouraged because she could not paint well, Woodrow replied:

146 Charles St.,
Balto., Md., Jan'y 8th, 1884

... You propounded a puzzling question in your last letter (by the way I've had only one letter from you *this year!*) If sensitive folk like ourselves find everything they do "simply execrable," whence comes the delight in work which urges one on, in spite of that supreme disgust, and in spite of the knowledge that the result *must* be "but the pitifullest infinitesimal fraction of a product?" That is a "riddle," and I can think of no solution, except that there is always satisfaction in hard, conscientious work, in the earnest pursuit of a clearly-seen, however distant ideal, and in the consciousness that one's hands are *acquiring* a skill and *learning* a cunning which may enable them some day to turn out forms of beauty such as will delight even our own eyes. We admire and strive after virtue none the less because we know we have it not.

As for your work, you are very unreasonable to be dissatisfied with it. I can find in it nothing but beauty and I am not blinded altogether by love of the hand that worked those faultless shadings. If you like my *writing* as well, and with as good reason, I shall be more than content! If I could tell you what I *would* do, you could appreciate my intense disgust for what I *have* done when you come to see it. I know that my careful compositions of to-day are vastly better than I could have written five, or even three, years ago—and that's very encouraging, but what is my style to what it should be! I have imagined a style clear, bold, fresh and facile; a style flexible but always strong, capable of light touches or of heavy blows; a style that could be driven at high speed—a brilliant, dashing, coursing speed—or constrained to the slow and stately progress of a grave argument, as the case required; a style full of life, of colour and vivacity, of soul and energy—of a thousand qualities of beauty and grace, and strength that would make it immortal —is it any wonder that I am disgusted with the stiff, dry, monotonous sentences in which my meagre thoughts are compelled to masquerade, as in garments which are even too mean for *them!*

Whew! What a tempest in a teapot! But the tragic affair has a ludicrous side to it, as what tragedy has not (for a man cannot mend himself after the damage of a fall from a railway car without the most laughable display of vanity!) Suppose you had to draw or paint your letters to me! If you did, you could appreciate my comical embarrassment at having to write poor letters to a young lady who knows that my chief study is the art of writing. . . .

In spite of his disgust, Woodrow had sent an article entitled "Cabinet or Committee Government" to the *Overland Monthly,* a national magazine. It was accepted, to his surprise, for he was not pleased with it. When it was published, he sent it to Ellen asking her to "judge it with love." *

A week later he moved to another boarding house. The small room at North Charles Street was gloomy in the wintertime, and very cold. It was heated by a diminutive coal grate which warmed only part of his anatomy at a time. And there were other, more important, reasons for leaving.

No. 8 McCulloh St., Balto., Md.,
Jan'y 16th, 1884

. . . But, there was another coldness besides the "winter's flaw" to drive me away from 146; I was lonely there beyond measure, for I was the

* Jan. 10, 1884.

only Hopkins man in the house, and amongst all the twenty boarders there was not one who took the least interest (except a *gossiping* interest) in me, or in whom I could find any attraction. One or two of the young ladies there showed a very evident willingness to become better acquainted, making all the advances that lady-likeness would permit— and they were very nice girls, well-bred and sweet-looking—but they talked with typical society soullessness, and I had neither the time nor the inclination, even if I had had the power, to feign an interest which I did not feel. Here I am much better off, established, as I am, in a larger and warmer room and surrounded by what I may, I think, call "picked specimens" of the University men, fellows of various characters, of course, but of equal enthusiasm in intellectual pursuits, sensible, well-informed, jolly and unaffected. It's a much more healthful atmosphere for me than that which I have left because it doesn't do for me to live for long periods together beyond the reach of congenial companionship.... I get to thinking too much upon that most unprofitable of all subjects, *myself*....

I am sure that you will be glad to hear, my darling, that the Western papers have praised my article in the "Overland" very highly and that it has met with a most favorable reception at the University. The men there whose opinions I value most have expressed their unqualified admiration of both the matter and the style of the piece. That they should commend the *style* is a ground of genuine surprise to me, for it is in my judgment too *staccato*. There are too many short, incisive sentences and in the effort at condensation, I have left the *transitions* of the argument much too awkward and abrupt. Trying to manage a six-horse team when there was scarcely room enough to do justice to the paces of a single steed has resulted in making the driving unnecessarily conspicuous. But nevertheless it's the style which has come in for the most unanimous plaudits. "Wilson," said one critic, "you've picked up a capital literary style somewhere" ("Picked up" indeed! Hasn't my dear father been drilling me in style these ten years past?) "Upon whose style did you form it? Did you come by it naturally, or have you consciously modelled after Macaulay?" (Poor Macaulay!) ...

I am immensely pleased that the style of "Cabinet or Committee Government" should have been considered good, because I'm sure that I can write much better prose than that, nay I am writing better upon the subject I opened upon New Year's day . . . because I can give myself room and drive with a freer rein.

I write to you freely and at large about such things because I can imagine that I see in your sweet eyes, the while, unbounded sympathy and love, whereas I know that when I talk to my companions about my literary difficulties, they suspect me of slyly doing that smallest and most contemptible of all kindred things, *fishing for a compliment*. Why can't we all of us be honest and straight-forward? Why should a fellow, when he asks to have the faults of his writing pointed out that he may correct them, be suspected as of course seeking flattery?

My success in literary effort has recently become much surer than it once was or promised to be, because until within a few months I lacked the true source of inspiration. I was then writing for myself, but now I am writing for *you!* This is no mere sentiment. The additional power is very real and very appreciable—and, besides, it was to have been expected. No man is complete until he has learned what perfect love for another is. His nature can't expand and get free play until it is bound up with another. I'm speaking the truest philosophy when I say that this 16th day of the month commemorates the date upon which I first became fully myself: for my love was not, and could not be, perfect until I knew it was returned and thereby sanctioned. You are in all the work I do, my love.

Ellen's father was growing steadily worse. She had not mentioned this to Woodrow, wanting to spare him more anxiety, but when, in February, Mr. Axson's mind began to fail, she wrote what must have been a very unhappy letter, for Woodrow went at once to Savannah. Back in Baltimore, he wrote:

8 McCulloh St., Balto., Md.,
Feb. 2nd, 1884

My own darling,

Of course, up here in the silence of my room, I've done a heap of thinking since my return. . . .

Ellie, I want you to make me a promise. Don't show me only your smiles in your letters, but tell me—won't you, my darling?—tell me everything that perplexes you or makes you sad: You told me last week that I looked at sorrow differently from other people and that I knew how to comfort you better than they. Well, then whenever you need comfort about anything, won't you come to me? You can find no better or surer way of making me happy; and you can invent no surer or swifter way of making me miserable than by with-holding your *whole* confidence from a mistaken desire to save me from pain or anxiety. You know it's a compact that henceforth we are to be one in hopes and plans and anxieties and sorrows and joys: that was the meaning of my visit; and I am bent upon keeping you in mind of the fact because I know from experience how hard, how well-nigh impossible it is to throw off your habit of trying to bear all burdens, small and great, *alone*....

The men at the Hopkins seemed to be very glad to see me back... I was missed most, as I expected, by the Glee Club, the remaining first tenor having without me a double burden to carry.... We expect to have our first concert next week... I wish you could hear some of the songs we are to sing.... Here's a specimen of one of them (to be sung to the tune of "I'm a pilgrim and I'm a stranger")

> "I wish I was a hip-po-po-tamus
> And could swim the broad Euphrates and eat grass.
> But oh! I am not; alas! I cannot
> Be a hip-po-po, hip-po-po-tamus
> *Chor.* But I'm a june bug
> And I'm a fire-fly
> I can buzz and bump my head against the wall"

The other stanzas are of a piece with this one, so you can imagine how chastely classical the song is as a whole! Why is it that the mere fact of being connected with a college gives grave gentlemen of almost thirty leave to sing in public songs which, under other circumstances, they would not dream of singing? For my part I rejoice in the chance. The older I get, the more does a boy's spirit seem to possess me and I chafe often, not a little, under the necessity of having to preserve the dignified demeanor of a man....

8 McCulloh St., Balto.,
Md., Feb. 5th, 1884

... You mustn't think, my darling, when I write you playful letters, full of absurd verses and other nonsense, as my last letter was, that I have

forgotten your sorrow. That sorrow is mine scarcely less than yours; but
it is part of my philosophy, my Christian philosophy, as you know, to
endeavor to learn lessons of self-discipline and purification, not lessons
of desolation and unhappiness, from the trials that come not through
my own fault—to follow, if only afar off, the beautiful example of cheerfulness set by your dear grandparents; and though my philosophy is
immensely superior to my practice, I feel that I am not violating its
principles when I sit down to amuse and divert you; for if you will
but smile and be happy, I am sufficiently blessed and can make shift to
be light-hearted myself. You see, the truth of the matter is that happiness consists of living for others—as a great many people have said,
but everyone finds out for himself without a definite trial at manufacturing happiness according to some philosopher's receipt. It's all
stuff to talk about its being self-sacrifice to live for others; it's a positive
luxury—albeit a very innocent and respectable luxury—for it makes
sorrows light and cares easy to bear. Now don't laugh! I know that you
think this the most amusing part of this letter ... because it illustrates
my tendency to talk big generalities—to drive a six-horse team to even
the smallest vehicle of an argument, when what I want to say is plain
and simple enough: that I am happy in your love. ...

I am no more addicted to looking for philosophical principles, however, than is a distinguished Harvard professor who has just left us,
after giving us a couple of lectures, and at whom you could not afford
to laugh as you do at me; though maybe there *is* this difference in the
two cases, that he usually *finds* the principles of which he is in search.
I wish that I could live near Dr. Royce * for a few months. He is one
of the rarest spirits I have met. He is one of those very rare minds which
exists in a perfectly lucid atmosphere of thought, having never a cloud
on its horizon, seeing everything with a clear and unerring vision ...
He has the faculty of bringing masses of detail into a single luminous
picture where they are grouped with a perfection of perspective and a
skill of harmonious arrangement which fills the novice, the would-be
historical painter, with despair. ...

Lew Wallace's *Ben Hur*, written in 1880, had been a best seller
ever since, but Ellen thought it was over-rated. Those who "raved
over it," she remarked, were chiefly "Episcopalians of an impression-

* Professor Josiah Royce.

able type." Woodrow had not read it, but did so now at her request and wrote that he was inclined to agree with her. Mr. Wallace's descriptions of the scenery of Judea "were rather too fine ... being coloured quite beyond the modesty of nature ... excellent examples of strong word-painting such as one would rather read than produce." "We dry fellows," he added, "can but look with amazement on such rhetoric. ... We must not dress our periods in such stately style, but must content ourselves with parading dull facts and talking plain sense." * Yet Mr. Wallace's style must have made him rebel, at least temporarily, against "dull facts and plain sense" for he indulged in some pretty fancy rhetoric himself in another letter to Ellen.

No. 8 McCulloh St., Balto., Md.
March 4th, 1884

My own darling,

I am in a somewhat comical state just now about my work. I have finished the essay upon which I have been at work for the last month and should be about beginning the next essay of the series; but my muse refuses to be forced. She never allows me freedom at the first in any undertaking. She reminds me that the first broadside is half the battle and that it is folly to waste my shot unskillfully at the opening of an action, and so tortures me for days together with debating various plans for the fight. It is my fixed rule to begin with directness, without manoeuvering or ado, and, consequently, I have to devote much care to selecting just the right point of attack in order that the action may become general without loss of time. But this belligerent metaphor isn't quite what I want, because it represents me as battling *against* my subject rather than *for* it, and because it is much too magnificent. One would suppose, from the tones and the tropes in which I speak of my arduous literary labours that I was writing at least an epic, or a system of philosophy, instead of some commonplace remarks upon a familiar subject.

I observe that I am much grander and more impressive when speaking *of* my subject than when speaking *on* it; for, though I have spoken to many of my companions about my work, only one of them understands just what it is. I discovered only a few minutes ago that one of them thought that I was engaged in writing a *history* of the Constitution ... I must talk very big and do very little to have given everybody so exaggerated an idea of the scope of my studies. I am much too young an

* Letter to E.A., Feb. 28, 1884.

eagle to try the long flight they expect to see me take. I am content for the present to explore the native mountains in the immediate neighborhood of the nest, reserving the pleasures of distant explorations to a time of stronger wings and longer pinion. I guess the truth of the matter is that I have spoken so knowingly of several distant peaks, which can barely be descried on a clear morning from the crag just over the next, that my innocent companions have concluded that I must have often been far abroad. I sometimes feel like a hum-bug rather than a royal bird. . . . It must be worth while to be a genuine eagle, born with an eagle's spirit. It's something, in the first place, to begin life on a mountain-top where the eye is not stopped in its view by your neighbor's stupid, square brick house with its chintz curtains at the windows. There's education in a ''bird's-eye'' view. Then, too, it's better to swing in independent flight from top to top than to be all your life flocking and nest-building and chattering with innumerable commonplace little birds in the branches of a tree which is, even at its highest twig, very near the ground after all. The only difficulty is that when you want company there are not eagles enough to make it. It's all well enough to make notable passages over wide continents and see noble stretches of the world, but it's lonely to do it all alone, and after it's done, nobody's the better but yourself. Eagle life is very selfish, as I've heard many an aged eagle confess, with a sigh, because he hadn't had a hand in dropping leaves upon the sleeping babes in the wood. It must be right chilly up in the dizzy crags when one gets old and feels his feathers growing thin! The war-horse that carries his spurred and belted rider to the field no doubt rejoices to smell the battle afar off and runs a short career of glorious excitement: but I suspect that his old age is not blessed with as pleasant and goodly memories as are the last days of some sturdy servant of the plow who can look back over long seasons of golden harvests. And so it is with the eagle . . . He's been a great, mayhap a famous, traveller; but travelling doesn't hasten the millennium. . . .

Ellen wrote to tell him about a lady who had disliked Woodrow Wilson when she had found him calling at the manse in Savannah.

My own darling,

I was infinitely amused by your report of what Mrs. Olmstead had to say about me.... Why, the dear, venomous lady! She hates with a spontaneity worthy of a more generous emotion. I never dreamed that she could be harbouring such feelings when she was saying her courteous adieux that evening. I am quite used to being taken for a minister. There seems to be something about the cut of my jib that leads a great many people to conclude that I am a missionary craft of some sort.... But it was very unreasonable of Mrs. O. to take such a violent dislike to me. It was quite natural that Dr. Axson should be entertaining a young minister and that young minister could not be blamed for falling in love with you.... Mrs. O. does not seem to be a very skillful reader of character. How did she come to believe so firmly, in spite of the ominous apparition of the young minister, that you would "shrink so" from marriage and "all that sort of thing?" This is really the most exquisite part of the joke!...

I am so glad, my darling, that you enjoyed the little volume of Ruskin's lectures which I sent you. Do you like the portrait? I do. It is a face of so much placid power. I have never read much of Ruskin—only enough to know that his wonderful prose has a great fascination for me—but I have read sufficient to enable me to appreciate what you say about the changes which have come since "Modern Painters" was written. I, too had noted the greater gentleness and tolerance of his later judgments. Age has mellowed him—has, too, made him broader and more tolerant in his sympathies. If he could have begun in such a temper, he would have been betrayed into much fewer extravagances....

Unconsciously, you have asked me a hard question when you inquire what I am going to call my series of constitutional studies. An appropriate title—one which is brief and at the same time sufficiently distinctive—is just what I have not yet been able to find. I might call them "Committee Government" since they concern chiefly the way in which Congress controls all branches of the government through its committees, but at least one of the series is to concern the organization and powers of the Executive departments, and such a title would not suggest such a subject. I don't want to bring the word "Constitution" into the title either, because I am describing the system which has grown up *about* the Constitution—a system made out of judicial decisions, statutes and unwritten precedents—rather than the Constitution itself. "The Government of the Union" is the best I have thought of yet, but it is altogether too vague. Maybe I can find the title I want when the series is done and the christening can no longer be postponed.

How Woodrow found time for all his activities is a matter of wonder. There were classes to attend every day, after hours of preparation; many more hours of research for his series of essays and their composition. In the spring there was exhausting "reading up" to be done for the examinations at the close of the term. "I am beset," he told Ellen, "by the worry of having more work to do than there's time to do it in." * Yet he did it, for he knew how to work, prodigiously and with a degree of concentration that was one of his most extraordinary and useful gifts. And he still managed to engage frequently in his favorite pastimes—singing with the Glee Club, long conversations with his friends, evenings at the theatre, writing to his sweetheart, and oratory. He was in great demand as a speaker and sometimes indulged in mild boasting about his successes in his letters to Ellen. She wrote:

Savannah, Georgia
Mar. 13, 1884

... [I] am *very* glad that Mr. Wilson, the critic, was so enthusiastically received. I envy the Hopkins Debating Club—lucky fellows that they are! I am *wild* to hear you speak, perfectly frantic! You wouldn't treat me as Mac † does Rose, would you? She has never heard him preach, though everyone else in Sewanee has. He won't let her....

Woodrow replied:

No. 8 McCulloh St.,
Balto., Md., March 18, 1884

... So you envy the Hopkins Debating Club and are "wild" to hear me speak? But reflect! These young gentlemen don't know what good speaking is. Of course I speak better than most of them do: I've had vastly more

---

* Letter, March 23, 1884.
† Ellen's friends—The Reverend and Mrs. McNaughton Dubose.

practice and have taken pains to train myself; but that is not saying I speak well. Moreover I must disappoint you by telling you that I entirely sympathize with ''Mac'' in being violently opposed to having my sweetheart hear me speak in public. I've frequently felt sorry for young ministers on the special ground that they couldn't in conscience refuse to let their wives go to church and so *must* face the ordeal of preaching before the person whom they love most in the world. I have never yet been persuaded to speak where there was any possibility of my parents hearing me.... You see, ... it's all vanity.... I want you always to be proud of me and I cannot be expected to stand in the way of my own wish by letting you hear me speak.

Of course I don't mean that I intend always to avoid letting you hear me. I mean that I will do nothing to make an occasion for you.... There is, on such occasions a terrible wear and tear on the speaker which I attribute to the fact that he has someone besides himself to carry through the race: that there is a heart beating as intensely as his own for his success. There is absolute joy in facing and conquering, a hostile audience, for example, or in thawing out a cold one, if the speaker feels that the hisses of the one or the critical stare of the other is hurting no-one but himself; while, on the other hand, he finds himself sensitive to all the movements of even the most friendly audience if he knows that there's someone present who cares more than he does when or how much he is applauded. Do you see what I mean? The very intensity of his sympathy with that loved auditor distracts his thoughts! It is as if he were both orator and audience....

Balto., Md., March 25th, 1884
No. 8 McCulloh St.

... Heaviness and formality are qualities which I sedulously seek to avoid in *all* my writings, but I have at hand evidence of the fact that I don't escape them. Sister Marion,* for instance, says in her last letter, after thanking me for the copy of ''Committee or Cabinet Government'' which I had sent her, ''How did you ever attain such a sedate, middle-aged style of composition, brother mine? You write as if further years and longer experience were hardly possible. Your whole *style* expresses the *dignity* of *age*.'' (The underscorings are her own.) Alas! alas! I suppose that my dear sister really thought she was saying nothing but what was

---

* Mrs. Ross Kennedy, Woodrow's elder sister.

altogether complimentary and calculated to gratify the author of the "middle-aged" style. But I am as much shocked as if she had said that mine was the style of the middle ages instead of that of the middle aged. What I am shocked at is, not the fact—for I knew that quite well before—but the *visibility* of the fact to uncritical eyes. The style of that particular article is, I know, more terribly "sedate" and stiff than most of my writing, because there a big subject is packed into a very narrow space: but why should Mrs. Kennedy, a Christian woman, remind me of the fact? You see, when a fellow is ambitious to acquire a crisp, fast-moving, brilliant, hard-hitting style—a way of putting things that will be very delightful to the palates of those who agree with him, but very acid to the taste of those who do not—he can't help wincing a little bit under the treatment of those adjectives "sedate" and "middle-aged?" I like wisdom but I like it *strong;* I like it militant, not mild and owl-eyed. . . .

Our Glee Club is looking forward to two rare disciplinary exercises—disciplinary to the patience of its members. On Thursday evening next we are to sing at "The Two-Hundred-and-fiftieth Anniversary of the Founding of Maryland." There is to be a great deal of tiresome speech-making by tireless speakers and we are to sing that dignified and patriotic, but none the less fatiguing "America" and that other national air, good for the throats of a brass band but not so good for the human voice, "The Star-spangled Banner." We had not a little difficulty in learning the latter, at our rehearsal last night, because four members of the Club ("one of whom I was which") had never heard it before, and it is by no means easy to acquire. . . . The other disciplinary action is to be an entertainment for the benefit of a "free kindergarten" in which a lady elocutionist is to play the principal role and we are expected to lift our voices in her support. What this thing is coming to is beyond human ken to divine. Presently we shall be travelling with the apostles of the "Woman's Christian Temperance Union" and singing at the polls wherever voting is to be done on a "prohibition amendment" to the State Constitution! It is considered the "proper thing" to sing only under some charitable "auspices". . . .

It was the fashion in those days for lovers to exchange locks of hair. The girls wore them in lockets, the men carried them in their wallets. Ellen and Woodrow did not scorn such sentimentality, although they did smile at it. Woodrow wrote:

... About the dark integument enclosed I have several remarks to make. It is not long enough to hang oneself with, but it is quite visible enough to serve as a fair specimen of the head from which it came. Again, on the one hand, it is an astonishingly small product of two months' persistent culture, though it represents locks long enough to get into their unhappy owner's ears and abundant enough to give him a desperately poetical aspect.... But, fortunately the value of this gift depends not on its size, nor upon the mechanical skill with which it was prepared. It has no intrinsic beauty or worth as have the beautiful silken strands you gave me. ...

The news from Savannah was heartbreaking. Edward Axson wanted his daughter with him constantly, yet relapsed into deep melancholy whenever she looked tired. He was afraid that she, too, would break down. There was nothing more important to Ellen than to serve and care for those she loved and, when the doctor told her that, for her father's sake, she must go away for awhile, it was almost more than she could bear. Woodrow realized that she had never needed reassurance as she needed it then.

Baltimore, Md.,
Easter Sabbath, 1884

... You have a very enviable lot in this world, little sweetheart. It is to make other people happy. What would your dear mother have done without your companionship? You were everything to her; and after her death you were all in all to your dear father—are so still—his comfort and his pride, his brave, loving, sunny-tempered Christian daughter. Not many people, my darling, have brightened the lives of those about them as you have. As for me! You have given me everything—your love—and have made me happier than in all my happy life I ever dreamed of being....

Try, my darling, to think of the possibilities of your father's case as little as you can. "Take no anxious thought for the morrow." Let us try to make our trust in God a real trust that will enable us to look forward without fear, in full confidence of ourselves one day seeing the mercy and the wisdom of the present dispensation. When there is anything to be done it is a *sin* to be passive; but when there is something to be endured, it is a duty for us to compel our hearts to be still in the presence of the doings of the Almighty. I hope for the best in this matter—I think that there is reason to expect an eventual recovery—but if hope is to be excluded in the end, let us pray God to give us strength and faith sufficient for that day. . . .

Ellen and Woodrow had been counting the days until Johns Hopkins closed for the summer at the end of May, for he had planned to spend the first week of his vacation in Savannah. What would they do now? Woodrow could not follow Ellen to the homes of the friends she planned to visit, because their engagement was still a secret. His spirits, always mercurial, were very low. Then his mother had an idea that sent them soaring again. He was going to spend the summer at home in Wilmington, North Carolina, and she would ask Ellen to come there for a long visit. Ellen was delighted with this plan, but after days of mysterious evasions, she wrote that she could not go. They had, it appeared, come up against an old-fashioned Southern idea of propriety. Woodrow protested:

> *8 McCulloh St.*
> *Balto., Md., April 11th, 1884*

That was a strangely sweet letter I received this morning, my darling, and yet it has left me in low spirits. . . . I have been reiterating the invitation of late for the purpose of calling forth your reason for not wanting to go and, now that the reason has been given, I am as much in the dark as ever. I find it hard to believe that your Grandmother and Aunt could regard your visiting my home as *improper*. Dear mother would be considerably surprised to learn that a plan which originated with her was so thought of. I am sure such visits are usually considered not only proper but *customary*. . . .

Yet, knowing that Ellen would not think of defying her grandmother, he let the matter drop and sent her long dissertations on the subjects which interested her most—Woodrow Wilson's opinions, ambitions and philosophy.

Balto., Md., April 20th, 1884

My own darling,

There are some orators in the world after all. I had heard one or two, but so long ago, and with so many disappointments intervening, that I had almost lost faith in the existence of such beings. I used to long to hear some man whom I would, because I must, recognize as an orator; I anticipated the coming of such a man as a revelation of power. I heard a man once, a man renowned for eloquence—so renowned that John Bright called our noble English language *his* language and Chatham's—and my heart almost stood still as my attention tip-toed to catch the first glimpse of his power: a tall, stately man who trod the stage with straightened figure and erect head like one conscious of a right to command men. His voice, too, when first it reached the ear, satisfied because of its full sonorous quality, its strength, its melody. But it never woke; it never left its first easy, leisurely pace; it lingered, finally it *droned*. What could be the matter? Had the man no life: did he always tire with that ponderous, monotonous cadence? Had his voice always that dull rebound when it struck the shallow bottom of that sluggish tone? No: he was repeating a memorized lecture, and so was a mere automaton, and not actor or poet enough to be kindled by old, familiar, oft told sentiments. What a mistake—what a suicidal mistake! Did he not know that the only fire which is the fire of true oratory is the fire of the orator's own *life?* Unless he gives his audience of himself, unless the audience now and again catch sight of the native, unartificial fires which burn in his heart, his finest phrases will fall cold and dead. What kindles an audience is no such enigmatical thing as "personal magnetism," though it is something quite as mysterious, perhaps: it is contact with the orator's inmost life—with his very soul. They have seen and touched his spirit, they have for the moment partaken of his power. His heart has gone into theirs, and the life of their sympathy has entered into him.

It is such thoughts as these, my little sweetheart, which dash my amusement with sadness when you declare your desire to hear *me* speak. I shrink from it most of all because of my unwillingness to have you so sorely disappointed as you will be: for not until I have rid myself of the accursed bonds of *self-consciousness* can I be an orator. Imagine a true poet self-conscious while writing his divinest verse, or a true painter self-

conscious while painting.... Oratory has much in common with poetry
and painting. The one thing that mars Thackeray, it seems to me, is his
self-consciousness. Self-consciousness is restraint: it shuts in the native
forces and makes of the would-be orator at best only an actor.

But why am I filling my letter with these commonplace reflections—
what brought on this attack, do you say? Why nothing, except that I have
again heard Dr. Duryea, the conjurer who used to conjure with my spirit
when I was a boy at Princeton and who is one of the true orators of the
pulpit....

I have been suffering my one-time delight in baseball—which was my
chief solace ten or twelve years ago—to draw me out as a witness to the
splendid games which one can see here at this season between the "crack,"
professional nines of the country; one witnessed yesterday afternoon. Just
before dinner my friend, Dr. Woods,* met me on the street, and, after
inspecting me critically, lectured me for "working myself to death," declaring that I looked about to break down, if I was not sick already: and
so carried me off *vi et armis* to dinner, and after dinner to a ball game.
His brother and sister and a young lady who is visiting the latter went
with us, so that we had a jolly time. I like good company as much as I
enjoy a good game of base-ball, and having both, I was immensely content,
so to speak, though it was marvellously like wasting time, considering all
I have to do before the close of the term....

Baseball and good company gave Woodrow the relaxation he needed,
but singing with the Glee Club brought out the boyish high spirits which
he usually—and reluctantly—tried to control. After the Club's last
concert he wrote:

Balto., Md., April 27th, 1884

... You will probably hear with deep regret that the great Johns Hopkins
University Glee Club met last evening to disband for the season: though
it will doubtless comfort you to know that the last act of its life was an
act of benevolence. One week ago it sang in the Methodist Church at Woodberry (a thriving suburb of Balto.) for the benefit of the "Woodberry
Workingmen's Library and Reading Room".... The "classical" pieces,
and even the milder sort of college songs, did not rouse much enthusiasm,

---

* Dr. Hiram Woods of Baltimore, Wilson's classmate at Princeton.

it is true; but the "three kittens" and the "Hip-po-pot-a-mus" went straight to their hearts, and will long be of sweet savour in their memories. After the concert we were treated to a very nice supper and came back to town in our four-horse "bus" in such high and musical humour that we doubtless made many peaceful citizens turn uneasily in their beds, as we went roaring and rattling thro' the quiet streets. . . .

A few days before this riotous evening he had written to Ellen enclosing a long quotation from one of his favorite poems.

Balto., April 22nd, 1884

I have copied for your delectation a few passages from Swinburne's "Tristram of Lyonesse". . . . I have been putting this wonderful verse to the use which I generally make poetry serve in my mental economy: to prepare me for composition. I had a speech to make the other night on the Blair Educational Bill, which Dr. Adams insisted upon having discussed and so I read Swinburne. From Shakspere, or from any finely figurative writing, I get a stimulus for extemporaneous expression, with either my tongue or my pen, such as I can get in no other way. It sets my mind aglow, seeming to make it nimble and strong, with a joyous strength fit for doing at its best any work it is capable of doing at all. But, for the matter of that, I think that the proper office of all books—even those dreary compendia which supply one with the innumerable facts of life and science—is to stimulate the mind. The man who reads everything is like the man who eats everything: he can digest nothing and the penalty for cramming one's mind with other men's thoughts is to have no thoughts of one's own. Only that which enables one to do his own thinking is of real value: which is my explanation for the fact that there are to be found in history so many great thinkers and leaders who did little reading of books—if you reckon reading by volumes—but much reading of men and their own times. "A little learning is a dangerous thing," but so is too much learning, also. Reason and understanding are the only things one cannot have too much of.

I have had a letter from sister Marion, in which she asks what I would think of a chair in the Arkansas University. Of course, I can't say until I hear more of the *character* of the chair, which she *thinks* might just at this time be procured for her interesting brother; but I shall write for

further particulars. What would my darling think of a home amidst the
pretty mountain lands of upper Arkansas?...

It sounded casual, this reference to his sister's letter, but he was, in
fact, excited by it. His father wanted him to return to Johns Hopkins for
another year because one was not, in the Reverend Joseph Wilson's
opinion, enough to prepare his son for the distinguished career he intended him to have. But the thought of having to wait another year to
be married was becoming more and more unbearable. He wanted a
job. He wanted it right away, and here was a chance to get one.

Part 3
The Search for a Position

"Sister Marion" and her husband, Ross Kennedy, lived in Little Rock, Arkansas. Ross had friends on the Board of Trustees of the State University and had boasted about his talented brother-in-law. Woodrow would, naturally, have preferred a position in one of the top-ranking Eastern universities, but anything would be better than putting off his marriage. When Marion's second letter came he wrote at length to Ellen, for he would not make any decision without her approval.

Balto., Md., May 1st, 1884

My own darling,

I must say that my sweet little lady-love is the most tantalizing young woman of my acquaintance. I ask her what she would think of the mountain lands of upper Arkansas as a home—for *herself* of course—and she replies: "I should think *you* would find the lands of upper Arkansas a very pleasant home!" Am I to understand then, Miss, that you have no personal interest in the matter, but intend to marry me without binding yourself to live with me? I had supposed, in my innocence, that in choosing a home for myself I should be choosing a home for you, and so turned to you to learn what you would think of going away beyond the Mississippi, far from both your home and mine: but, if I am not to have your companionship, I am quite indifferent as to what sort of place I go to!

There's not much to tell about the Arkansas institution:... It is called "Industrial" because its chief endowment consists of a large quantity of land granted that State by Congress, as other public lands were granted other states, for the partial endowment of mechanical and industrial schools.... Like the University of California..., the Arkansas institution is *co-educational*, admitting women to its classes as well as to its faculty.

Of course not all of the features are agreeable to my tastes; but the

63

same features are common to all of the new and most of the old colleges below the very first rank ... and one must face the fact that it is impossible, as it is undesirable, to start at the top, in just such a berth as one could wish for. Such places have to be won from the foot-hold of places lower down: and even any foot-hold is extremely hard to find; for very few colleges care as yet as much as they should for good teachers of history and political economy ... and a good offer is not to be despised wheresoever it comes. The offer from the Arkansas University *is* a good one for a beginner in the professorial field, though it is by no means superlative. Sister Marion says, "The salary is $1700 a year." ...

The probability ... of there being a vacancy for me arises from the fact that the President of the University has just resigned and an entire reorganization of the faculty is expected, in consequence, before the opening in the Autumn. ...

In short, taking the circumstances all together, as far as I have learned them, the opportunity seems as favorable as any other that is likely to offer, and my only desire now is to learn what my darling thinks of the case. ...

If the vacancy expected should occur, brother Ross seems quite sure of his ability to secure it for me; and, if the chair be given me, I should doubtless be expected to enter upon its duties next September. That would, of course, break in upon the plans which I have so far had, but no great harm would result. A man learns best what he is under the immediate necessity of teaching, of making his own in order that he may impart it fresh to others ... I should not mind how long I had to study here and wait for "something to turn up," were it not for a simple circumstance, which is that *I want you*—with a longing whose intensity seems like to break my heart. ...

Desperately anxious for her approval, he did not wait to hear from Ellen before writing again.

Balto., May 4th, 1884

... I hope that my darling will not answer hastily. ... Of course this Arkansas matter is as yet wholly "in the air"; it may, and possibly will, come to nothing, and I have suspected since I wrote you last Thursday, that I was hardly justified in troubling you by building on so slim a foundation the request that you would decide, conditionally at least, so grave a matter. My inclination now is to beg that you will withhold your reply until I see you in vacation : for you can hardly know ... how much depends upon that reply. The first year of my work in a professorship will be the critical year : and the conditions of that work are within your control. . . . The first year will be the most trying because I will have to pass it among strangers, who, besides receiving me without sympathy, will watch me, as a youth and a novice charged with important duties, with constant criticism : it will be the season when my situation, my standing, will be altogether *a-making* ... I long to have the support of your love and companionship from the very start. They would be simply *invaluable* to me, saving the *wear* and *tear* of the trial. Now, I know that my darling loves me well enough to interpose no objections on her own account, but does she think that her duties to others stand in her way ? You know, don't you, ... that our marriage wouldn't at all change your relations to Eddie, if you should want still to keep him with you.

But enough of this for the present ! I wanted only to give you plenty of time to think about it ... I am quite willing to trust all your heart's dictates. . . .

Ellen's level head did not approve of his going to Arkansas University, because she thought it the wrong environment for a writer of history and political science. But her heart could not resist his pathetic eagerness. She told him that if he liked the Arkansas plan, she did too, although the final decision, as far as their marriage was concerned, must depend upon her father's health.

Balto., May 8th, 1884

... Of course it goes without saying, my darling, that I had not forgotten your dear father in sketching possible plans : *everything* must depend upon his condition ; my whole object was to prepare you for what I *might* be in a position to do, provided it were at all possible. . . . As for your brothers—"your boys"—my darling, it is part of my strongest purpose and dearest hope to stand in your place towards them as regards money matters—to espouse your duties as well as your sweet self. . . . The only thing, therefore, for us to think of after I shall have obtained a place with adequate salary will be your dear father's condition: nothing else shall stand in the way of that union which will perfect our happiness and so add to our usefulness. . . .

I think it very probable, dearest, that your father, were he consulted in the matter, would wish our marriage to come as soon as possible, knowing, of course that it would in no way take you away from the boys, but would only add to your life someone who would love them and care for them to the full extent of his ability, as if they were his own brothers by blood; for that was just the interpretation I put upon a passage in one of his letters which you sent me. In language that touched and gratified me he expressed his thankfulness for the fact that . . . he could safely commit you to my love and care. . . . You can imagine, therefore, my precious one, how anxiously I await the issue of this Arkansas affair. . . .

"I am quite certain," Woodrow had told Ellen,* "that at my birth no poet was born." Two days before her twenty-fourth birthday he proved this conclusively. He wrote fifteen verses in praise of his lady-love, entitled, "To E.L.A. on Her Birthday," of which the first verse is a sample:

> I cannot tell, my lady fair,
> What thine own thoughts may be,
> When that thou comest once again
> Thy natal day to see.

Before he mailed his verses a disturbing letter arrived from Ellen. She had been struggling for some time with her conscience and had lost the struggle. Her grandparents were carrying a large share of the expenses of their son and his family and it was her duty, she felt, to relieve the situation a little by earning a living. She might also be able to save part of what she earned so that, when she and Woodrow were married and her brothers came to live with them, she would not have to depend entirely on his "noble" offer to support them. She had, therefore, applied for a position as art teacher at a school in Augusta, Georgia. Woodrow was miserable.

Balto., Md., May 13th, 1884

My own darling,

I had completed a birthday letter to you, in rhymed and metrical prose, before your letter reached me this morning (you will probably be as

---

* Letter of October 30, 1883.

puzzled at I am to decide what induced me to adopt the *form* of poetry.
I can only say that my mood was poetical, though it did not produce in
kind) ; but the contents of your letter demand an immediate reply. . . .

I must confess . . . that your letter has given me a terrible case of the
"blues." It almost breaks my heart to think that there is not now at hand
any means of preventing the consummation of an arrangement which will
take my darling away from her friends to enter upon trials such as she
dreams not of, and such as it should be my duty to relieve her from. And,
though I dare not stand in the way of what she deems her duty, this thing
shall not be done if I can prevent it. My darling, listen! You must promise
me that you will take no final step (such as the definite *acceptance* of a
position—no application is final) in the matter *for one week from this
date—before,* i.e., *the 20th of May* for my sake, my darling, sacrifice everything but a last or an only chance, rather than do anything final before
that date!

. . . That's rather an odd philosophy of yours . . . that whatever comes
of this will be *"right";* it is almost too near to saying that "whatever is
is right", which is very far from being true. I have full faith in the right
ordering of Providence ; but we cannot be too careful in seeing that we
do our duty, not only, but that we do it *in the wisest way.* A false step on
our part would not be right because it belonged to the fore-ordained order
of events. . . .

Ellen agreed to wait, but three days before the deadline he released
her from her promise :

Balto., Md., May 17th, 1884

. . . My somewhat mysterious insistence upon delay till the 20th must have
puzzled you not a little and I ought to explain at once. . . . This is the whole
of the mystery, my darling. I was in hopes that certain letters I was expecting would contain more definite news than I have yet had about the
progress of my schemes for a settlement next year, and that I could ask
you to forego your own projects for something more definite than an "if."
But, alas, I have learned nothing more than I knew before and can no
longer plead for any delay. This last manoeuvre of a wilful man bent upon
having his own way has proved a dismal failure : and, if the fuss he has
made about it and the interruptions of plans it may have cost have not

distressed my darling, no harm has been done. You see, if you *will* go and engage yourself to an intense individual who takes everything to heart too deeply, you must nerve yourself to abide many extraordinary vagaries with patient allowance until you can take him in hand and teach him more moderate ways.

... I dread seeing you undertake a teacher's duties because I know quite enough of the conditions of such a situation as you seek to wish most earnestly to keep my darling from its wearing, harassing trials.... Besides ... I have some ambitions stored away in odd corners of my heart. I have never yet been of any use to anyone: I have yet to become a bread winner; and I should find unspeakable delight in taking upon my shoulders the burdens you have to carry. The reward would be two-fold. It would, in the first place be *yourself*—and you can't form an approximate guess as to how much that means to me—and, in the second place, the novel indulgence of affording aid to those near and dear to me. I am quite willing that you should think the proposition a ''noble'' one—I confess myself quite ready to tolerate the very nicest things you can think of me—and I can't object to your calling me ''rashly generous'' for I have stoutly determined to let you call me what names you will—but I must insist upon being allowed to think of it as just what it is, a self-indulgent purpose from which I will not be retarded by such names as ''Atlas'' and the like. Your Aunt Ella never said a truer thing than that ''you can't expect people to wait until Eddie is grown and married''—at least, if *I* am the ''people'' she had in mind. ...

His last letter to Ellen, before he left Baltimore for his summer vacation, cleared up a misunderstanding.

Balto., Md., May 25th, 1884

... Do you really think, my precious ... that I was trying to persuade you that all things do *not* work together for good? I would as soon try to persuade you that there is no God. I meant only that your little piece of philosophy, as you put it in one of your letters, would justify one in letting things drift, in the assurance that they would drift to a happy result. I was simply expressing, too awkwardly, no doubt, my idea of *how* all things work together for good—through the careful performance of our duty. ...

Two days later at the manse in Wilmington, he had what he called "a solid loaf" before going to work on the last of his essays. He was tired and very glad to be home. His was a devoted and passionately loyal family, and home to this sensitive young man was a small citadel of peace and harmony. Loneliness, introspection, self-distrust and despondency—his familiar demons—never tormented him there.

His sisters, Marion and Annie, were both married, but his parents and young Joseph, the brother who was ten years younger than Woodrow, welcomed him like a returning hero. Doctor Joseph Wilson, handsome, powerfully built, with a thick shock of hair and piercing brown eyes was, Woodrow believed, the wisest and most stimulating man in the world as well as the most lovable. And Joseph returned his love and admiration in full measure.

"You deserve the place which you occupy in the house of my soul," he wrote in 1889, "and even a bigger place were it a bigger soul. How I have enjoyed the presence of that dear son whose love I trust so implicitly and in the wealth of whose gem-furnished mind I so delight!"

Jessie Woodrow Wilson, from whom her elder son inherited his gray eyes and his shyness, was his ideal of what a mother should be. "She was one of the most remarkable persons I have ever known," he wrote to a friend * many years after her death. "She was so reserved that only those of her own household can have known how lovable she was, though every friend knew how loyal and steadfast she was. I seem to feel still the touch of her hand, and the sweet steadying influence of her wonderful character. I thank God for such a mother!"

On the day he left Baltimore the president of Johns Hopkins University, Dr. Gilman, had told Woodrow that he had won a fellowship for his second-year term. This was considered a high honour, but Woodrow was in no mood to rejoice. He wanted a job. What good were honours if they did not make an early marriage possible? He wrote to tell Ellen about it and added:

Wilmington, N.C., May 28, 1884

... A fellowship carries with it a stipend of $500.00, besides various valuable privileges and the twenty fellowships given in the several departments (there are two in ours) are competed for very sharply every year, not only by the best men in the University but even by honour-men of the German universities; so they are regarded as the great prizes. I have the additional satisfaction of knowing that I was picked out by both the faculty and the students of our Seminary as having full title to the ap-

* Rev. Wm. J. Hampton, Sept. 13, 1917.

pointment. . . . Complete success, such as I have had at the Hopkins, has
the odd effect upon me of humiliating me rather than exalting me: for I
can't help knowing how much less worthy and capable I am than I am
thought to be. I am not so clever at deceiving myself as I am at deceiving
college companions and Roman girls. . . . It's satisfactory to have a fellowship awaiting one if a professorship be not offered or desired. . . .

On the twenty-ninth of May, Edward Axson died. When the news
reached Woodrow in a letter from Ellen's cousin, Mary Hoyt, he wrote
at once.

Wilmington, N.C., June 1st, 1884

Oh, my precious Ellie, my poor stricken darling! how shall I tell you the
things that are in my heart today. Miss Hoyt's note . . . came this morning,
and ever since it came, my heart has been aching as if it would break—
not for *him,* my darling: for surely it was a blessed, gracious relief from
the sorrows of his condition; but for you, and for Stockton and Eddie. The
very fact that you did not write to me yourself, but got your cousin to
write for you, indicates, in a way that frightens me, the effect the news,
coming, as it did, so suddenly and without warning, must have had on you.
Try to bear up, my darling. Remember how many there are left who love
you and to whom your love is all in all. Your dear father, however sad or
tragic his death may have been, is happy now. His Saviour, we may be
sure, did not desert his servant at the supreme moment; and it is a joy to
think that he is now reunited to the sweet noble woman who went before
him . . . and as for us, have we not each other—have we not, above all
things else, the blessed privilege of living for the service of God, in a glad
performance of duty? Oh, my darling! I love you, and my heart is almost
broken at the thought of your unspeakable sorrow. . . .

I am ready to come at once if you want me and think it wise and best
that I should come. I long to come, but will wait to learn your wish: for
I want to come for your comfort, not for my own indulgence. . . .

It was characteristic of Ellen Axson to write that she wanted him to
come only if it did not interfere with his work. Woodrow assured her
that it would not, and left the next day for Rome, where Edward Axson was to be buried. He stayed there for two weeks after the funeral
and told her, one day, that he wanted his own private name for her.

He had been thinking about it for a long time and had finally chosen "Eileen." There was Irish, as well as Scottish, blood in his veins.

When he went back to Wilmington, Ellen found forgetfulness in hard work. Her father's furniture and books had been left in the parsonage in Rome, but now they must be packed and stored until she and her brothers could use them. Trying hard to be cheerful, she wrote:

Rome, Georgia, June 28th, 1884

... I have had such a week of it that writing to you seemed, like all the other pleasures of life, "a thing to dream of, not to do;—something forever out of reach".... Such a task as it is! And the books are the worst of all. I didn't suppose that anything could make the sight of books so hateful to me. I feel rather spiteful in thinking of the authors! They might have been better employed. I am even inclined to think that—say—three volumes would contain all that was worth saying in the whole lot. But such experiences teach one several useful lessons,—among others the undesirableness of riches—of dragging about with one too much "impedimenta"—in short of playing, in the journey of life the part of the laden donkey, whose own share in his burden is only a cabbage leaf, or so, to satisfy the need of the moment. I am convinced that I have too many "things" entirely....

I was very glad to know that you had a pleasant journey and that you hadn't "the blues." That's right, and I shall try to follow your good example. Indeed, I don't think that any thought of *you*—even the thought that you are not here—has power to give me the blues. I am too glad that you are *somewhere!*

The joy it gives me to love and to be loved by you is too deep and entire to be affected *beyond measure* by accidents of time and place. And yet I do miss you so much—more than I ever did before. "What shall I do with all the days and hours that must be counted ere I see thy face?" Don't you think I am unreasonable to begin thinking already about the next time? It certainly isn't because thoughts of the last time have been exhausted, or have lost their charm. But perhaps I am a little like certain children I know, who, about a week after Xmas begin to lament that they must start their calculations all over again—that they can no longer say it is one, or a dozen, days away, but three hundred and sixty! They find the pleasures of anticipation at a discount. But, for all that, your visit,

dear love, made me happy. If it "did good" to you, what do you suppose
it did for me whose need was so much greater?...

For some months a controversy had been raging in the Southern
Presbyterian Church. Woodrow's uncle, James Woodrow, had gone to
Harvard in 1853. He had studied under Louis Agassiz, become fascinated
by Darwin's *Origin of Species,* and had gone to Heidelberg for further
scientific studies. Heidelberg gave him his doctor's degree, *summa cum
laude,* and since 1861 he had been famous in the South as the most brilliant and popular professor on the faculty of the Presbyterian Theologi-
cal Seminary at Columbia, South Carolina. He taught science and,
because he had a passion for truth as he saw it, dared, finally, to teach
the doctrine of evolution. He maintained that evolution was "God's plan
of creation," which, to orthodox Presbyterians, was nothing less than
heresy. The storm was slow in its approach, but when it broke, it almost
tore the church apart.

His nephew, very like him in many ways, was fiercely on Professor
Woodrow's side. He wrote to Ellen in great indignation:

Wilmington, N.C., June 26th, 1884

My own darling,

The attack on uncle James Woodrow which I predicted has begun.... It
must be reckoned wicked to bring upon God's church such reproach of
spite and bigotry....

If Uncle J. is to be read out of the Seminary, Dr. McCosh * ought
to be driven out of the church, and all private members like myself ought
to withdraw without waiting for the expulsion which should follow belief
in evolution. If the brethren of the Mississippi Valley have so precarious
a hold upon their faith in God that they are afraid to have their sons hear
aught of modern scientific belief, by all means let them drive Dr. Woodrow to the wall....

Ellen had told him, in Rome, that she had been offered employment
as an art teacher and would have to accept. But Ross Kennedy wrote
that there was still hope that Woodrow would receive an offer from
Arkansas before the end of summer, and again he begged her to wait.
Ellen, however, had become convinced that he should have another year
at Johns Hopkins. It was essential to his career, she insisted, and surely
they could wait one more year to be married. They were still young and

* Dr. James McCosh, president of Princeton. An enlightened and original scholar.

certain of each other's love. And she would enjoy teaching painting. Besides, what was so terrible about a girl earning her own living? Woodrow thought it was very terrible, so she promised to wait a little longer. Then, a few days after he returned to Wilmington his hope was permanently shattered.

Wilmington, June 29th, 1884

My own darling,

The question as between Arkansas and Baltimore has been decided for me. . . . The Board of Trustees decided *not to reorganize* the faculty: so that I did not even become a candidate. There was nothing to become a candidate for; and the whole scheme is as though it had not been. This news came to me this morning and I had to sit down at once, with as good grace as I could assume, and write to dear President Gilman that I would accept the fellowship and pay my respects to him in due season at the opening of the next semester of the "greatest Educational Show on Earth."

And now; . . . are you satisfied? For my part, I am deeply disappointed, because I firmly believe that the sooner I get to work in the faculty of some comparatively small college, with my darling for my help-meet and loving companion, the sooner I shall reach usefulness and achieve the highest success. . . . The indefinite postponement of our marriage is, for me, the greatest element of disappointment. It seems to me that I can wait for anything more patiently than for that! I am not talking mere lover's sentiment when I say that my life, and consequently my success, is bound up in you, and that I cannot live or work at my best until I have, not your love only, but yourself, your companionship, as well. I have never had a more earnest conviction than this. . . .

I have a request to urge, Eileen, my precious darling: believe me, all my heart is in it, and I make it, therefore, without any apology for returning to a matter about which you have already expressed what would seem to be a final judgment and decision. I could not beg even a friend with such persistent reiteration, but I can beg *you* . . . to reconsider your refusal to visit Wilmington. . . . There is nothing here, dearest, from which your bashfulness need shrink; nothing but love and love's consideration: and I think that you would face a great deal more than a transient embarrassment for my sake. . . . We have set our hearts on having you come to us. Can you refuse? . . .

But obedient Ellen still refused to go to Wilmington without her grandmother's permission. Then Mrs. Wilson, as stubborn as her son when she set her heart on anything, wrote to Mrs. Axson and the old lady relented. The wife of a minister knew, apparently, just what to say to a minister's wife.

Wilmington, July 13th, 1884

My sweet Eileen,

Hurrah! I knew Mrs. Axson, after all, better than you did, my darling. You may imagine the delight with which I heard dear mother read the enclosed! I went down to the P.O. to mail the letter to my sweetheart which I finished about half an hour ago, and brought from the office this delightful note from Mrs. Axson, in which the dear lady actually expresses the wish that you should visit us! My darling, I can't tell you how happy this has made me because ... it assures us of having you with us during propitious September. What strides I can take to-morrow in essay "No. 4!" How impossible it will be for headaches to come or for appetite to go: For Sept. is coming! My darling, I am not only glad but thankful.... You will give us a generous portion, if not all, of Sept., won't you? The time will be gold to me and its length will measure my preparation for successful work next year!...

His spirits rose another notch when Ellen wrote that she did not have to earn a living after all. Her father had left her and his other children enough money to live on, very modestly. Her elder brother, Stockton, was going to college, young Edward would stay with relatives, and Ellen had decided to do what she had dreamed about for years— study at the Art Students' League in New York. Woodrow was a little worried when he thought of a young and pretty girl, quite unaware of the wickedness of the world, living alone in the big city. But he knew that it was no use arguing with Ellen and rejoiced with her in the fact that New York was only a few hours, by train, from Baltimore.

He tried to work on his essays—No. 4, "The Senate," and No. 5, "The Executive"—but what with helping his father with the minutes' he was preparing for the next meeting of the Presbyterian Assembly, daily "buggy-rides" with his mother and long letters to Ellen, he made very slow progress. He also found it hard to concentrate because Ellen did not write as often as he did.

... So you ''can't take it in'' that *your* letters *could* ''make such a difference to anyone,'' can't realize that anybody's life stops for want of
a letter from you and want to know if you're ''*really* to believe'' that my
not hearing has such an effect upon my spirits? Well, you *are* a little
goose, a very desirable and surpassingly lovable little goose, with whom
one would wish to live all his life, but a goose for all that, about some
things. *In primis*, about *yourself*, not to know how much you are to
some people, and notably to a particular person not necessary to mention.
The simple truth, Miss, in my case, is that if the intervals between your
letters be long—and how long a few days seem now!—or if a letter confidently expected at a particular time is in the least bit delayed, everything in my arrangements gets off its hinges: I can't write a single
sentence about the Senate, can't be decently sure of an appetite—am a
nuisance to myself, and doubtless to everybody about me....

There was another reason for his lack of concentration. Grover
Cleveland and James G. Blaine were engaged that year in a dramatic
struggle for the Presidency and, after sixteen years of Republican ad-
ministrations, Woodrow believed that the American people were ready
for a change. It was not easy for a man who had longed, ever since he was
a boy, to be an orator and to go into politics, to sit quietly writing political
essays while other more fortunate men expressed their opinions on public
platforms. There was an evening when he pushed his calligraph aside
and went to a mass meeting where fire-works competed with a thunder-
storm and the Governor of North Carolina made a speech. Afterwards
he went home and wrote to Ellen.

... Barring interruptions made at my elbow by some silly girls who were
conspicuously out of place in such a crowd, not only because of its nature
but also because of their desperate ignorance of the matters the speakers
were talking about, I enjoyed the speech-making and the scene to the
top of my bent. Gov. Jarvis, who made the principal address of the
evening, was admirable. I had expected a good deal of him; but I received more than I had expected. In the first place he *looked* like a man,
which is almost half the battle with a public speaker; in the second place,
he had the *voice* of a man, full, round and sonorous; and in the third

place, he spoke the words of a man, earnest, moderate, eminently sensible. The principle draw-back was the audience, which was big and dull.... It cheered the name of Gov. Cleveland, but let the great principles which his name represents pass without any show of cordial greeting.... Governor Jarvis therefore deserved the greater credit for preferring to dwell on arguments which were worthy to be applauded rather than on sentiments which were sure of applause.... He is not an orator, but he seemed to me to illustrate the advantages which the powerful speaker, even if he be without unusual talents, must always possess over the forceful editor, even if the latter be endowed with genius. The well-commanded voice, the manly bearing, the earnest manner of a capable speaker trick men into listening with pleasure ... to things which they would not think of reading in print, even though they could read them in half the time. Those people who talk about the press having superseded oratory simply shut their eyes to the plain evidences to the contrary exhibited in all parts of the world.... I never yet read a great speech without regretting that I had not heard it.... I have read nearly all the published speeches of John Bright ... but does that compensate me for never having been within sound of the voice of the greatest of living English orators? But hold on, my dear Woodrow! All this argument you are rushing into may be very good, but it is altogether gratuitous. There's nobody on the other side.... Let's have a little peace and quiet in a letter!...

At the end of a long letter devoted entirely to telling Ellen how much he loved her, Woodrow wrote:

Wilmington, Aug. 26, 1884

... In looking over this letter, I am constrained to recognize the fact that it is really scandalous. You have enough love talked to you to spoil all the least spoilable girls in a kingdom! My next letter shall be all about the stupidest news of the town, about parties and fires, political meetings and baseball games, market prices and novelties in ship-rigging. Or else it shall be redolent with all the most pungent thoughts of certain (would be) famous essays now in progress. Look for it with fear and trembling!...

He tried, in his next letter, to keep his promise by describing a writer's frustration in a small Southern city in 1884, reminding himself of it, regretfully, after four pages of "love-making":

Wilmington, August 31st, 1884

... I've been forgetting the post-scriptural promise of my last letter! And yet, maybe it would be heartless to write you a proxy epistle, full of dull news and commonplace comment upon it, such as I write to those correspondents ... whom I will not permit to know me except in my company garb, set down to entertain a guest, strenuous in insisting upon topics of passing interest—even joining Gordon in the Soudan rather than let the conversation flag—but never vouchsafing more than a glimpse of the thoughts and impulses and affections which are part and parcel of myself, and so sacred, not because they are great and rare, but because they are private, personal. . . .

Then, too, the specifications of that promise were ill-advised ... I write from a *Post Office*—rather than from a *place* bearing description. . . . There is not enough striking individuality about the people in Wilmington to furnish picturesque material. Too many are like my friend, the book-seller, and my five-minute acquaintance, the librarian. The other day I wanted to verify my recollection of a passage in Buckle and I went down to the book-store to see if I could find there a copy of the "History." Mr. H., the book-seller, had never heard either of the book or of its author's name. He insisted upon calling poor Henry "Bockle," and wished to know if his book had appeared recently! I left him abruptly, lest I should too plainly betray my inordinate admiration for him, and went up to the public library to search there for the work, or for any traces of a knowledge of it. The handsome young damsel in charge there heard my inquiries with a smile of ill-concealed incredulity as to the existence of any such work—much as if I had asked for "Snooks on the Moon-Beam." They had, she said, no history of civilization but Guiz*otte*'s (so she persisted in pronouncing the honoured name of poor dead M. Guizot). It was like being told that the library contained no work of *art* save a history of idol-worship, and that, so far as was known to my informant, that was the only work upon art extant! Of course not all Wilmingtonians are like this hardened book-seller and that unhappy

girl. Like every town of its size it has its proportion of culture and
scholarship. . . .

Ellen made a great hit with the Wilson family when, in September,
she came to Wilmington. "I am so glad that she came to us," Jessie Wilson wrote afterwards to her son, "for now I am *sure* you will be happy
in each other. She is very lovely—so intelligent and in every way attractive." Unsentimental Joseph went overboard—"That dear Ellie,"
he wrote, "whom we both love paternally and maternally." *

At the end of September Ellen went to New York and found, after
days of searching, a room in a boarding house on West 11th Street which
suited her. The rent was low, the landlady a Southerner, and the other
boarders eminently respectable. She went happily to work at the Art
Students' League, and every Sunday to a Presbyterian church, called
"The Broadway Tabernacle." The minister had been highly recom-
mended by Woodrow's father. An acquaintance at Ellen's boarding
house had made a suggestion in regard to her choice of a church which
shocked her. Woodrow wrote approvingly:

Balto., Md., Oct. 13th, 1884

. . . I don't wonder that you object to Miss Lester's proposed Sunday
plan of sampling all the churches in the city. That would not only be
very unsatisfactory, but, it seems to me, would also be more like sight-
seeing and diversion than like worship. . . .

He had found when he returned to Baltimore that his classes had
all been "bunched in the middle of the week," which gave him time
to get his essays in shape as a book which he had finally decided to call
Congressional Government. He then composed "a letter of consummate
tact (!) to the publishers to whom it (the MSS) is to go first" † and
tried not to be too hopeful that they would accept it. In the meanwhile
he read the essays, by request, to his fellow-students at Johns Hopkins.

Bluntschli Library, Oct. 17th, 1884

. . . I am to read the third of my Essays at the Seminary tonight—"to
set a high standard of work for the new men," says Dr. Adams' ‡
blarney—it is the one, you remember, on "Revenue and Supply," the

* W.W.'s letter of October 13, 1884.
† W.W.'s letter of Oct. 6, 1884.
‡ Dr. Herbert B. Adams, professor of international law at Johns Hopkins.

driest of the lot. . . . I read the first two last year and Dr. A. now wants the rest in order, at intervals through the year.

I am quite well—hurried, as usual, but in excellent spirits—and every day more in love. . . .

When the first excitement of her adventure in independence had worn off, Ellen confessed that she was lonely, and Woodrow dashed off immediately to see her. They had three happy days together, but when he left, his own loneliness was harder to bear.

Balto., Oct. 22nd, 1884

My own darling,

It was *terrible* to have to come away! I didn't know *how* terrible it was until the parting was over. I won't say that the pain of separation was greater than the joy of being together—because it wasn't. That joy is beyond all measure, is worth all that can be paid for it. But the leave-taking *is a big price.* I felt desperately forlorn as I sped away from the great city which contains my treasure. And I was brought away with such unrelenting vigor that one might have imagined that the railroad authorities knew the temptation I was under to turn back and were determined to give me no chance to do so. We made never a stop between Jersey City and Philadelphia, making those hundred miles in two hours! . . .

Woodrow Wilson knew very little about women in those days of his youth.

Balto., Md., Oct. 25th, 1884

. . . Tell me, love, isn't it so that the plain girls whom men can't love are often, if not generally, disinclined to love men? However much of the woman and the woman's characteristic affections they may have— isn't it true that they seldom "fall" in love by an irresistible impulse? Or, does this only *seem* to be so because the consciousness of being unattractive to men drives them within themselves and disposes them to cynicism. You were *made* to win somebody; but they are made not to win, aren't they? To come down to instances: do you think that Miss Anna * is

* Another of Ellen's boarding-house friends.

really as indifferent to men as she seems to be? For my part, I liked Miss Anna and feel that she could attract if she would: but her manner is *hard* toward men. How different it was when I first met you! I used to think, "how this little lady can love if she will, if she find anyone worthy!" "What a sacred and boundless treasure has been, or is to be, found by some fortunate man!" And to think that *I* found it! How shall I ever be able to show how I prize it? I have adopted the only plan I know of: to give in return for it all that is purest and best in my own heart. . . .

Woodrow Wilson made friends easily, when he wanted to. He needed friendship and returned it wholeheartedly. There was a group of his classmates at Princeton whom he especially loved and trusted and with whom he remained friends all his life. Charles Talcott, who had joined him in his "solemn covenant" at Princeton, Robert Bridges, editor of the *Evening Post* and later of *Scribner's Magazine,* Cleveland Dodge, of the Phelps-Dodge Corporation, and Hiram Woods, who was practicing medicine in Baltimore when Woodrow was there, were all in this group. And his friendship with his former partner, Edward Renick, whom he once described as a "lovely being," lasted for many years.

There were also several men in the Graduate College at Johns Hopkins whose companionship he cherished. Among these was Charles Shinn, a warm-hearted and erratic young man, and one of the few people to whom Woodrow confided the secret of his engagement. Shinn went to New York and called on Ellen to find out for himself if she was the right girl for the friend he admired extravagantly. She was, he told Woodrow in a letter "penned in wild enthusiasm." *

Yet even Woodrow's closest friends never understood him completely, for his entire confidence was given only to Ellen.

Balto., Md., Oct. 28, 1884

. . . Since I have loved, and been loved by you, my darling, I have been able to appreciate as I never did before the exact place which friendship occupies in one's life, as distinguished from that love which only one person in the world can accept and return, in the case of each one of us. My intercourse with my friends is freer, less artificial, much more of the heart, than the intercourse I hold with the rest of the world, but it, after all, differs from the latter in degree rather than in kind. It's just Browning's idea that I am beginning to appreciate:

* W.W.'s letter of October 30, 1883.

"God be thanked, the meanest of his creatures
Boasts two soul-sides, one to face the world with,
One to show a woman when he loves her!"

When Shinn talks to you about me (if he does) don't you feel that there is a part of me he doesn't see at all which only *you* see, or ever have seen? And yet I have probably shown him as much of myself as I have ever shown to a friend. Friends, take them at their best, are outside of my individual, my secret, my inmost life. You alone are part of that. You alone may know me altogether, at my best and at my worst. You alone may look my heart full in the face and see without reserve the lineaments which others only guess at. And *this,* my Eileen, is *the* delight of my love for you. I did not know what it was to live until I found you for whom to live, in whom to live. Not even the precious, the inestimable love of my mother gave me a foretaste of this joy. This is *why* you are "all the world to me"—and yet this proves that very phrase a poor lying phrase, because you are to me what not all the world could be: you are the keeper of all my heart secrets. You are my very life. You are the one person in the world whose heart is mine, who stands with me, as against the rest of the world. Ah, my darling, my darling, what would I be without you!

The man who was later to approve the Women's Suffrage Amendment to the Constitution wrote:

Balto., Md., Oct. 31, 1884

My own darling,

Yesterday Mr. Wright * and I, in obedience to a sudden impulse of curiosity, went down to the *Y.M.C.A.* and attended the afternoon session of the Woman's Congress. We viewed the remarkable assembly from the gallery.... Barring the chilled, scandalized feeling that always comes over me when I see and hear women speak in public, I derived a good deal of whimsical delight, mixed with not a few instructive suggestions as to character and the like, from the proceedings. Mrs. Julia Ward Howe was in the chair—a most attractive, motherly old lady, born, apparently, to control rather by affection than by the exercise of presidential au-

* Johns Hopkins friend.

thority—but possessed of less mother wit, I should say, than round, jolly
Mrs. Cheney * who rolled herself on to the platform to make the only
natural, spontaneous, graceful remarks that relieved the stiff, self-assertive tone of the proceedings. The only noticeable "orator" who spoke
from the floor was a severely dressed person from Boston, an old maid
of the straitest sect of old maids. Not trousers and a Prince Albert coat
could have made her more manly in her bearing. She was a living example—and lively commentary—of what might be done by giving men's
places and duties to women—a very dialectic Amazon! I enclose the
programme in order that you may read the queer address to the people
of Baltimore which it contains. What an odd mixture of deprecating explanation and almost defiant self-assertion!...

Woodrow had confessed to loneliness, despondency and discourage-
ment over his work in his letters to Ellen, but not to the sickening sense
of failure that sometimes tormented him. Now, no longer surrounded by
his admiring family, he had such a serious attack of self-doubt that he
could not conceal it from her.

Balto., Nov. 1, 1884

... May I confess to you, my darling, that I have been fighting against
the blues all morning?... Perhaps you have not seen enough of me yet
to find out just how foolish I am: but you will discover that, when I
confess that a very frequent cause of despondency with me is an overwhelming doubt about my ability to do anything worth doing. Now and
again I lose all faith in my own talents and am possessed of the conviction that I am nothing better than a dull fool, with a vain knack for
counterfeiting thought and am ashamed that anyone should admire me.
Of course I could not confess this to anyone but you. I should be taken
to be doing that most contemptible of all things, courting a contradiction,
"fishing for a compliment!" But I can own to my Eileen, who loves me
and therefore has faith in me, that I often absolutely *suffer* under a
sense of being a *humbug,* pretending that I possess [a] mind and really
possessing nothing but the skill of concealing the absence of it—or, at
best, possessed of only a single mental muscle, and for the rest utterly
without sparkle or versatility, a heavy one-sided creature unable to find

* Edna D. Cheney, Massachusetts suffrage leader.

the simple hole in life into which he might be made clumsily to fit. Perhaps it is not quite exact to call these the blues: it is better to say that I am filled with a sort of supreme self-indignation, or self-pity, as a man whose education, so far, consists in being able to express clearly the poverty of thought that is in him. I have studied the art of expression without being equally careful—possibly without being able—to have something to say. I blush to see other men less pretentious and more solid, more real. But I must not work the thought into feverishness by trying to force it into language. . . . I must wait for tomorrow to come with its return of my comfortable normal conviction that I may, if I find work, be an ordinary useful man— or, mayhap, of my occasional conviction (or delusion), brief but enjoyable, that I have a message for the world and the ability to deliver it.

My darling need not distress herself because of my folly in manufacturing such doubts out of the desire to be something different from what I am—a brilliant instead of merely a serviceable man. It does me good to confess. . . . And the privilege of confessing to you is like a cool, refreshing breeze, to blow away the clouds that oppress and stifle me. . . .

On Sunday, November the second, Wilson and Shinn, two ardent young Democrats, sat for hours reading the newspapers and worrying about the Cleveland-Blaine Presidential election. Reading the Sunday papers was frowned upon by all good Presbyterians.

Balto., Md., Nov. 2nd, 1884
4:20 P.M.

. . . Shinn has been with me ever since church this morning. . . . We have been sitting up here in my room since dinner doing what my conscience does not approve of, but what you will see to have been almost inevitable under the circumstances. We have been reading the *Times* and *Herald* of this morning and canvassing all the possibilities of next Tuesday. I am exceedingly hopeful, though so anxious as to be thankful that there is to be only a day or two more of suspense. Only my profound trust in an over-ruling Providence will keep me from the profoundest despondency, my darling, if Cleveland should be defeated. God only knows what will be our political destiny if the Republican machine should triumph again! . . .

Three days later Grover Cleveland's election and a letter from his love banished most of his dejection.

> *Bluntschli Library, Nov. 5th,*
> *1884, 11:10* A.M.

My own darling,

You may imagine how profoundly thankful I am for the apparent result of the election. I say "apparent" because of course we are as yet far short of confident assurance of victory. But all the indications point to Cleveland's election and I hear no *claims* of success for Blaine. It *seems* as if our hopes were abundantly realized, my darling, our prayers for the country answered. If so, a great cloud is lifted from my heart, and I can turn to my work with unanxious zest.

I am *very* tired, having been out of bed 'till three o'clock this morning, standing in a dense, yelling crowd and am painfully dragging myself through lecture hours as best I may....

I have just received your Monday night letter. How can I sufficiently thank you for its sweet comforting words of cheer and confidence! I *will* try, my precious, to "look on the bright side of myself." It is altogether the wisest thing to do: and it ought to be easy with such help as I get from my darling's unfailing love. And yet it is terribly hard work to thaw out this present frost of despondency about my gifts, their character and amount. The *facts* really seem to be against me—on the side of knowledge at least, if not on that of capacity for using it, if I had it. After all, however, it *ought* to content me that I can fit myself for useful labour and can faithfully do my best without any special concern as to whether that best will be remembered outside of my own family or beyond my own generation. The whole matter revolves about the question: Is it right to foster a longing to do immortal work and to encourage a conviction of the possession of power to do it; or should one school himself to be content with mediocrity?... Of course, with such content supreme, the highest sort of enthusiasm must be thrust out to die. But how is one to know that he has strength to go as far as such enthusiasm sees in its visions of new worlds of thought? How is one to tell a castle in the air from a sober, achievable purpose? These are the questions

that vex my thoughts—and which I *allow* to vex them in the face of my
determination to *do* simply what my hands find to do and to let the
perfect performance of that be the present rule of achievement. That is
the rule of common sense: but I am not confessing common sense: I am
confessing *myself* to *you*, who will not think me a mere doubting, weak-
kneed fool for my pains. I shall *act* as if I had no doubts, but I can let
my darling see, the while ... what my inner history is. . . .

There was an important question to decide. Should Woodrow try
for a Ph.D. degree at Johns Hopkins, or continue to concentrate only
on the subjects that interested him most? Joseph Wilson, after he and
his son had discussed the question in letters for some time, decided
against it. Woodrow had always valued his father's judgment more than
that of anyone else, but now he wanted Ellen to make the final decision.

Balto., Md., Nov. 8th, 1884

... As for the degree, my pet, father advises me not to try for it: and
since his advice coincides with my own coolest judgment in the matter,
I have concluded to make no special effort in reading for it. ... I am
quite sure that I shall profit much more substantially from a line of reading of my own choosing, in the lines of my own original work, than I
should from much of the reading necessary in the Ph.D. course, though
my *inclinations* will take me through the most important topics of that
course. The difference will be that I will read, *outside* of the prescribed
lines, a great deal that will be of infinitely more service to me than the
volumes of another sort which I should perfunctorily peruse, to the
mortification of my own tastes and desires, were I to goad myself to the
tasks heaped upon the degree candidate. Do you approve? You certainly
have a right to be consulted, because it is probable that a degree would
render me a little more *marketable* next June than I shall otherwise
be. ... I must put myself up to the highest bidder at the end of this col-
legiate year: and it is probable that I would fetch a bigger price with
a Ph.D. label on me than I can fetch without. It's a choice, apparently,
between pecuniary profit and mental advantage—with the mental sacrifice perhaps small enough to allow one to think of risking it. Tell me
just what *you* think about it, darling. I *want* your advice ... you are

nearer to me than anyone else in the world. I want you to feel about all my affairs that they are yours as much as mine. . . .

Ellen, too, advised against his trying for a Ph.D. She was certain that he was destined to be a great political writer and saw no reason why he needed a degree for that. As for the "marketable" value that a degree would give him, she tossed that aside as unimportant compared to his health, which she was afraid might be undermined by the extra work involved in procuring it.

There is an apparently indestructible myth concerning Woodrow Wilson. He was, according to the myth, cold and unapproachable, an intellectual snob, a cloistered scholar, unaware of, even bored by the hopes and fears of ordinary human beings. He had emerged from his ivory tower to become a politician only because he was ambitious and loved power. But, smooth-tongued and clever, he managed to convince the masses that he was their friend and advocate. So runs the tale. The truth is clearly seen in his letters to the woman he loved. Woodrow Wilson was only twenty-seven when he wrote:

Balto., Md., Nov. 9th, 1884

. . . I have returned to my normal senses now, and shall strive not to stray from them again. I have in my mental mechanism somewhere a weight of commonsense which is generally sufficient to keep my thoughts at their proper balance. It is only when I handle that mechanism roughly out of impatience for its small capacity, that this weight gets displaced. I doubt it's not so much morbid introspection as the influences of the atmosphere in which I live here that explains my unhealthy states of mind. A man who wants to put fresh thought into the minds and fire into the purposes of his fellow-men of the everyday world naturally feels stifled in a thick, scientific atmosphere. He lives in uneasiness when he realizes that every person and everything about him is intending to make a mere student of him. A mere student can make himself understood only by students. He thinks the thoughts and speaks the dialect of a class, a caste; he can touch neither the sympathy nor the interest of the community at large, which is made up of unstudious people of plain, workaday opinions and simple, practical, unlogical, hand to mouth judgments. If one sees men only through and in books, he sees only the *simulacra*, walking qualities, labelled emotions, catalogued feelings. If he lives all his life in a room, if he feels more at home in a library than in conversation with his carpenter, if he understands Latin better than the sentiments of his coachman, if he wouldn't turn from his constitutional history to watch the games of light-hearted children, he is, to the fullest extent of the meaning of each of those "ifs," unfit to have anything to say to his fellow-men.

The whole effort of University life is to make men interested in books and in the remote interests which books discuss; to make them technically accurate; to make them prefer Greek accent to English pronunciation. And it is this spirit against which I struggle. I want to be near the world; I want to *know* the world; to retain all my sympathy with it—even with its crudenesses. I am *afraid* of being made a mere student. I want to be *part* of the nature around me, not an outside observer of it. John Wilson had a great deal to say because he was a splendid animal; he admired and celebrated virtue because he could be tempted by vice. An ascetic could never become, by any ingenuity of training an effective temperance lecturer. Jno. B. Gough was a drunkard. Milton lived apart from flirting girls, constructed an ideal love—and wrote pamphlets in favour of divorce. Carlyle could not understand a man who did not have dyspepsia. It's not so much eloquence as "fellow-feeling" that makes Henry Ward Beecher attractive to all classes of hearers. Disraeli knew nothing about the true principles of politics: but he knew *men*—especially House of Commons men. Calhoun read the Constitution as the schoolmen read Aristotle—and the world ran all over his doctrines. Burke lived too much with books to know what the French Revolution meant. And so it goes. You'll never find in a *cloister* a fulcrum for any lever which can budge the world!

Here's the problem, then: How get fresh air in this world of book-research? how learn to ride a live horse on a hobby-horse? How discover by reading heavy books the quick, direct, certain way to inform and influence men who read only entertaining books—books which touch with a practiced hand their own ordinary lives—books which can be understood without conscious effort? I want to write books which will be read by the great host who don't wear spectacles—whose eyes are young and unlearned! I don't care how much contempt may look upon my pages through professors' glasses!...

Ellen must have been shocked by his criticism of the "atmosphere" at Johns Hopkins, for he wrote in another letter:

Biological Room, J.H.U.,
Balto., Nov. 13, 1884
8:45 A.M.

...I am waiting here for Dr. Hall to begin his weekly lecture on peda-
gogics. ...

I think you misunderstood my argument about the effects of University life. For a man whose wish it is to perfect himself in the physical
sciences or in technical scholarship—for the chemist, the biologist, or
the classicist—and such men constitute the majority of University students—the Hopkins has, I am sure, no drawbacks, save only those which
are characteristic of *every* human institution. But this majority creates
the *atmosphere* and sets the methods of the place: and that it is which
makes me uncomfortable. My chief interest is in politics, in history as
it furnishes object lessons for the present—the University professor's
chief interest is in the accurate details of history—in the precise day
of the month on which Cicero cut his eye-teeth—in past society for
its own sake. At least that is the tendency—towards scholasticism. Knowing how and why I like to read of past times, you can see that for me
the specializing mania of life has its *special* drawbacks.

Ellen's soft Southern drawl and gentle manner had won the hearts
of most of her fellow-boarders—in particular the heart of Mr. Goodrich,
whose first name is not revealed. She never used it, either in his presence,
or to Woodrow. Mr. Goodrich liked to read aloud, especially to Ellen, and
had joined a "reading club" at the boarding house. Ellen, perhaps to
test Woodrow's statement that he was not jealous, wrote him at some
length about her new friend.

New York, Nov. 11, 1884

... We decided to have another meeting [of the reading club] close upon
the last, and a very pleasant time we had too! No formality or stiffness
whatever. Mr. Goodrich read from Bret Harte's stories, while Miss M.
and I sketched her cousin and Mrs. Jenkins. Mrs. J. is perfectly lovely!
and so is Mrs. Weiler!! and so is Mr. Goodrich!!! his loveliness consisting in the fact that he is going to take me to see Irving and Ellen
Terry. To go out with a boarding-house acquaintance isn't exactly what
I should have anticipated doing; but it hasn't taken a whole month,

by any means, to obtain satisfactory evidences as to Mr. Goodrich's character and antecedents. He is a thorough gentleman, born and bred,—of
good old Mass. puritan "stock"; one who has been most carefully
trained up in the way he should go. He is quite a young man—only
finished at Andover last year—fresh and unspoiled, yet very intelligent, entertaining and well-read. You would have been amused the other
night, when he asked me to go to hear Irving; he was very awkward
and embarrassed and, as you will readily understand, I liked him the
better for it—"Miss Axson, would you object?—may I—ah!—I would
like so much to ask—if I only *dared!*—for the pleasure of taking you,
etc."

Woodrow tried to be generous about the lovely Mr. Goodrich.

Balto., Md., 13th, 1884

... I am delighted, my pet, that you are to see Irving and Ellen
Terry.... I am sure that you will think, as I do, that Miss Terry is
infinitely better than Irving—at least if you see them in parts anything
like those in which I saw them—namely Hamlet and Ophelia. His strut
is almost as execrable as his pronunciation. She is beyond comparison
the finest actress I ever saw. Ah, Eileen, what would I not give to see
her *with you!* I envy Mr. Goodrich *with all my heart!* Wouldn't *you*
rather go with me than with him? ...

Ellen had written that she sometimes refrained from saying in her
letters things she had "fancied" she would like to tell Woodrow.

Balto., Md., Nov. 16, 1884

... It is my greatest *desire*, that you should say just anything and everything you fancy you would like to say—even to putting into words
what you think of me! I can imagine my taste revolting if you were
to say *conventional* things to me ... because you thought policy or po-
liteness constrained you to do so ... but nothing that is prompted by
an impulse to open your whole mind to me can seem to me unnatural
or in bad taste. You need never pause to speculate, "What will he *think*
if I say what I am tempted to say?" Just remember that *I love you
with all my heart....* Speak to me, darling, as to your other self....

You are not apprehensive of my criticism? If there were anything in your sweet letters to criticize, *I* shouldn't find it. I esteem much more highly your opinions than my own: and I am yours, darling, in *everything.*

Ellen replied,

New York [undated]

No darling, I am not afraid of criticism—as these scrawls which I am constantly sending abundantly show—because I have no appearance to keep up with you. Before all else I want you to know the truth, to see just what a foolish little creature I am. I know *now* that such knowledge won't cause you to love me less, or it would have had that effect long ere this, for there has been no lack of sincerity in our dealings with each other. And, if you will only love me, all *must* be well with me. For the rest, though your approbation is more precious to me than all the world beside, your praise sweeter to me than all else, I am too low in my own esteem, especially when I think of myself in connection with you, for criticism to gain any sting from wounded pride. Ah, darling, I love you. I love you as my own soul. Why can I not be, for your dear sake, all that I wish to be, all that your love ought to be?...

She asked in another letter:

New York [undated]

...By the way, what do you know about the "Society for Ethical Culture" and Felix Adler? Mr. Brush * belongs to it and so does a pretty *young* girl in our class. It is said that they don't believe in God or even in the immortality of the soul. What a terrible faith—or no faith!—and the idea of a young *woman* adopting it!

With this letter she enclosed, without comment, her answer to Woodrow's request that she should "put into words what you think of me," letting a poet speak for her, as she so often did.

"And wilt thou have me fashion into speech
The love I bear thee, finding words enough,

* George DeForest Brush, famous artist, then teaching at Art League.

And hold the torch out while the winds are rough
Between our faces to cast light on each?
I drop it at thy feet. I cannot teach
My hand to hold my spirit so far off
From myself—me—that I should bring the proof
In words of love hid in me out of reach.
Nay, let the silence of my womanhood
Command my woman-love to thy belief." *

Mr. Goodrich, Ellen wrote, had given her a copy of a new poem which had made a great hit—"Rubaiyat by Omar Khayyâm," with illustrations by Elisha Vedder. The stern young Presbyterian did not approve of the poem.

New York, Nov. 18, 1884

... I was wild to see it, for I have read and heard of nothing else, it seems to me, for weeks past.... Mr. Goodrich has been trying to obtain possession of it for some time; he brought it up and read it to me.... I really believe that Vedder has more genius than any other American artist; he is not merely a great workman, like so many French artists, but he is equally great on the intellectual and imaginative sides. It seems a pity, does it not, that such noble work should be expended on such a heathenish poem—that he should add any attraction to such miserable philosophy. Why could he not have chosen a subject worthy of his art!...

Woodrow wrote to tell Ellen that he had asked Robert Bridges to call on her.

Balto., Md., Nov. 20, 1884

If I have any *best* friend in the world, that friend is Bob Bridges.... I have for a great many years felt towards him as towards a brother: and if we have drifted apart of late years it has been only because of the necessity which has separated our *lives*. It has never weaned my heart from the dear, genuine old Scot. None of Bob is on the surface, but the deeper you dig the finer they are. He and Charlie Talcott and Hiram

* Elizabeth Barrett Browning.

Woods were the *real* friends whom college life gave me for an inspiring possession: and if I keep any friends, I shall, before all others, keep them. . . .

The "genuine old Scot" told Woodrow afterwards that he was "delighted" with Ellen, but she thought he was bored because she was not "intellectual." She was, as she had told Woodrow, "low in her own esteem." By the same token Woodrow's next letter worried her. It contained a long quotation from Walter Bagehot which, briefly summed up, stated that Shelley's first wife was an "ordinary woman" with a "common female mind," who, like all such women, preferred ordinary men rather than men of genius. She could, therefore, have made "an everyday person—a gentleman, suppose, in the tallow line"—happy. But not Shelley. Woodrow wrote:

Balto., Md., Nov. 22, 1884

. . . Here is an extract I have just hit upon and which I know you will appreciate and enjoy . . . because it is from an essay on Shelley by my master, Bagehot—the most vivacious, the most racily real of writers on life—whether the life be political, social or separately intellectual . . . . This is a long quotation to burden a short letter with, but I know that you will not begrudge it the space. This is the only way in which I can even come near to realizing the luxury of carrying the best, the most suggestive passages of my favorite authors to my best loved companion. Of course the explanation of Shelley's mistake in this unfortunate marriage is simple. Mistake was inevitable when he chose to marry a girl because her beauty had won his fanciful love at first sight and because her name was Harriett—a name of tender associations with him because it was borne by a cousin whom he had loved and lost—to another man! When a man marries off-hand he can't count on anything as certain, except extreme danger. It's like *dying* off-hand and blindly running the chances as to climate in the next world. But to marry thus is just what the man of genius . . . is exceedingly likely to do, and his only protection is to be found in the rule which Bagehot points out: that an essentially ordinary woman is not likely to want him! . . .

The problem of choosing a life-companion is, therefore, a serious one for everybody out of the "tallow line," though there's more tragedy in it for the genius than for lesser folk. Perhaps it is fortunate for the race that there are so few geniuses in it. The average man would be monstrously uncomfortable if the wife of his bosom were of this rare make —not less uncomfortable, I take it than a woman would at the incomings and outgoings of a husband who was afflicted with the disease of being unlike anybody else she had ever known or heard of, and consequently altogether, hopelessly, unaccountable. . . .

Ellen, quite certain that Woodrow was a genius, replied:

New York, Nov. 24, 1884

. . . Many thanks for the very interesting and suggestive passages from Bagehot. I would like to read the essay on Shelley, both to obtain in full his very sensible views on the "intellectual marriage," and also to see what he has to say in Shelley's defense for it seems to be to some extent an apology for him. What a very keen observer he—Bagehot —is! And what a very fortunate thing it is for the world that it *is* so largely regulated by the law he points out; a most natural law, too, for everybody knows that "birds of a feather flock to-gether," and the rarer sort, of which there are not enough to make "flocks," dwell apart—to themselves. It is a cheering reflection from one point of view, for it shows that the poor helpless men of genius are not *utterly* unprotected, after all.

Yet it is, for me, a very uncomfortable reflection too, if it be absolutely essential to the happiness of an extraordinary man that his choice should be an extraordinary woman;—but I won't tease you with such talk now, when it will do no good—and after all I am not quite as "ordinary" as the type Mr. Bagehot describes, for she, it seems, is too essentially commonplace even to *appreciate* or understand anything above the average. I can and do, and I love you, my darling, beyond the common.

> "And love, mere love, is beautiful indeed and worthy of acceptation.
> Fire is bright, let temple burn, or flax! An equal light
> Leaps in the flame from cedar-plant or weed.
> And love is fire—and what I *feel* across the inferior features
> Of what I *am* doth flash itself and show
> How that great work of love enhances Nature's." *

I have been trying all day in vain to recall what I wrote in my

* Elizabeth Barrett Browning.

letter of Thursday night which I wouldn't dare say to you.... I remember reading long ago what professed to be a thoroughly true and tried receipt for writing a "perfect love letter"—it was, "to begin without knowing what you mean and end without knowing what you have said." So far as that goes mine are all right!...

Woodrow protested. She *was* extraordinary. She was that rarest of all creatures—a woman with a fine mind and a great heart and, besides all this, she was an artist, which he had always longed to be. He had written on that subject, before her letter arrived:

Balto., Md., Nov. 23rd, 1884

...I have never suspected myself of possessing artistic talents, it is needless to say, but I have always known myself capable of entering into the artist's feelings and of understanding his delights. I have always reverenced the power of artistic creation above the power of poetic creation. I suppose that it would be idle for me to hope ever to be an orator if I did *not* have these artistic sympathies. It has been one of the peculiarities—one of the few grave misfortunes—of my life that I have hitherto *known* least of the two things that move me most, poetry and painting. My sensibilities in those directions seem to be like a musical instrument seldom touched, like a harp disused....

His ambition to be an orator was showing signs of realization. Young Woodrow Wilson—now called the "Hopkins genius" by some of his colleagues—was in great demand as a speaker in Baltimore. He made fun of himself, told Ellen that he "posed as a professor of things in general and nothing in particular," but he loved it.

Balto., Md., Nov. 25, 1884
9:30 A.M.

...Well, I made my speech last night, and my auditors actually seemed delighted. I could not have been more flatteringly listened to or more heartily applauded. This does not argue much for the taste of the Hopkins Literary Society. It is, indeed, only another way of saying that its members are young and haven't heard many speeches from men who enjoy speaking as an intellectual exercise. That's the secret, undoubtedly, of what little success I have had as a speaker. I enjoy it (speaking) because it sets my mind—all my faculties—aglow: and I suppose that this very excitement gives my manner an appearance of confidence and self-command which arrests attention. However that may be, I *feel* a sort of transformation—and it's hard to go to sleep afterwards. . . .

That year at Johns Hopkins should have been very pleasant. Woodrow was not only a success as a speaker, but also as a scholar. And his reputation as a brilliant conversationalist made him much in demand at dinner parties and social "functions." But he was not happy. The lack of even the prospect of a professorship spoiled everything for him. So when Dr. Adams told him that the board of trustees of a woman's college, to be opened soon at Bryn Mawr, was interested in him and his "historical work," he was excited. Dr. Adams arranged a meeting with Miss Martha Carey Thomas, Dean of the new college, and Dr. Rhoads, one of the trustees. He wrote to Ellen the next day.

Balto., Md., Nov. 27th, 1884

. . . You never heard of Bryn Mawr College? Well, neither did I. The fact is that Bryn Mawr College has not been started yet. A wealthy "Friend" of Philadelphia, recently deceased, left $800,000 for the establishment of an institution for the higher education of women, to be conducted under the auspices of the Society of Friends—or at least under the direction of certain members of that Society whom he named as executors and trustees—but to be non-denominational in its teachings and government. . . . The trustees have been using the income which has accrued since the founder's death in the erection of the necessary buildings at Bryn Mawr, near Philadelphia. But they have also been gradually getting a faculty together and perfecting their organization with a view to opening the college next autumn. They are, of course, choosing their teachers with great care because each teacher chosen will have to lay the foundation of his, or her, department—will have to *organize* it, and give it direction and plan. You understand, then, the object of the introduction in Dr. Adams' office. Bryn Mawr is to have a department of history and the Dean and trustees are in search of someone fit to organize it. My lecture was about to begin, so Miss Thomas simply invited me to lunch in order that Dr. Rhoads might have an opportunity to talk with me. Miss T. was not at lunch herself, but I had a delightful talk with Dr. R. He is every inch an "Orthodox Friend" and I was "Thee'd" at a great rate: but he is a genuine, earnest, intelligent man and I enjoyed talking with him, notwithstanding the novel nature of the interview. The Doctor's object was, not so much to discover what I knew as to get a key to my character and an insight into my views on certain points which he considered vital. He was glad to find that I believed that the hand of Providence was in all history; that the progress of Christianity was as great a factor as the development of philosophy and the sciences; and that wars were to be justified only by necessity: and he was careful to ascertain my views as to personal religion. What will come of the interview I can't tell. He gave me his address and asked me to think over what he had said as to the kind of position offered and to write to him within two or three days, accompanying my letter with a statement of the courses of study I have pursued, etc. In the meantime, he supposed, Miss Thomas would want to talk with me and ask me to meet Mr. Francis King, one of the trustees.

There are several things that would make a position at Bryn Mawr very advantageous for a youngster who wants to gain a reputation and make his work tell as soon as possible. To work there would be to work under the eyes of the Hopkins. Miss Thomas is the daughter of one of our most influential trustees, Dr. Jas. Carey Thomas, and Mr. King is a trustee of the University as well as of Bryn Mawr. Indeed the University is very largely under the control of the same "Friends" to whom the government of the college is entrusted.... Reputation under their auspices would be reputation *well placed,* so to speak. At any rate to serve them would be to serve enlightened masters. I don't know what chances there may be for my election, but I should certainly accept any offer from them that included salary enough for us to live on. Before the negotiations go any further, tell me what you think, my darling. I have told you all the essential facts that I know myself—so please don't plead insufficient information, but write as my Eileen, my pledged wife....

The girl who had been raised in the South of the 1860s and 1870s, replied:

New York, Nov. 28 /84

My darling Woodrow,

I have just been having some interesting conversation with my Quaker friend below stairs, Mrs. Wright, of Phil. I was anxious—owing to my deep interest in the higher education of women!—to learn something of Bryn Mawr and the new college there! So she has been telling me all about it,—about the beautiful village and buildings and the wonderful "Dean": Miss Martha Carey Thomas, whom she knows very well indeed.

This is a very interesting letter of yours, dear, and has certainly given me a good deal to think about today.... There would seem to be many things in Bryn Mawr's favour.... And perhaps the greatest circumstance in its favour, to my mind, lies in the fact that you would be the *first* professor—that you would enter on the work untrammelled by precedent. It would give you more opportunity to do as you please— to carry out your own views. The work of organizing, while, I should think, more difficult than the mere carrying on of another's plans, must be also much more interesting and inspiring. I should imagine, too that it would be a more important work—one involving greater responsibility and therefore one which would gain a higher reputation for him who did it well.

But, do you think there *is* much reputation to be made in a *girl's school*—or, an it please you, a "Woman's college?" Can you be content to serve that sort of an institution? That is the only objection to the plan in my mind, but I must confess it seems to me a very serious one. Can you bring yourself to feel thoroughly in sympathy with that kind of thing—with the *tendencies* and *influences* of such an institution? Can you, with all your heart, cooperate with the strong-minded person who conducts it?—The *"Dean!"* how ridiculous! If they are going to have "prudes for proctors, dowagers for deans" it would be more consistent to follow Tennyson's scheme to the bitter end and exclude men altogether—on penalty of death! Seriously, dear, I fear you would find it very unpleasant to serve, as it were, under a *woman!* It seems so unnatural, so jarring to one's sense of the fitness of things—so absurd too.

I may be very silly to say so, but it seems to me that it is rather beneath *you* to teach in a "female college,"—that last is a "vile phrase," but it suits me at present! However, as you perceive, I am merely telling you how I *feel* in the matter; these are not matured, deliberate, settled *convictions,* on my part. If you are *sure,* after careful reflection, that it is the best thing for you to do—if *you* are *entirely* satisfied and pleased with the prospect, you need not fear but that I will be equally pleased and satisfied. I am only anxious, my darling, that your impatience

for a position of some sort may not lead you to decide hastily in favor
of a disagreeable one. . . .

On the day she wrote this letter something happened which drove
Bryn Mawr temporarily into the background. Houghton, Mifflin & Co.,
had received the manuscript of Woodrow's book, *Congressional Government,* early in October. Now, at last, they wrote that they would "take
great pleasure" in publishing it and paying the author ten per cent in
royalties, "if this was agreeable and satisfactory."

Balto., Md., Nov. 28th, '84, 12:15 A.M.

My own darling,

As you will see by the enclosed letter from the publishers, I have some
exceptionally good news this morning for my Eileen, and I know that
she will be as happy as I am about it. They have actually offered me as
good terms as if I were already a well-known writer! The success is of
such proportions as almost to take my breath away—it has distanced
by biggest hopes. . . . There is not much doubt about the terms being
"agreeable and satisfactory" to me, as I shall let them know at once.
. . . Your love, my precious little sweetheart, makes this first success
sweet; because you share it and you will be glad! . . .

Ellen's letter in response to this great news is missing, yet it is
clear, from his reply, how she felt.

Balto., Md., Dec. 1, 1884, 10:35 A.M.

My own darling,

How shall I thank you for the sweet letter you wrote on Saturday night!
My success with the publishers is not worth half so much to me as your
delight in it. One ounce of love is worth many tons of literary reputation: and one word of *your* love is sweeter to me than anything and
everything this world can afford. My darling! I am so glad for *your*
sake that Houghton, Mifflin, & Co. accepted my *mss!* I trust that their
action means an *opening* for me: if so, all that goes through that opening
hereafter shall be made better by the inspiration of your love. . . .

No, I did not send the dedication with the *mss,* but with my letter
accepting the terms offered. Do you know how the dedication runs? "To

his Father, the patient guide of his youth, the gracious companion of his manhood, his best instructor and most lenient critic, this book is affectionately dedicated by the Author." Do you like that, my darling? I want it to be a surprise to dear father, and so shall leave the secret to be revealed to him and to dear mother by the book itself. . . .

Woodrow was not, however, too elated over his success to come down to earth again. The Bryn Mawr matter had to be decided in two weeks. He was disappointed by Ellen's "earnest protest" against his acceptance of the offer. He would, he assured her "not be under a woman." Miss Thomas was only the Dean. Dr. Rhoads was the president. And there would be several men in the faculty.

Baltimore, Md., Nov. 30th, 1884

. . . Dr. Adams seems to think that an appointment at Bryn Mawr would be an exceptional honour, especially in the department of history, since several of the best known of the young teachers of the country—such as Wm F. Allen, the historical critic of the Nation—have been spoken of in the past. Whatever else it might be, the position would *not* be *beneath* me, my darling—you may rest quite easy on that point. . . .

I have none of the same objections to a school such as that to be opened at Bryn Mawr that I have to a *co-educational* institution: and the question of the higher education of women is certain to be settled in the affirmative, in this country at least, whether my sympathy be enlisted or not.

. . . At Bryn Mawr I should probably receive a very comfortable salary (I am prepared to refuse anything less than two thousand dollars); should have more leisure there than here or elsewhere for private study. . . . It is not my purpose, you know, my darling, to spend my life in teaching. It is my purpose to get a start in the literary work which cannot at first bring in a living. I should, of course, *prefer* to teach young men and, if I find that teaching at Bryn Mawr stands in the way of my teaching afterwards in some man's college, I shall of course withdraw. But Dr. Adams did exactly the same thing before coming here—he was first of all professor at just such an institution, Smith College in Mass. —and, besides beggars cannot be choosers. . . . The whole question, therefore, is reduced to this: do I think I could gain the object of my ambition in teaching women? The question as to whether it will be *agreeable*, or not, I leave out altogether. I could do my duty fully, without fretting, provided my ultimate object is not interfered with or postponed meanwhile. . . .

My anxiety to do what is best in this matter has cost me both sleep and ease of mind. I have not attempted to argue away your objections: they stand with a force of their own . . . I have merely desired to point out other considerations which, to a certain extent—perhaps altogether—counterbalance them. And if my darling, after further consideration, continues to think that the position . . . is one which she should be sorry to have me accept, I will at once and without hesitation withdraw from the candidacy. I will not take, contrary to her choice and judgment, this first step that we shall take together! . . .

The matter seemed to have settled itself when Woodrow was informed that his salary, as professor of history at Bryn Mawr College, would be $1200 a year. He was indignant:

Balto., Md., Dec. 5th, 1884

. . . I am to dine this evening with Miss Martha Carey Thomas. She will, I fear, find me in a somewhat grim humour. . . . They must offer me *some* inducements to go to Bryn Mawr—not a meagre stipend which would be barely enough to live on, and leave absolutely no margin on which I could collect a small library and make our escape from B.M. in the summers. They would not value me if I were to "let" myself cheap: so that, unless they choose to increase the offer considerably, the negotiations are at an end. If my book makes any sort of a hit, it ought to give me prestige enough to get something better than a $1200 position.

But Miss Thomas was surprisingly amenable.

Balto., Md., Dec. 6th, 1884

I dined with the "Dean" last evening and had a very interesting experience. When I arrived she was critical and a whit superior; when I left, she had quite admitted my intellectual equality and was ready to defer to me in everything. Finally, she seemed really to enjoy hearing me talk. Her critical temper had melted into sympathy: and she was anxious to know if I would come to Bryn Mawr if the trustees were to offer me such and such a salary—for I had told her that I had written to Dr. Rhoads declining twelve hundred. I think that they *will* offer me more, with a prospect of an advance both in academic rank and in salary at the end of two years, and such terms would undoubtedly be better than I could expect to make elsewhere at present, since I am known to have had no experience in teaching and must submit to be taken *on trial* at first. . . .

His hopes rose and fell in the days that followed while he waited to hear from Bryn Mawr's trustees. To quiet his nerves he worked hard at his studies and wrote only love letters to Ellen.

Balto., Md., Dec. 7, 1884

. . . There surely never lived a man with whom love was a more critical matter than it is with me! . . . With *all* of your love life will be easy and full of promise of the highest, worthiest success: without all of your love life will be hard beyond endurance and full only of irksome duty grimly done, like prison labour. I dare not think what would become of me if your love were taken away from me—and yet I wonder at myself for telling even you these secrets—these bottom-secrets of my nature. . . . Pride plays so prominent a part in my disposition that probably my companions would not more than suspect *some* change, were my *heart* to die. But pride has no place in my dealings with you, my darling! . . . You are not a "companion": You are *mine*—are you not, darling?— my heart's mistress, my sweetest comforter, my promised wife! Do you think that you can be happy living with *such* a chap—so given to odd moods—so prone to break out suddenly in unnecessary self-revelations? Say again that you love me and trust me with all your heart and I will ask no more such foolish questions. . . .

Balto., Md., Dec. 9th, 1884

Mr. Bowen * (one of my new intrusive friends, the American political economists) is very interesting, but he is cold-blooded: he discusses marriage from the *economic* standpoint, as intimately connected with the question of *wages*, and it is, therefore, an *immense* relief to turn from

* Francis Bowen, professor of natural religion at Harvard—1835 on.

him for a little while, to give one's *heart* a chance to think a bit. Wages *have* a most uncomfortable, imperious way of commanding the question of marriage: but so does the body incommode and often dominate the heart: and that does not disprove or throw the slightest doubt upon the conclusion to which everybody who *has* a heart must accede—that the body was made for the heart, not the heart for the body. Marriage isn't in any *true* sense an *economic* question. I mean to marry my darling—provided she continues of the same mind as at present!—simply and only because I love her with all my heart and need her at every turn of my life, and not because I expect some day to earn more money than I need for my own support.

You dear little bewitcher! Do you think it's fair to thrust yourself into all a fellow's studies so? How can he understand political economy when he is thinking of a pair of soft loving brown eyes ... how can he remember when Crecy was fought or hope to comprehend the German Reformation? The only hope for him is to be with you always, because these thoughts will not interfere with—they will help—his studies when the element of anxiety and lack and loneliness is taken out of them.... My private opinion is ... that he was meant to have somebody to spend his life for—and yet was meant to be taken care of by a woman's aid, a woman's tact and sympathy. He needs to be loved and believed in with that unbounded, unquestioning love and belief which only a woman can give—which it is a woman's glory to give, even when she gives it unworthily! ...

The attack on Professor James Woodrow had finally reached a climax. He had been tried by the Southern Presbyterian Synod, convicted of heresy and dismissed from the Seminary. Woodrow wrote, in distress:

Balto., Md., Dec. 16, 1884

... If what the clipping I sent you says is true, the trustees of the Seminary have, at the bidding of the Synods, not only eaten their own words but put themselves utterly in the wrong, and the Seminary in imminent jeopardy of ruin. They have left Uncle James the moral as well as the controversial advantage. They cannot do him any real injury. Distressed as I am at the turn things have taken and at the thought of the terrible anxiety and pain Uncle James must have suffered, I cannot help seeing that the victory really lies with him, and that the *disgrace* of the affair falls upon the church. That is the terrible part of it. . . .

Ever since the day when twelve-year-old Tommy Wilson wrote a constitution for the "Lightfoot Club" in its secret meeting place—his father's stable in Augusta, Georgia—he had been fascinated by this democratic instrument. When he was seventeen he went to Davidson College, became a member of the "Eumenean Debating Society," declared that it needed a constitution and wrote one. It began with a declaration that "the object of the Society shall be the acquirement of literary knowledge, the promotion of virtue and the cultivation of harmony and friendship." From Davidson he went to Princeton, organized a "Liberal Debating Club" and performed the same service. "This society," the preamble stated, "shall be founded upon the fundamental principles of Justice, Morality and Friendship." When he attended the University of Virginia Law School, the "Jefferson Society" elected him president and, very soon thereafter, he appointed a committee "for revising our constitution," and directed the revisions. Now, at Johns Hopkins, the man who was eventually to draw up a covenant for the world, wrote his fifth constitution. In his letter to Ellen, telling her about it, he reveals a side of his nature which may explain his inability to win the support of the "little group of wilful men" who prevented the ratification of that covenant by the United States Senate.

Balto., Md., Dec. 18, 1884

. . . Well, I have given the Hopkins literary society a new name, and a brand-new constitution of my own composition. I even wrote a set of by-laws for them and presided over the meeting at which they adopted all the new methods. They have fallen in with my plans with remarkable unanimity: it remains to be seen how they will operate them. It will require some parliamentary talent to infuse real life into the "Hopkins House of Commons."

It is characteristic of my whole self that I take so much pleasure in these proceedings of this society. It reminds me of the time when I piloted a new constitution to adoption in the society at the University of Virginia. I have a sense of power in dealing with men collectively which I do not feel always in dealing with them singly. In the former case the reserve of pride does not stand so much in my way as it does in the latter. One feels no sacrifice of pride necessary in courting the favour of an assembly of men such as he would have to make in seeking to please one man. . . .

Mr. Goodrich's name was appearing too frequently in Ellen's letters for Woodrow's peace of mind. He trusted her implicitly, but he did not trust Mr. Goodrich. He cautioned her gently that it was unwise to accept the gentleman's escort too often, but when she replied that her friend was not only a gentleman but a New Englander and therefore thoroughly trustworthy, he used sterner methods. After a preface that would have softened a much more stubborn girl than Ellen, he dared for the first time—in a post-script—to assert his authority as her fiance.

Balto., Md., Dec. 18, 1884

. . . You are the only person in the world—without any exception—to whom I can tell *all* that my heart contains. I believe that I am only just beginning to appreciate fully the consequences of this. One of these, which has been once and again forced upon my recognition, is that I am more affected by your opinions than by those of anybody else. With everybody else I am willing that it should be a matter of "give and take": if I cannot convince them that I am right, I am willing that they should differ with me as widely as they will: it's simply a question of mastery. But I have found, to my cost that it isn't so when *you* reject my judgments and opinions, when *you* set my conclusions aside as over-wrought or foolish. I will not undertake to name or to analyze the difference. . . . It does not grow out of anything so small as *pique* that you should not always think me right. I have no special *amour propre* as regards my own judgments: I am quite conscious of being extremely fallible. Nor does it spring from a desire to rule your opinions except by reason: I have never found it agreeable to deal with persons who invariably agree with me. But I have long had the habit of recognizing my own feelings quite frankly—without any attempt to hoodwink *myself*—and I can't make an exception, if I would, in the case of this feeling that takes hold of me when my Eileen prefers other conclusions to mine. . . . It's odd that circumstances should be able to play such tricks with character. . . .

P.S. I had meant to say something about Mr. Goodrich, in answer to your letter of this morning; and though it *is* very late, I will even now add a few words while the matter is on my mind. You were quite right in your forecast of my opinion on the subject of his attentions to you. I do *not* believe in the possibility of the "platonic schedule" *at all.* Of course I have *perfect* faith in your discreetness; but you must remember that he is in ignorance of your engagement, and that not the broadest hints conceivable can make him "understand" so long as you continue to wear your ring as you have been wearing it. Not to wear it on the significant finger is in effect to *conceal* our engagement, my pet, and nobody can be expected to understand hints in the face of the testimony of his senses. Your faith in the power of the New England climate to change human nature may be well founded; but I think it would be much fairer to me if you would wear your ring as an engagement ring. I have not insisted upon this before ... but now I trust that my darling will see fit to observe my wishes in the matter, if she has not done so already. . . .

Ellen's reply is missing, but it evidently calmed his anxieties for a while.

Balto., Md., Dec. 20, 1884

What sweet things you say to me in your letters, my darling! My letters "surround you with brightness and warmth" and "furnish the whole day's supply of sunshine?" ... When I read these sentences, ... I feel as I suppose a man must feel who has suddenly come into such a fortune as he had long eagerly wished to possess and with which he thinks he can do all the great things his heart has devised. Here am I who have been waiting all these long years for the love of someone to whose happiness I could devote my life, and I have been given more than I dared hope for. I have been given the perfect love of the woman of all the women in the world to whom I can render perfect allegiance: the woman whom I knew the world contained, but thought Fortune too niggardly to give me. . . .

It would be impossible for me to live *alone*, without home companionship. . . . But, if I had not found you, I should simply not have known what real love was: I should have gone all my life long mistaking homage and loyal affection for it, and wondering why I was not satisfied.

When I found you I found asserting itself within me a new self I had never recognized before. I had admired other women ... because I had discovered in them womanliness, tenderness and sympathetic intelligence. ... But I was always able to study them from an attitude of dispassionate criticism. I saw their faults distinctly and felt mildly amused by them. ... I could regard their faults with that lack of annoyance, that affectionate pity, which one feels with regard to the shortcomings of a sweet child. The feeling was just one side of that instinct of protection which I suppose every man feels toward women. ... There was a part of my mind and heart which I kept to myself and felt that they had, and could have, nothing to do with: which must, so far as they were concerned have *always* been kept to myself. But once, by what seemed a chance, I discovered my real heart. I found a woman who moved me as I had never been moved before; whose eyes told me, almost from the first, that there was nothing in my heart which she could not sooner or later find out, if she chose; who made me think of *her* instead of myself, the centre of my world ... I felt that unless I could gain leave to live for her instead of for myself all that was best in my life would be ruined: because she had awakened in me that love which a man feels only once—and which had hitherto slept in me—only to leave it forever unsatisfied. ...

The Christmas holidays that year were in sharp contrast to the lonely days Woodrow had found almost unendurable the year before. He went to New York, rented a room in a boarding house near Ellen's, and spent every day with her. For a week after he returned to Baltimore he tried to tell her how happy she had made him.

Balto., Md., Jan. 2, 1885

... How shall I tell you what the past eight days have been to me! They have been the happiest days I ever spent. They have given me my darling all over again. They have not so much increased as *confirmed* my love for her by showing me how completely it renews all that is noblest and best in me to be with her, with what unspeakable tenderness it fills me,—with what courage and what a sense of power it endows me to feel the loving presence that is to make my life bright and healthful and strong—that is to keep my mind fresh by keeping my heart young. Oh Eileen, my treasure! I love you, and it is my strength that I love you! ...

Balto., Md., Jan. 3, 1885

... The future seems to have received a new meaning, and I can't find it in my heart to be any longer so anxious about it as I was. This new taste of your love seems, by some logic not to be understood, to have made it certain that I shall be offered, before next Autumn, such a position as I want. ...

Balto., Md., Jan. 4, 1885

... When I get weary, or discouraged, or perplexed, or when my loneliness threatens to become desperate, it is an inestimable solace to me to know that you love me with all the wealth of your love ... that you think of me with keen sympathy with my work, with a woman's pride and trust in the object of her love, with a woman's loving desire to be by my side. ... My heart is in *your* work—is in all your life, down to its least details; my thoughts follow you through every day's routine. My love is surely of the sort meant for everyday wear, for the *smallest* sympathies and services, as well as for the greatest. ...

Balto., Md., Jan. 9, 1885

... Love has worked wonders for me. The love of the dear ones at home kept my disposition from souring when I was a youngster, and prepared my heart when I became a man for that supremely great love which has come to make my life both possible and complete. Love is the greatest —incomparably the greatest—fact of my life. Without it, my heart would starve and my mind become parched and arid. ... I trust you with all the faith ever given man to spend; I love you with all the love ever given to a single man to bestow; I have found the end of restlessness, the solution of doubt, the perfection of hope, the sweetest gifts of happiness. ...

He must have persuaded Ellen, during those days in New York, that teaching women would not after all be "beneath him," for he wrote:

Balto., Md., Jan. 10, 1885

... The Bryn Mawr decision is to be taken [by the Board of Trustees] on Monday and I am waiting for it as a criminal might wait for the answer to his appeal for release. If I am elected, the next six months of work will but speed my happiness; if I am left out in the cold the coming months will simply punctuate my anxieties and the weary waiting....

He had also finally convinced Ellen that Mr. Goodrich must be told that she was engaged. She wrote that she had done so, but that he had begged her to let him continue to see her and had promised to "acquit her beforehand of any possible consequences to him." Would Woodrow mind if she still saw him once in awhile? He minded—so much that on the day he heard from Bryn Mawr's Board of Trustees he wrote five pages of protest before telling her the good news, relenting only so far as to say that he would not object to her accepting Mr. Goodrich's escort to church. "Though I shall pity him and fear that he won't derive much benefit from the church services," he added with uncharacteristic sarcasm. Then, at last, came the news.

Balto., Tuesday morning,
Jan'y. 13, 1885

... I have heard from Bryn Mawr, little lady! I have been elected "Associate" in History for two years at $1500 a year. This is the lowest rank, and men who are no older than I, but who have received their degrees and had a single year's experience in teaching, are put in the grade above; but I have no substantial grounds for objecting to that. There will be no real subordination. "Associate" means nothing. There is to be but one instructor in history and he is to be the head of the department, of course. I suppose that there can be no question about the advisability of my accepting the offer. Small as it is, it is quite as much as I have any reason to expect would be offered me elsewhere. I have written to father about it, and shall tell Dr. Rhoads that I will take a few days to consider the matter. And now, what say *you?* ... You have the first right to be consulted, and your judgment in the matter is more vital to me than anyone else's can be. Would you be altogether satisfied to have me accept? The election for two years means that at the end of that time, my services in the meantime having been satisfactory, I would be promoted to the next rank—"Associate-Professor" and to a larger salary. Tell me without reserve *exactly* what you think, my darling. You are now, and always shall be, my chief counsellor....

But ... I haven't broached the real subject of my letter yet! Can you

guess what that is?... Is there no immediate consequence to my acceptance of the position at Bryn Mawr? If I decide that in the affirmative—as I shall, if you and dear father approve—there is something,
you know, which *you* will have to decide! Why, my darling, my heart
beats so at thought of that decision that it is actually hard for me to
write about it! My precious Eileen, won't you be thinking of ways to
make our marriage possible in June?... Bryn Mawr opens on the 15th
of September. We wouldn't want to make the first weeks of our married
life correspond with the first weeks of college work in a strange place,
would we?... Oh, my darling! How shall I tell you of the flood of ex-
ultant, tender, passionate feeling that comes in upon me at thought of
so near a fulfillment of the sweetest, the holiest, the strongest, the most
selfish and most *un*selfish wish of my life. I *cannot* wait for anything but
an imperative necessity—that is wherein I am selfish—I long to give
myself, *all* of myself, to my darling's service—that is wherein I am
not selfish....

Ellen gave her consent to his acceptance of Bryn Mawr's offer, and
said that she would take a June wedding under consideration.

Balto., Wednesday afternoon,
Jan'y. 14, 1885

My own darling,

What a sweet, what a *precious* little document that was that I received
this morning! It was so full of your love—which is my delight and my
strength! And may I not wish *you* joy, little sweetheart, on my Bryn
Mawr election? I know that you are glad ... but are you glad, Eileen,
altogether on my account? Tell me, darling, isn't there a little joy for
your*self* in what that election promises us? Oh, my darling, if it is to be
—and I don't believe that you will have the heart to refuse me—how
am I to wait the six months with even a *show* of patience!—But I must
not talk of that any more just now. I am so excited about it that were
I to dwell on it too long, I think I should go to New York to-night....

I went last night to hear Beecher's lecture, and was splendidly entertained for an hour and forty minutes, though he was constantly offend-
ing my tastes and denying my opinions. His subject was "The Reign of
the Common People" and he sent through it a stream of strong, shallow,

noisy, irregular, evident, picturesque, taking talk. Nobody wanted him
to stop; nobody failed to admire the skill and popular force of the man;
nobody carried away much instruction. He proved that dilute sense may
fill a hall with intent listeners; he did *not* prove that much greater
eloquence, much stronger reasoning, much more compact sense could
not fill it quite as full. Dan'l Webster could have had as great success,
but Beecher paid much less for his. . . .

Now he could calm down and write again about Ellen's favorite
subject—Woodrow Wilson and his work.

Balto., Jan'y. 20, 1885

. . . I feel a much greater affinity for the busy rush and the practical talk
of the outside world that don't read than for the noiseless, level, monotonous talk of a book, whose life seems inseparable from a seat indoors.
These bright, inviting days . . . tempt me every moment to throw down
these heavy volumes and run out into the glories of the open air. But a
man can't find *all* the necessary food for thought in the streets of a great
city, or even in the free inspiration of the noble country-side. To be a
heeded, a trustworthy, a conscientious thinker nowadays, one must dig
into books. He can't find history anywhere else; he can't understand
present experience unless he knows the experience bound up between
the covers of ponderous books or recorded on the faded faces of old
manuscripts; so that he *must* focus all his senses in his spectacles, and
strive to forget that he was not meant to sit all day in a hard chair at a
square table, pouring all his energies out in deciphering stiff print.
There's duty in drudgery as well as in love and laughter. It's quite as
necessary for the Christian to work as for him to be glad. If he finds
himself now and then quite worn out, he deserves sympathy, but not
release. . . . In short, if a man does not find duty agreeable, he does not
deserve gratification. . . .

Ellen Axson, artist and lover of poetry, was, at the same time, an
exceedingly sensible and practical woman. She had given her consent
to the Bryn Mawr appointment, because she could not bear to disappoint
Woodrow, but when she sat down to examine facts and figures, she was
worried. Two people could live on $1500 a year, but Eddie and probably
Stockton would eventually come to live with them, which would mean

that they would have to rent two rooms. Rents at Bryn Mawr boarding houses, she had found out, were very high—ten dollars a week for room and board for one person. Forty dollars a week for four! With royalties from *Congressional Government* and her own and the boys' small incomes, they could manage, but Woodrow must continue to write, and a successful writer on politics and government needed more than merely food and lodging. Much as she hated to disturb his happy dreams, she pointed this out to him and suggested that they put off their marriage for another year. The two long letters he wrote in reply may not have lessened her anxiety, but they stopped any further objections.

Balto., Jan'y. 22, 1885

... You may be sure that I have thought over the matter often and most carefully with an eye to its *business* side alone, as it was clearly my duty to do—and after such views repeatedly taken, I can say without hesitation and without bias from sentiment, that there would, in my opinion, be nothing *imprudent* in our going to Bryn Mawr on $1500 a year for two years. In the first place it will not cost us ten dollars per week apiece necessarily.... I have not had any correspondence with the boarding-house keepers at Bryn Mawr, ... but their charges would be unlike any I have ever heard of if they demanded twice as much for two persons as for one.

But suppose they do, what then? I admit that a thousand dollars being paid out for board, no margin would remain for books or for the necessary (?) journeys to Washington; but I think that enough would remain for our other necessary expenses: and I am sure that there is something that is more needful for my success than books and trips to the capital, namely, peace of mind. *That* will come to me, not with abundant means, but with *you!* I am not saying this, darling, only as a lover: I am simply putting into words a deep, deliberate, rational conviction—a conviction which antedates my meeting with you; for I knew then that I could never have true peace of mind until I found the companionship which I have since found in your love!

How does the case stand, then, with me? If I am to spend another year without you, it will be simple prudence to decline the Bryn Mawr offer and spend that year *here*. I would only break myself down by undertaking such a situation alone. Pecuniary anxieties, should I be weak enough to yield dominion to them, could not torment me half as much as the double burden of novel responsibilities and loneliness.

The reason I asked in one of my recent letters, about your plans concerning dear little Eddie was that I wanted to have a definite correspondence with the Bryn Mawr landladies; and, if I found that their charges were beyond the capabilities of $1500, it was my intention to decline the position there. It is hardly *possible* for me now, however, to withhold my decision any longer—I have already been quite too slow about arriving at it—and I shall sign the two year contract in the full assurance that it will be possible for us to make satisfactory arrangements. Of course I shall not do this to force your hand, my precious ... I want to leave you absolutely free to make your own decision: my only desire is to *help* you in this, as in all other things. Take counsel of your *heart,* darling, not of your fears. And above all have no fears for *me!* ... Have you so little faith in love that you think the inconveniences of imperative economy, which can have in it no actual *want,* enough to outweigh it with me? ... Why, I am not *at all* of your creed in this matter. I believe that it gives love *wings, not* chains, to lay upon it the necessity of self-sacrifice—and the sharper the sacrifice, the longer and stronger the wings! ...

He knew Ellen very well by now, as his second letter proved. If she believed that she could help him with his work, she would say no more about putting off their marriage. So he told her how she could help, foretelling the beginning of a partnership that lasted all their lives.

Balto., Jan'y. 23, 1885

... I know that the help and companionship of a loving wife are more necessary to me a thousand fold than a private library or means for travels of investigation,—provided the only woman whom I *could* marry will consider it not too great a sacrifice to accept, for my sake, a very scant living. ...

I have been, very naturally, thinking a good deal of late about the practical details of our life at college next year—I mean as regards my work ... and there seem to me to be several very simple, feasible and delightful plans by which you can give me the best possible aid merely by doing, as my proxy and for my benefit (you see how selfish I am!), such reading as you delight most in doing. I shall have to work away unceasingly in one or two rigid specialties; my darling can find out for me what is going on in the world, what subjects are commanding the most space in the magazines (for the library will contain them all), what is being written that would be suggestive to me; can recite to me the plots and read to me the choice parts of the best novels of the day, and fill my too prosy brain with the sweetest words of the poets; can, in short, keep my mind from dry rot by exposing it to an atmosphere of fact and entertainment and imaginative suggestion. We will purvey for each other in separate literary fields, if my darling is pleased with the idea, and she may add to her talents in the art which she already excels in that other equally great accomplishment of making pictures for the mental eye of the man who loves her with all his heart. . . .

Ellen's response to this letter exceeded his hope. She wrote at once that she would marry him in June and he could hardly believe it.

> *Balto., Sabbath afternoon*
> *Jan'y. 25, 1885*

. . . The crowning, the most precious sentence in this sweet note is "So it must be as you wish." As I wish! *Can* it be true that I am to have, as my heart's most inestimable treasure, the loving wife for whom my life has so long waited? . . . Are you really to be my bride, my life-long sweetheart, the joy and pride of my manhood, and, if God will, the comfort and strength of my old age? Yes, you have promised! And I? What will I give in return? There is very little that I can give—except love. That is much—and you shall be rich in that. . . . If love can make a true husband, I will be one to my darling. . . .

The following Sunday, he wrote:

> *Balto., Jan'y. 29, 1885*

. . . Shall I tell you . . . what I like to think about on Sundays? I like to look forward to the time . . . when we shall go to church to-gether and feel our love for each other sanctified by our common love for the gracious God who brought us to-gether; when we shall pause from the week-day work to talk, as we please, the sweet confidences of love, to look each other in the eyes and know that we are the same sweethearts as of old, only with *more* love, and a more precious intimacy, and to commune with the Father in Heaven whose children we delight to be. . . .

January, 1885, was an exciting month for Woodrow Wilson. Shortly after Ellen had settled on a June wedding and he had signed the contract to teach at Bryn Mawr, two copies of *Congressional Government* arrived from the publishers. And he felt the thrill that every author knows, when he sees the actual, bound copies of his first book. He sent the first copy to Ellen with a note enclosed.

Balto., Jan. 24th, 1885

I received two copies of ''Congressional Government'' last evening and immediately reversed the wrapper about one of them and sent it off to you . . . I took time only to write your name upon the fly-leaf: but that cost some ten minutes, because it was so hard to know what to write! Of course, however, I had to refrain from putting anything more . . . I had to say everything or nothing—and what I wanted to put would have been out of place on the public face of a book. I *wanted* to say that everything in the book was yours already, having been written in the light and under the inspiration of your love; that every word of it was written as if to you, with thoughts of what you would think of it, and speculations as to your delight should it receive favour from the publishers and the public; that, as your love runs through this my first book, so it must be the enabling power in all that I may write hereafter, for without your entire love and faith and sympathy it must be also the *last* book into which I could put any of *myself;* that, in presenting it to you, I was presenting it to one whose praise and approval are a thousand times sweeter and more essential to me than the praise and approval of the whole world of critics and readers. In sending you my first book, darling, I renew the gift of myself. . . .

He sent the second copy to the Reverend Joseph Wilson, to whom the book was dedicated.

Congressional Government was a success from the start. The first edition was sold out in a few weeks. It ran, eventually, through more than thirty editions. The first straw in the wind appeared when the author, like many another, strolled into a bookshop—anonymously— and asked for a copy.

Balto., Jan'y. 26, 1885

... I had a comical experience.... The first clerk I approached did not know of the book and asked me if I "remembered who it was by." I simulated an air of difficult recollection and told him that it was written by a man named Wilson. He inquired of an elderly gentleman about Wilson's "Congressional Government" and was told that all the copies had been sold, but that more had been ordered. ...

A day came when Woodrow's worldly wisdom was confirmed and Ellen's faith in the power of the New England climate to change human nature rudely shattered. Poor Mr. Goodrich, unable to control his emotions, proposed to her. She told him sternly that he could never see her again, and described his reaction in a letter to Woodrow, whose indignant response arrived by the next mail.

Balto., Sabbath afternoon
Feb'y. 8, 1885

... So Mr. G. sought his fate, did he? My brave, true little sweetheart! You have acted just as I would have you act. But what shall I say for him? If he pleaded and protested, and thought himself unjustly treated, I don't wonder that you saw how weak and unmanly the whole thing was on his part! Why, Eileen, I can't conceive of a *man's* making it *necessary* that you should have a "scene" with him.... He is either a fool or a knave; but I have no inclination to abuse him. I can only pity and despise a man who hasn't the manliness to see that he *owes* it to you to *anticipate* your wish to have nothing more to do with him; and I cannot sufficiently rejoice that you are finally rid of the attentions of a man whose lack of true gentlemanly instinct must have exposed you to repeated mortification. I sincerely hope that you *will* leave the house. ...

In the same letter he told Ellen that he had gone to Bryn Mawr to talk to a Mrs. Hawkins, owner of a boarding house. The lady, he reported, "charges enormous prices, with *such* assurance," but it would silence Ellen's "unselfish objections" to hear that "it would cost *one* person *almost* as much for board there as it would cost for *two*," since Mrs. Hawkins wanted "ten dollars apiece for two and 'about fifteen' for one!"

In February reviews of Woodrow's book began to appear in magazines and newspapers. Most of the critics were enthusiastic and many expressed surprise that a man of twenty-eight, still a university student, had written it. When he heard that the famous essayist and biographer, Gamaliel Bradford, was going to review it in the *Nation*, the author was elated. Yet, although Mr. Bradford wrote that it "was one of the most important books, dealing with political subjects, which have ever issued from the American press," and compared it favorably with Bagehot's *English Constitution*, both Woodrow and Ellen were annoyed when the review was published.

Balto., Feb. 15, 1885

My own darling,

I was disappointed in the *Nation's* notice just as you were and for the same reasons. I knew that responsible cabinet government was Mr. Bradford's hobby; but I did not suppose that he would ride it into this review with such extraordinary demonstration; and of course he misjudges my purpose altogether. If the conclusion drawn from this book is so evident and so irresistible, why not let its readers draw it for themselves? They will like it much better if it seems to be their own than if it were thrust in their faces. I do not consider constitutional amendments necessary *at first*, to make way for a *beginning*, any more than Mr. Bradford does; but I think they would be necessary eventually, as he does. A magazine article is a proper enough place to advocate such a change, but such a book as I tried to write is not; and Mr. B. has done it a great disservice by bringing in my *Overland* piece to supplement it.

I suppose that it is ungracious to take exception to the warm praise of my work, but I may confide in you the fact that it seems to me almost ridiculous. I should like above all things to be able to write something comparable with Bagehot's "inestimable work"; but of course it will be evident to every one who has read both my essays and his that I am as yet *very* far from having approached the excellencies of my master; and this critic's rhapsody will, I fear, be read with elevated eye-brows and a smile of disbelief. The publishers will find it useful for their advertisements, but it will scarcely advance the fame of the book.

Probably no author is ever satisfied with any review of his writings —because critics are seldom or never of the number of those bosom friends of the author to whom alone the real *spirit* of his work is revealed—and doubtless these three columns in the *Nation* contain infinitely more of appreciation and sympathy than most writers can ever hope to get from contemporary criticism; but I may pour into *your* ear the disappointments which come to my sensitive, secret heart. . . .

I am conscious of being in all things *too* sensitive. Most men of my age and in the earliest, most critical stages of their careers would be willing to pay any price for such a notice from such a paper as the *Nation;* and would enjoy very keenly such congratulations as it has brought me. But the object that I have placed before myself is so dear, so sacred in my eyes that anything that in the least obstructs it or diminishes the chances of achieving it hurts me like a slap in the face. I want to contribute something substantial to the political knowledge and the political science of the country, to the end that our forms of government and our means of administration may be perfected. Since I am shut out from realizing my first ambition, to become a public servant and actively participate in the direction of affairs, it is my heart's dearest desire that I may become one of the guides of public policy by becoming one of the guides of public thought. . . .

Woodrow Wilson's reputation as a remarkable young writer was now so well established that he began to get some interesting offers. Houghton, Mifflin & Co. asked him to write another book, and Wm. F. Ford of Bradstreet's "begged" him for "something worth while about the course of things in the last session of the Forty-eighth Congress."

Ellen was delighted. She wrote that, in her opinion, "of all the world's workers those which take by far the highest rank are the writers of noble books." But she was not at all sure that Woodrow agreed with her. She suspected that his early ambition to become a statesman and an orator was still his "dearest desire." He had told her that speaking in public "set his mind all aglow," that he felt "a sort of transformation," * and she knew that he was usually dissatisfied, coldly critical and often exhausted when he was writing. Hoping that her suspicions were unfounded, she asked some searching questions and received two long, very honest letters in reply.

Balto., Feb'y. 24, 1885

. . . So you did not find a satisfactory answer to your questions in that early letter † of mine? Well, my precious, it is very easy to supply the

* Refer W.W.'s letter of Nov. 25, 1884.
† Refer W.W.'s letter of Nov. 30, 1883.

missing parts of the confession; and although I would ever so much rather wait till I might *say* such things to you, when I could *feel* and *see* what you were thinking and what you were wondering upon the subject, and how much you were loving me the while, I will try to satisfy my darling now upon her points of doubt. These are *not* "foolish words," little sweetheart, into which you have put your questions, but very sensible, womanly words, which demonstrate your *right* to know all my thoughts . . . you have the title both of love and of understanding.

Yes, darling, there is, and has long been, in my mind a "lurking sense of disappointment and *loss,* as if I had missed from my life something upon which both my gifts and inclinations gave me a claim." I do feel a very real regret that I have been shut out from my heart's *first* primary ambition and purpose, which was to take an active, if possible, a leading, part in public life, and strike out for myself, if I had the ability, a *statesman's* career. That is my heart's—or rather my *mind*'s—deepest secret. . . . But don't mistake the feeling for more than it is. It is nothing *more* than a regret; and the more I study the conditions of public service in this country the less personal does the regret become. My disappointment is in the fact that there is no room for such a career in this country for *anybody,* rather than the fact that there is no chance for *me*.

Had I independent means of support, even of the most modest proportions, I should doubtless have sought an entrance into politics *anyhow,* and have tried to fight my way to predominant influence even amidst the hurly-burly and helter-skelter of Congress. I have a strong instinct of leadership, an unmistakably oratorical temperament and the keenest possible delight in affairs; and it has required very constant and stringent schooling to content me with the sober methods of the scholar and the man of letters. I have no patience for the tedious toil of what is known as "research"; I have a passion for interpreting great thoughts to the world; I should be complete if I could inspire a great movement of opinion, if I could read the experiences of the past into the practical life of the men of to-day and so communicate the thought to the minds of the great mass of the people as to impel them to great political achievements. Burke was a *very* much greater man than Cobden or Bright; but the work of Cobden and Bright is much nearer to the measure of my powers, it seems to me, than the writing of imperishable thoughts upon the greatest problems of politics which was Burke's mission. I think with you, darling, that "of all the world's workers those which take by far the highest rank are the writers of noble books." If one could choose between the two careers, *with the assurance that he had the capacity for either,* "it would seem to *me* that there would be no room for hesitation even."

But my feeling has been that such literary talents as I have are *secondary* to my equipment for other things; that my power to write was meant to be a hand maiden to my power to speak and to organize action. Of course it is quite possible that I have been all along entirely misled in this view: I am ready to accept the providential ordering of my life as conclusion on that point. Certainly I have taken the course which will, with God's favour, enable me to realize *most* of what I proposed to myself, and I do not in the least repine at the necessity which has shut me out from all other courses of life. It is for this reason that I have never made these confessions so fully before: I did not want even to *seem* to be discontented with my lot in life. I shall write with no less diligence of preparation, both moral and mental, and with no less effort to put all that is best in myself into my books because I have had to give up a cherished ambition to be an actor in the affairs about which my *pen* can now be busy. The new channels of work shall not clog my enthusiasms, and nothing shall lower my ideals or make a pause in my effort to realize them. One thing there is which I have now that I did not have when I dreamed and planned about a career as statesman and orator; one thing that I had no conception of then, and which is more to me than the strength and inspiration of *any* ambition: that one priceless, inestimable thing is *your love,* my Eileen! But continue to love me as you do now, and I shall stop short of nothing noble of which my powers are capable. I accept your judgment: the writer's career *is* the highest: and you shall help me to write truely and worthily, to write so that every page shall testify, by its honesty, by its clarity, by its unsoured temper, that I have lived in the light of your love. . . .

If it had not been for one passage, this eloquent letter might have put an end to Ellen's "points of doubt." "I have a strong instinct of leadership, an unmistakably oratorical temperament and the keenest possible delight in affairs." How could she believe that with these gifts, this temperament, Woodrow would be content to sit on the side lines?

In a moment of prescience she wrote that some day the conditions which
now made it impossible for him to enter public life would change and
that his great gifts would not be wasted. But Woodrow, after modifying
his earlier opinion, presented another which seemed unanswerable.

Balto., Feb'y. 27, 1885

You certainly know, my matchless little sweetheart, how to answer my
letters in the way of which my heart most approves.... I am afraid,
however, that I cannot agree with [your] conclusions concerning the
probabilities of my future career. I have not given up all idea of entering public life because I have given up all hope of seeing the conditions
of public life bettered before I am too old to go actively into politics:
but because I see very clearly (and entirely without regret) that I shall
all my life be under the necessity of *earning a living*. I expect to see a
very rapid as well as a very early reform of our methods of party government—a reform which will open the doors to the most honourable and
the most gifted; but I do *not* expect to inherit or to earn an independent
fortune. The lawyer's office is much nearer Congress and the cabinet
than a professor's chair, and money-making is possible in the former,
impossible (or next to impossible) in the latter. I should have stayed
where I was if I hoped to enter politics. But I saw that in every *electoral*
system, and especially in ours, there are innumerable chances of defeat.
It is often—particularly for a man of independent action—easier to
lose than to hold a constituency: and men in this country are, by long-
settled policy, allowed to have no constituency but that which lies immediately around them, are suffered to represent no district but the one
in which they live. And to lose his political place is, for the poor man, to
find himself without *any* place. In his business—in his private profession,
whatever it may be—he finds himself forced to begin over again. Nobody
wants a man who has tasted of political office, and so gotten political
excitement into his blood, to manage the delicate details of his law
business for him—and certainly no university or college board wants a
politician on its faculty. For a man who has no independent means of
support, the chances of defeat are the chances of *poverty*, are the chances
of financial ruin. The youth who plans a one-day entrance into political
life had better begin early to earn and to hoard, to acquire and multiply,
money. He cannot afford to trust the salary of political office for a

livelihood: he cannot afford to be elected to-day unless he can afford to be defeated five or ten years hence.

Of course an unusual combination of fortunate circumstances may open a public career for me and give me a chance to find out whether or not I really do possess the peculiar talents which I have imagined myself to have; but that is an extremely remote contingency, and is by no means worth looking forward to. And you must not distress yourself with the belief, darling, that my regret at having been shut out from the life toward which my first and strongest desires drew me is accompanied with anything like *pain,* or with a sense of failure, of having taken that work which I can do second-best and missed that for which I was intended. As I said in my other letter, I am quite ready to believe that it was simply strong desire, not *instinct,* upon which the ambition was founded. I accept my new profession with a profound impression of being providentially directed, and accept it with pleasure, enthusiasm and hope. If the circumstances which have shut me out from politics had been of my own making, I might feel differently: but, as it is, I obey cheerfully the plain dictates of prudence. I have not suffered defeat—I have not lost my proper birthright—I have simply been corrected in my views of myself, and my talents and directed to the path which is the only one that leads to the successes I was meant to attain.... I thought once that my ability to write clearly, my familiarity with the use of the pen, was merely to aid me as an orator and a statesman: it turns out that the latent powers of oratory and statesmanship which I possess—if, indeed, I possess them at all—were intended to complete my equipment as a *writer* on politics—in order that I might *see* as a statesman and might tell what I see with words that live and inspire. I am content; I am not baffled. Doubtless I have been pointed to my truest and best victory....

Joseph Wilson loved the English language, used it superbly and trained his children to express themselves clearly and correctly. His elder son, the one who sat entranced on a hard pew while Joseph preached, was his prize pupil. It was not only his father's voice but the words he used that fascinated Tommy, and he was not so much hurt as ashamed when Joseph corrected him sternly. When he used the wrong word or muddled a sentence, Joseph always demanded, "What do you mean by that?" Tommy would explain and Joseph would bark, "Well, why didn't you say so?" To Woodrow Wilson, writer and orator, this training was invaluable, and he always gave his father the credit when, eventually, he acquired a vocabulary that was larger than Shakespeare's. But Joseph Wilson used the flat "a" and Woodrow was eventually convinced that this was incorrect. At Johns Hopkins, among his other activities, he trained himself to use the broad "a," but without exaggeration.

Ellen was interested and asked him to send her a set of "rules and lists" so that she might speak as nearly as possible like her beloved. She never succeeded. Her soft Southern drawl made the broad "a" seem ridiculous and the drawl was incurable. But she carefully preserved these rules and lists.

The broad, Italian sound of "a" (as in father) seems to be most common:

1. Before "th": path, bath, wrath.

2. Before an "l" sound is merged in that of some neighbor consonant: e.g., half, calm, balm, palm, psalm, etc.

3. In *au* before an "n" or "f" sound: e.g., laugh, launch, vaunt, flaunt, aunt, etc.

The *intermediate* sound of "a" (the Italian "a" uttered with a very light touch) between the "a" in fat and the "a" in father, is most common before "f," "s" or "n." Here are a *few* samples: advance, after, am*a*ss, answer, ask, basket, branch, chance, chant, class, plaster....

These will be enough to practice on for the present, won't they?

Ellen's conscience was bothering her. She was enjoying her work at the Art Students' League enormously. She spent many happy hours at art exhibitions and was thrilled by occasional evenings at the theater, but life to this daughter of the manse was a serious matter. Innocent pleasures were all very well, but life's chief object was to be of service to other people. She decided to teach two evenings a week at a "missionary school" in one of New York's slum districts. Woodrow had protested:

Balto., Feb'y. 9, 1885

... It will not add to my peace of mind on Sabbaths that you have undertaken missionary labours.... One who is not a New Yorker must be ... exposed to risks in the work to which city-wise and city-hardened persons would not be subject.... I entirely sympathize with your feelings in the matter, but I can't help questioning the wisdom of the arrangement. . . .

But Ellen insisted that it was her duty, and taught at the school for the rest of her stay in New York. She had no fears for her own safety, but some of the "new thought" she heard at the Art Students' League made her feel that the very foundations of society were in danger. Woodrow wrote in reply to one of her letters on this subject.

Balto., March 1, 1885

. . . I don't wonder that you can have no sympathy with that false talk about "a woman's right to live her own life." If it means the right of women to live apart from men, it is as untrue to the teachings of history, to the manifestations of Providence, and to the deepest instincts of the heart, as would be the other proposition that *men* have a right to live outside of the family relation. The family relation is at the foundation of society, is the life and soul of society, and the women who think that marriage destroys identity and is not the essential condition of the performance of their *proper* duties—if they think so *naturally* and not through disappointment—are the *only* women whom God has intended for old maids. Their sex is a mere accident.

In my opinion, a woman proves her womanliness, a man his manliness, by longing for the companionship of marriage, and for all the duties and responsibilities that marriage brings. I have no words in which to express my contempt for the view which would have it that marriage *belittles* a woman! It no more belittles her than it belittles a man. If it be a marriage of love, it *ennobles* her as nothing else could. If she cannot preserve her individuality in the family—if she cannot make it more felt there than anywhere else—she simply has no individuality worth preserving. It is simply ridiculous to argue as if women were now what they once were, the mere drudges of the household: and, in order to make the creed, that women must take care, for the sake of their independence, to live exactly the same life that men lead, a creed which will allow society to exist [only if] it first be provided that men be enabled to assume the sex and the duties abandoned by the mother and the housekeeper! Oh, it is a shame so to pervert the truth! For these people *are* very near a *great* truth—only their little souls are too soiled by selfishness to hold that truth in its *purity*. Women *have* a right to live their own lives. They have mental and moral gifts of a sort and of a perfection that men lack: but they have not the *same* gifts that men have. Their life must *supplement* man's life: and it cannot supplement man's life without being in closest wifely communion with it. This is not putting their lives in a position *subordinate* to the position allotted to men. The colours of the spectrum supplement each other, but without *all* of them we should not have the full splendour of the sun.

And here ... we can find the true rule for analyzing our own case. You do not merge your life in mine from any doubt about your own being worth living separately, or because of any assurance that mine is full of the best uses and the best ambitions, but for that other, that glorious, reason, which makes our love for each other so sacred and so real, because neither of us would be *complete* without the other. I know that my life would be stripped of the great part of its worthiness and its power to achieve if I did not have you to love and to serve, and from whom to receive that love and sympathy which are the life of my heart. And our love warrants me in concluding that it is just the same with you, that it has been my privilege to make your life complete....

An old German philosopher, who used to search for—and in most cases find—the fundamental psychological facts of society, used to maintain the apparent paradox that no man ever fully realized his own identity until he lost it in the service of love for another; that duty performed at the promptings at the heart was the only true *freedom*. ... A heart is no heart in isolation and self-absorption. It is hard to express the idea without seeming to indulge in subtleties; but the *fact* is plain enough. We were not at peace with ourselves until we, in a sort, gave those selves away, pledged them in each other's service. ... It is not peculiar to women, my darling, to fail "to find contentment in living for themselves." Men are quite as unable to satisfy themselves with self-service. True-hearted men ... consciously or unconsciously, testify to Hegel's beautiful conception that they can find their true selves only in the love and devotion of family life. ...

Interest in *Congressional Government* kept growing steadily. "Our book," Woodrow called it, and told Ellen everything anybody had said or written about it. His friend Shinn, now working for *Overland* in San Francisco, had written that he was very happy about Woodrow's "transcendent and well deserved success. You are going straight to the

front. God bless you, and your dainty, loving genius of a wife-to-be.''
Charles Dudley Warner had ''complimented'' the book and said that he
had sent a copy to Matthew Arnold recommending it to him as ''the
best book on the subject.'' Houghton, Mifflin had asked Woodrow to
write a volume on North Carolina for their series, ''American Com-
monwealths.'' The University of Michigan invited him to read a paper
before a meeting of the Political Science Association, and hinted that
he might be asked to join their faculty. A newspaper suggested that he
write a series of ''letters'' on government, and this tempted him, but
he refused. He explained why in a letter to Ellen.

Balto., Mar. 21, 1885

... I should *like* an occupation which would leave me free, living on my
wits, as it were—free to take up any other task that offered to meet my
ends better. But these are likings ... at which Prudence laughs. This
excellent conservative mentor says reprovingly, ''Wilson, keep your
head! Don't let your love of active affairs tempt you to hover on their
outskirts. You know well enough that you can't *enter* them ever. If you
understood the practical side of Government and extracted a bit of its
philosophy as a college pupil, there's no reason why you should not hope
to do more and better of the same kind as a professor, if only you keep
out of scholastic ruts and retain your sympathetic consciousness of the
practical world, where prejudices never refrain from meddling, where
passions never manage to keep out of mischief, where ''horse sense'' is
always at a higher premium than learning, where practicable ''business''
is everything. . . .

Since Ellen could no longer accept Mr. Goodrich's invitations to go
to the theater, she went, instead, to matinees with some of the Art
League girls. They sat in the gallery, usually paying only twenty-five
cents. ''Very nice people'' sat there, too, Ellen assured Woodrow, in
case he should fear for her safety. The day after she saw Ellen Terry and
Henry Irving in *Much Ado About Nothing*, she wrote:

New York, March 22, 1885

... I believe they say that Beatrice is her best part,—she was certainly
exquisite in it—while Irving made a *capital* Benedict. . . . He was so
unusually free from affectations too. . . . But that play always makes me
so cross—to read it even, while to see it acted is, of course, many times

worse. The idea of having for its *hero* such a mean, base, contemptible, ignoble wretch as that Claudio!... And to think that Hero should marry him after all! Why do you suppose Shakspere made his men *such* poor creatures as a rule and his women such paragons!...

She had been promoted from "black and white" to the "paint class" at the Art Students' League and wrote that she was "altogether fascinated." Her letters were filled now with talk of methods, models and masters, although she seldom failed to include the "love-making" Woodrow longed for.

New York, March 24, 1885

... How can I ever tell you how I prize this tender, watchful love of yours. Every smallest proof of it is treasured up in my heart of hearts and will be all my life. What a happy woman I am and shall *always* be! I can scarcely believe sometimes that it is really I who am so blessed— blessed more than I ever thought to be even in my dreams.

Yours forever,
Eileen

Her pleasure in her work at the League finally brought a troubled letter from Woodrow:

Balto., March 27, 1885

... I don't believe that even you, my Eileen, can have any idea how much I am wrapt up in your studies—for your sake of course, above everything else, but also for their own sake. You know what I believe with regard to your powers in portrait painting: I believe that you can do some really *great* work in that which seems to me one of the very highest departments of art; and I am *so* glad to see every *technical* obstacle taken out of your way: so that, if you want to paint hereafter, you can be free to realize the very best results—so that you can satisfy yourself.... Of course there's that fact, which sometimes makes me feel so guiltily selfish, that marriage will take away almost all your chances for work of that kind; but my heart will be in any arrangement you choose to make by which time may be found for your studies, even after I have appropriated you to myself. Do you know, Eileen,... that I have often wondered what you thought on this point? Won't you tell me, darling? That is now the only point of importance upon which my little sweetheart has never said *any*thing to me—the interference of love with her profession—the sacrifice of that profession involved in giving herself to me. In that sweet talk we had about my stealing gold to be a foil for my silver I learned only the wonderful perfection of her love, which made no sacrifice made for me seem a sacrifice at all. But have you no plans concerning your art studies after June?

Ah, sweetheart, this thing has torn my heart more than once! I *hate* selfishness; it hurts me more than I can tell you to think that I am asking you to give up what has formed so much of your life and constituted so much of your delight. And yet that is what is involved in becoming a wife: we shall want to go to house-keeping as soon as possible.... I would give my life for you, and yet I am asking you to give your life to me—for me, to be merged into mine. Does my darling want that?...

Ellen replied:

New York, Mar. 29, 1885

...I think you do my love a great injustice. I have a great respect for it, because it has shown such sapience and fine judgment: it is so well able to render a *reason* for the faith that is in it. I have never seen anyone who can be compared with you for good and great and delightful qualities. So when head and heart unite in telling me that this is the man whom I most honour, admire, look up to as well as the only one I can love, it would be strange indeed if I did not wish to spend my life with him—and for him. The really strange thing is that you should choose to spend your life with *me*. You know Carlyle says that "let but the rising of the sun or the creation of a world happen twice and it ceases to be marvellous." But this is one great mystery that even use and wont cannot make less marvellous....

It is common to lovers, of course—the sense of inadequacy, the fear that they may disappoint each other—but Woodrow and Ellen never quite outgrew it. Again and again each must reassure and praise the other. One day after Woodrow sent her a quotation from Ruskin, Ellen wrote:

... How well and truly it describes the difference between the self-conceit of a little man and the self-reliance and self-respect of a great man. I believe it is true that only men who are great in soul at least can look at themselves in that calmly impersonal fashion and make a full, just estimate of their powers, yet without any trace of vanity as the result. It must be because they are able to rise above self-consciousness. With the majority of people there seems to be small choice in their attitude toward themselves; they are either consumed with self-conceit or they are the victims of a paralysing self-distrust. It may be that the self-distrust is well founded. And yet I don't know—we were all given *some* work to do and the problem is simply to find out what our portion is, and then, whether great or small, to quietly go ahead and do it. And I suppose that if we knew the commission to be Heaven-sent and did it to God's glory rather than our own, we would be content with the work whatever its nature. I imagine that the ministering spirits feel equally honoured, in their *great* humility, whether they are sent on the humblest or the grandest missions. And then of course, if we could be sure that God had set us the task, we should be no less sure of our power to do it.

But there's the rub—the problem isn't a simple one **after** all. It is easy to *say* that to "know thyself" and then *forget* thyself comprises the whole secret of living, but it isn't so easy to *do*. Strange that it should be so hard to find oneself out— But how I run on! What I started out to say was that I think these words of Ruskin's describe *your* spirit, exactly, my darling, and it is one of the things which I admire and love most in you, that rare combination of power and modesty. One must be conscious of this power to *use* it effectively,—you know your power and it spurs you on to do great deeds, yet leaves not a trace of self-conceit. ...

Yet, even in her humblest moods, Ellen was certain that in all the essential ways they were meant for each other.

New York [undated], 1885

... I hope we will always remain too young to "long for rest" as the chief of blessings: I grow so tired of hearing people talk of heaven as if it were nothing but a place of *rest*. ... Of all the imaginings of heaven which I have heard or read, I think I like best that of the noble woman, who when asked how she best loved to think of it, answered quickly, "As a perpetual service without weariness."

And, my darling, I want to tell you that when you speak of ours being kindred spirits you touch one of the deepest sources of the ever-growing joy which fills my heart to overflowing. I too, have had an ever-deepening sense of the inborn sympathy there is between us in all matters of importance; we look at life in the same way, our ideals and aspirations are in harmony—and our thought is so often the same about those things that make it a great and sweet, though solemn privilege to live; and it is this sympathy which, together with the greatness of my love makes me hope now that, in spite of all my unworthiness, I was indeed meant for you,—that I may do you good and not evil all the days of my life....

Woodrow, although he loved her humility, tried to convince her that it was unreasonable.

Balto., March 30, 1885

...You do not recognize your genius for thinking and loving in just the right way. It shall be my mission to lure you away, by love and trust, from your self-distrust and make you see some part of the discovery I have made, that *your* powers are as great as—as your *love*. I shall not fear to destroy the *beauty* of your humility: I shall hope to remove its *blindness*. My darling's heart is too great for anything but humility, and too true to hold anything but the truth: and the truth is that her gifts *both* of mind and heart are such as *any* man might be proud to do homage to....

Before she met Woodrow, Ellen had not been particularly interested in politics, but no one close to him could escape the contagion of his absorption in the problems of the time or his interest in the statesmen who dealt with them. Yet her point of view was sometimes very feminine. When President Cleveland reappointed a Republican office holder because he had a fine record of efficiency, and hungry Democrats howled in protest, she wrote:

New York, April 1, 1885

... What a *stone wall* Cleveland is! My respect and admiration for him increase daily,—and to tell the truth I didn't like him very much, except

by comparison with Blaine; I never liked his *looks*.... I am really enthusiastic over the man's strength of character, his stern regard for
principles before all things. People must believe in him as a reformer
now. That seems to have been a great test case. But ... do you think it
will "dismember" the Democratic party? ...

On the same day that Woodrow wrote, "your pen has acquired new
powers of speech of late," Ellen was proving this to be truer than he
knew. She did not, that day, need the poets to help her. She revealed
her heart to him as she had not done before in a rapturous, unrestrained
song of her own.

New York, April 3, 1885

... There is no sort of happiness which you have not made me feel—
tumultuous joy, sweet peace too deep and still for words and light-
heartedness and the passionate heart-throb which is almost akin to pain,
—I know them all—and more than all else, a solemn, prayerful, awed
feeling at the thought of the way in which God has blessed me, and of
what He demands of me in return;—of all that it means to be a true
wife,—and to such a man as you, my darling.

You must admit, sir, that in the case of some men I know, it would
have been a much simpler affair, because their conceptions of a *wife,* as
of a *man*—and of life itself—are all lower and narrower. Such a man
deserves less of a woman too, because he gives so much less. She *couldn't*
be so in debt to him as I am to you. But there is one thing I *know,*
darling—I have yet to learn whether the most perfect love, the tenderest
service, the most passionate loyalty can make me, without certain qualities which love cannot give, such a wife as yours should be. But I know
that, notwithstanding the demand is so much greater, I will be a better
wife to you than I could ever have been to a small man, because no other
but yourself could have so stirred my nature to its utmost depths, could
have inspired me with such passionate longing toward my own ideal of
womanhood, or have given me so strong a motive for earnest unflagging
effort for attainment. I am afraid all this is very wrong, it sounds almost
as if I were putting the human love above the divine as a motive for
well-doing, but you will know I don't mean *that;* I am sure that my love
for God and desire to serve Him haven't grown *less* in these two years.

But it would be strange if a great love did not exert some great power upon one's life and nature....

Woodrow's self-revelation had not been quite complete. There still was something which he had been afraid, until now, to enlarge upon.

Balto., April 5, 1885

... I have reminded myself of one of my standing perplexities: which is that there's one whole side of me whose acquaintance you have never made, and to which I have always been awkwardly unable to introduce you—though I *have* had sense enough to speak of it once or twice in my letters. It may shock you—it ought to ... to learn that I have a reputation (?) amongst most of my kin and certain of my friends for being irrepressible, in select circles, as a maker of grotesque addresses from the precarious elevation of chair seats, as a wearer of all varieties of comic grimaces, as a simulator of sundry unnatural burlesque styles of voice and speech, as a lover of farces, even as a dancer of the *"can-can"!* How you have reformed me, I can't divine; but I know that I could not so much as imitate the sound of a cornet in your presence in Savannah, and that not a single trace of the comical vein which used to make my letters so dear to sister Marion's heart has found its way into my correspondence with you. I am not conscious, however, I assure you, Miss Eileen, of having been at all *saddened* by my acquaintance with you; and, though it's natural that an engagement of marriage ... should have made me realize as never before that boyhood's responsibilities were behind me and that all the highest strivings of manhood were at hand ..., I did not feel robbed thereby of boyhood's *gaiety*. I received, rather, a notable augmentation of *that*. It must be that most of my letters to you, and all of my thoughts when we have been together, have been full of my love for you, which has seemed too holy, too wonderful a thing in its perfect joy to be *played* with. I have been a little awed by it.... But you'll find out soon enough what an overgrown boy you have taken as your "lord and master (?)" I suppose that I shall not *always* be awed in your presence! ...

Ellen's doubts about her ability to qualify as an ideal wife for a scholar no longer troubled her. Believing now that perfect love and understanding would compensate for her lack of erudition, she could afford to indulge in some humorous comment on purely intellectual marriages.

New York, April 5, 1885

... Do you suppose it is possible for any human soul fully to reveal itself even when it most wishes to do it? I fancy that our knowledge of that great mystery never comes from tracing step by step its hidden processes, but from inferences judiciously drawn from telling facts gleaned here and there,—from hints and suggestions,—that we pursue the same process that the scientist does in trying to unravel the secrets of nature. Only, of course, in our study of *human* nature we have a great advantage in that it is our *own* nature,—our knowledge is an intuition. And when to that we add the knowledge which comes from great love and perfect sympathy we need not despair of fully understanding one another in spite of the difficulty about words. ...

But query!—if you know a woman so well that you are sure beforehand what she is going to say, or what she would *like* to say on any given subject, what special interest do you find in hearing her say it? Why isn't she an unmitigated bore? When you have seen through her even down to the "vacuum" which somebody says lies beneath all our talking and thinking, what next? That is a question which seems to have disturbed even so sensible a man as Hamerton,* who in discussing "the intellectual marriage" suggests, I believe, as the only remedy, that "they renew themselves" constantly for the other's benefit. I am inclined to think it would be hard to find any way to ward off that danger from a *purely* intellectual marriage. ... If one married a Macaulay simply to hear him *talk*, one would grow tired of it in the course of years, if one didn't exhaust his resources. The novelty would wear off and the flashes of silence would be like balm to the suffering. But I know *now* that a true man and woman never weary of true love and sympathy. It is a possession which time doesn't cheapen. I remember when such questions as those I asked you above seemed to me among the greatest difficulties in the way of marriage. What *do* they talk about! I should think they would wear each other out or suffer from a most embarrassing dearth of remarks! What a foolish school-girl's idea it seems to

* Philip Gilbert Hamerton, British essayist and author of "The Intellectual Life."

me now! As if marriage were like an evening call where long pauses are awkward and must be avoided at any cost. And as soon as both feel themselves "talked out" it is time to part;—only in the former case the inability to *part* renders the situation truly deplorable! A never-ending evening call!—*horrible!* ...

Balto., April 7, 1885

... No, my sweetheart, I do not "suppose it is possible for *any* human soul fully to reveal itself even when it most wishes to do it," if its *purpose* be self-analysis and self-revelation; but if its purpose be to love as it would be loved and to speak that love as it would have love spoken to it, it may succeed, if the purpose is such as guides all its life. Love lives not in oneself but in the object of one's love. ...

Gamaliel Bradford, whose review of *Congressional Government* had annoyed Woodrow, wrote that he was coming to Baltimore and would like to "have some conversation" with the author. Woodrow wrote Ellen about the impending visit and added:

Balto., April 13, 1885

... So we will meet, and discuss oppressively heavy topics, doubtless, much as if all the weight of government were on our mental shoulders. Verily there are penalties connected with writing a book! ... I can amuse myself by putting Gamaliel, old boy, through his paces. I can see what sort of feet he has to sit at. ...

Mr. Bradford's feet turned out to be anything but clay.

Balto., April 16, 1885

My own darling,

I ought in conscience—and I must as a gratification of my own feelings—make this letter a tribute to Mr. Bradford. I have spent most of the day with him ... and I have enjoyed him more than I should have enjoyed an old friend. ... He is natural, he is earnest to the pitch of enthusiasm in things worth thought, he is full of knowledge *and* full of affairs; he is cordial, he is delightful. ... His sympathy and his power to stimulate thought have done me as much good as a week's vacation! I feel that I have gained a friend worth having and that I have had my thinking apparatus loosened and lubricated again just as it was in peril of growing rusty. I have met a *man,* and I am excited over the event. . . .

Ellen had set the month for their wedding, but not, in spite of Woodrow's urging, the date. Now, at the end of a long love letter she mentioned an approximate date and he wrote, joyfully,

Balto., April 18, 1885

. . . Somehow it seems to me that the sun shines brighter today than it ever did before. For does not this precious letter close with one of those "By the ways" which often serve my lady to introduce the most important things she says? . . . Do you think, Miss, to escape in that way the embarrassment of fixing a particular day? To say "any day between the 24th and the 31st of June" means that we will be married on the 24th; for I shall certainly take the earliest date you offer. . . .

But it was not so simple as he supposed to fix a date for the wedding. Ellen's grandparents and Stockton Axson, Woodrow's parents and sisters had to be consulted, not to mention numerous aunts, uncles and cousins who would never get over it if they were not present. There was also another difficulty which had not occurred to Woodrow. A bride must have a trousseau and Ellen's would take more time than usual to assemble for she had been in mourning ever since her mother's death and needed an entirely new wardrobe. And, because she could not afford to buy it, she planned to make all her dresses herself when she went back to Savannah. But she had paid her tuition fees at the Art Students' League in advance until June and she was appalled at the thought of spending money and getting nothing for it.

New York, April 19, 1885

. . . Being a man it is probable that you think three weeks more than time enough for *anything!* Perhaps I should make some concession to masculine ignorance and explain more fully. There is a great deal of sewing which I *must* do. I can't afford to have it all done for me. Here in New York the material for an inexpensive dress costs just *half* as much as the making of said dress, and in Savannah it is almost as bad. It is positively ruinous to "put out" anything but a handsome dress. So you see my predicament—one must have some time to prepare even the most modest trousseau....

To her great amusement, Woodrow had something to say about her trousseau.

Balto., April 21, 1885

... Don't it take less time and trouble, darling, to make straight skirts with perpendicular pleats, or like devices, and bodies of the same style, than to make flounced skirts with skewed over-skirts (you must let me use my own terms, however untechnical) and bodies with stiff necks? You know, as I confided in you when we were only friends that I have very decided tastes in ladies' dress (else I would not dare to venture into this department of inquiry where I don't know the language).... I know that for some reason the close-fitting, high-necked body of your black silk dress is not at all becoming to you.... Is it because you are best suited by square yokes, open necks, simple pleated skirts, and—but dear me! I must get out of this just as soon as I can. What temerity!...

Ellen wrote, after reading this letter:

New York, April 22, 1885

... Would your feelings be deeply hurt, if you knew how I have been laughing over it? You have Bible authority for not liking "stiff-necked" people but what *is* a stiff-necked "body"?... You didn't tell me what sort of hats you like! Pray write full descriptions of them! You do it *so* well! It will afford me such exquisite delight to read it. Really I think it is *very* nice in you, dear, to take an interest in such things, and since I find you have such decided opinions about them, I am more than anxious to have them. All suggestions thankfully received! Do you like little bonnets tied under the chin or broad-brimmed hats or "turbans" or "pokes"? And perhaps I had better take your opinion on the colour question....

Balto., April 23, 1885

My own darling,

So I am to write another letter on the dress question! Well! You display a splendid temerity in asking me to do this: but I'll do it ... even at the risk of being laughed at again and poked in the ribs with such sentences as "you do it *so* well!... I find that I do not like *any* close-fitting silk bodices. The material is so stiff that it gives, when fitted, a *rigid, stayed* appearance to the figure—and the straight, round of military collars with which such a fabric is usually crowned suits only persons of military fulness of bust, for whom a suggestion of *drill* is not out of place. Consequently what seems to be needed is relief of the stiffness by means of some perpendicular arrangement (how language does fail me in this great undertaking!) of some more pliant material in front, shirred, or something of the sort, at the throat and at the waist. A *basque* form that goes below the waist and is reinforced with whalebones, or the like, is terrible to look upon. There is the real beauty that delights my eye only in those fabrics out of which bodices can be made which *suggest,* rather than outline, the figure. ...

I don't like *too much* black, I confess. ... Of course since I have never seen you dressed in *any* colours, it is impossible to be sure of my opinions in this matter. My imagination prompts me very strongly to the idea, however, that very deep blue or a rich maroon, purple or (for the heresy will out!) crimson would suit you best. ...

Concerning what he called "the great bonnet-hat question" Woodrow's tastes were equally definite. He did not like turbans, or bonnets that tied under the chin. He did like broad-brimmed hats, but preferred the "poke"—"with a sort of peek-aboo effect for the upper part of the face."

Ellen had been on the verge of buying a bonnet when this letter arrived. The next day she bought a poke after "a battle royal" with friends who said it wasn't stylish. But she was adamant on the colour question.

New York, April 24, 1885

... Think of *me* in crimson or purple! Oh my! I can wear no colours but golden brown and soft greys, dove colours or fawns.

While she painted and shopped, Ellen began to worry about those odd women at Bryn Mawr who had taken up "higher education." They would probably be condescending because she did not know as much as they. When Woodrow sent her Bryn Mawr's first catalogue, she wrote:

New York, April 26, 1885

... Truly they have a masculine standard "sure enough." Oh dear me! What a little goose I am! This brings it home to me afresh. I think I had better go to school there—only I couldn't get in. ...

She received in reply two reassuring dissertations on education. Woodrow had some novel ideas on this subject—ideas which had begun to germinate years before under his father's influence. Joseph's striking phrase, "the mind is not a prolix gut to be stuffed," had made a lasting impression upon his son. When Woodrow was a student in Princeton, he had chosen to concentrate on the subjects that interested him most— methods of government, political theories, history, and the lives and opinions of great political leaders—giving only cursory attention to other scheduled courses. As a result he graduated fiftieth in his class, which did not trouble him in the least. At Johns Hopkins he had per- suaded Dr. Adams to release him from what he called "cut and dried courses" so that he might master his study of comparative politics. Now, in language more refined than his father's, yet equally striking, he outlined his theories to Ellen. It is noteworthy that seventeen years later, when he became president of Princeton University, he still held these theories and convinced the faculty that they were sound.

Balto., April 27, 1885

... Sweetheart, I shall agree with you that you *are* a little goose to be- moan the fact that you don't know as much as the Bryn Mawr girls are expected to know! What do you think of *my* case? I am to be one of their instructors, and yet I not only could not pass the entrance ex- aminations, without special preparation, but could not even be an ad- vanced student, much less a Fellow in my own department—because I can't read German at sight! But that by no means indicates that I am not infinitely better educated than my pupils will be. Both you and I have what is immeasurably better than the *information* which is all that would be needed for passing Bryn Mawr, or any other college examinations! We have the power to *think,* to *use* information. For my part I want to carry as little *information* in my head as possible—just as (to use some one else's illustration) I want to forget the figures in the column whose *sum* and *result* I have ascertained and want to keep. I must *scan* information, must question it closely as to every essential detail, in order that I may extract its meaning; but the meaning, once mastered, the information is lumber. It is enough if I know where to find it; for corroboration, for illustration, etc. Of course one *can't* make himself familiar with facts for such a purpose without remembering some of the most essential of them: but it is sheer, barren, ignorant waste of energy to try to remember a fact *for its own sake*. It is like eating for the sake of eating. If you mean to get into sympathy with my mental processes, you must learn not to feel at all disturbed about the small amount you "know." Be glad, rather, that you are past that—that drill, that *exercise* at digestion, that preparation for the period when memory's *burdens* can be—and should be—thrown off and the mind be brought into the glorious liberty of *choosing* what it shall know—the liberty of exchanging plethora for *health!* ...

Balto., April 30, 1885

...I would have you understand that I am going to marry a girl who is...in a very *true* and large sense educated.... Why, my artless little lady, you yourself prove my case for me...for you avow your taste for the good things of the mind, your earnest curiosity as to all things worth knowing.... If you are not educated then I am not: for I have always found you quick to appreciate the things that constitute the staple of my thoughts—of such thoughts as I could not think were I not educated. Cultivated tastes may be said to be almost synonomous with education; and my darling has gotten from her friends, the poets, the painters, the essayists—from all her book companions—as great—nay a much greater—power of sympathy, of stimulating sympathy with my work than she would have had if she had spent a score of years systematically reading history and political economy....

In the interval between these letters Woodrow wrote on a subject close to his heart—the ideal emotional relationship between man and wife. It is, particularly at the end, a remarkable letter, for few men acquire such wisdom before marriage.

Balto., April 29, 1885

... Your disposition is very different from mine, you know, sweetheart. My impulse is to tell *everything*, even the trivial ills of my experience, to the one I love—to make my mind an open book to her. But your life has been one of self-withdrawal—one long effort to wear smiles for those you have loved and keep your tears for yourself alone. You have ... schooled yourself in self-repression, for the sake of others, and because you thought so to command your sorrows. It was only the other day that you were wondering if you would ever learn to bear the ills that affected *me* with the same "philosophy" which you had compelled yourself to practice with reference to your own. I pray God you never may! It shall be my life-long effort to convert you to a different philosophy with regard to *yourself*: that to keep sorrow kills, while to *share* it with those whose love makes them capable of sharing it indeed, is to change it from a poison into a blessing. . . . I shall never feel that you have accepted my love in its fullness until you have learned to cry in my arms. . . .

To which Ellen replied with equal wisdom:

New York, May 3rd, 1885

... I am one of the few who are most fortunate,—more fortunate even than children, for I am not only happy, but I *know* it. Ah, dearest, your love falls short of nothing. . . . I well know that, if this love of ours is to fulfill its sweet promise, we must see to it first of all that it be without dissimulation. My love has no secrets from you, darling. If I have not told you *all* the story of my love and joy and faith in you, it is only because I cannot. I am ever seeking that great heart's word which will say to you all that my heart says—vain search, for only a lifetime of love and service can tell the tale aright. With God's blessing, love, I will keep that which you have committed to me with a true woman's steadfastness of love and singleness of devotion. You may well trust my love—as I trust *yours,* for I do know the blessedness of that assurance, the strength and joy it gives. . . .

Woodrow sent her a parasol for her twenty-fifth birthday and a long letter in which he promised to make all of her birthdays with him "sweeter and more hallowed" by his "life-long devotion."

New York, May 15, 1885

... I can't thank you enough for your lovely gift ... and for this precious letter. ... What can I do more than pledge you once again my little all —my *great* all of love in return! I pray God to give me wisdom equal to my love. ... I trust that there *is* a wisdom which is the direct result of love, and of my absorbing desire to serve you well, to be a true help-meet for you. Otherwise there would be something terrible in the thought of such a life as yours, with all its wonderful possibilities for good, being at the mercy of one foolish little woman. Ah! You must believe in us, you men, before you trust us with such power to work you weal or woe—a power which even the most thoughtless woman—though she may not recognize it—cannot escape from exercising. Darling, if I am to have your life-long love and devotion, you need have no fears for my future birthdays; their happiness is ensured, for there *is* no trial, pain or anxiety which it cannot lighten or dispel. ...

Ellen's amusement over some of Hamerton's observations did not prevent Woodrow from quoting him again to prove a point. The omissions are his:

Balto., May 15, 1885

... It is not by adding to our knowledge, but by understanding us, that women are our helpers. The intellectual life is sometimes a fearfully solitary one. ... The man devoted to that life is more than all other men liable to suffer from isolation, to feel utterly alone. ... Give him one friend who can understand him, who will not leave him, who will always be accessible day and night—one friend, one kindly listener, just one, and the whole universe is changed. It is deaf and indifferent no longer, and whilst *she* listens, it seems as if all men and angels listened too, so perfectly his thought is mirrored in, the light of her answering eyes! It requires only love and just the sort of education and sympathetic intelligence that you have to enable a woman to realize *that* ideal. ... I am too sensitive, too intense, too anxious, too selfish, too open to any influence that stirs anywhere near me, to escape having a great deal of suffering at every turn of my life. ... Love, *your* love, is to keep the experiences which cut me—from cutting me to the quick. If I find in you a love that is boundless, which is altogether mine, which is unquestioning and ever ready to respond to the utmost claim that can be made upon it, I shall have found the most satisfying companion that man ever had. Does *that* frighten you?...

Now, at last, the long wait was almost over. On the thirtieth of May, when his second semester at Johns Hopkins ended, Woodrow left Baltimore and went to Columbia, South Carolina, where his parents and young Joseph were staying with his sister Annie and her husband, Dr. George Howe. And, on the first of June, Ellen returned to her grandfather's manse in Savannah. They still wrote to each other every day, letters filled with joyful anticipation of the future and plans for their wedding. Should it be in the church, or in the manse? Must all the parishioners be invited, or only relatives? What should the groom wear? A dress-suit or what Woodrow called "a dressy walking suit"? "Will you give me your instructions, if you please, my dearest, and I will follow them to the letter." *

Columbia, S.C., June 10, 1885

I don't know, Eileen, my precious one, *how* am I going to behave myself that day! Maybe the excitement will make me unusually quiet—as excitement generally does—but I never before experienced excitement so mixed with overpowering delight as the excitement of that day will be: and so there's no telling....

The day came when Ellen and Woodrow wrote to each other for the last time, or so they hoped and believed. They were sure that they would never be separated after their marriage, never again have to depend on words to express their love. Each tried to capture the essence of the moment.

Columbia, June 21, 1885

My own darling,

It seems altogether too good to be true that our bondage to pen and paper is at last at an end!... This letter will reach you on Monday, and on Tuesday I shall go to my darling to *carry* the words of love with which my heart is so full,... to consecrate to her my life, that it may be spent in making perfect the fulfilment of all the sweet promises in which our

* W.W.'s letter of June 4, 1885—from Columbia.

love for each other is so rich. Ah, my sweetheart, I wish that I could show you *some* of the gladness with which these thoughts fill me. But it is literally unspeakable. It is not translatable into anything but high spirits and a tumultuous throbbing at the heart....

I wish that I could put into this letter, my precious, some words of love that would make you treasure it more than you have ever treasured any of my other letters. I feel as if this last love-*message* were in some sort sacred. My deepest, strongest desire in marrying you, darling, is to make you happy, and I would put into this letter some word of love which would seem to your heart a sort of sweet preface to the book of love which we are about to open together, to read new secrets of sympathy and companionship. I would have you catch a glimpse of my purpose for the future and of the joy which that future contains *for me,* of the gratitude I feel for your priceless gift of love, and of the infinite love and tenderness which is the gift of my whole heart to you.

And think, my sweet one, with what unmixed delight we can look back upon our love for each other in the past. What a sweet preparation we have had for our wedding day! How *precious* the experience of these months of our engagement has been!... I shall not be able to look back over the last two years without seeing that, whether I deserve it or not, this supreme good fortune was all along meant to be mine—through the marvellous goodness of God, who gave me a nature which needed above all things just such love and companionship as you alone could give me ...and then brought you to me to satisfy that need: and not only to satisfy that need, but also to make me a better man through the gracious influences of your lovely womanhood.... It cannot be *chance* that brought us together. Surely a man and woman who can love each other as we love must have been born for each other.... In finding you, I found not only the woman to whom I could give perfect love, but also the woman whom I had been loving, in my imagination, for I knew not how many years! How sweet it is to go back in thought to that time of this wonderful discovery!... It seems a sort of seal and sanction of the future, that you should have come to me, as you did, as a verification and justification of all my longings in the past....

Good-bye, then, sweetheart till Tuesday. God willing, I shall come to claim a part of your welcome then:... the next time that I hold you to my heart will be the happiest moment of all my life, and the delicious prelude to still happier hours when you will be constantly at my side to tell me of the love that is more than life to me. Darling, once more I pledge you all my love and honour. I *love* you. With all my heart, in all my thoughts and hopes and purposes I am

Your own

Woodrow

Savannah, June 20/85

And can it really be possible, my darling, that this is my *last* letter to you? I did not realize the fact until just now when I began to count up, and perceived that a letter written tonight or tomorrow would reach Columbia after you leave on Tuesday. How strange it seems to think that we will have no more need of letters!—how strangely sweet! And yet the letters have been *so* dear to me, and will always be my carefully guarded treasure even when I have you too. They have made so large a part of my life for so long that I daresay I will still be listening and watching for the postman many a time when I am even at your side.

You say well, dear, these are solemn thoughts as well as sweet ones,—thoughts which give me always the desire to fall on my knees and pray the Father to prepare me for whatever he is preparing for me; to give us His blessing in all things, to choose all our changes for us, and to teach me how to be all that I *wish* to be to you, all that your wife *should* be. And I am sure, love, that He *will* bless us, because we are *His*—because in spite of all our failures we *do* desire above all else to be under His guidance in everything,—to love and serve Him well and truly. Therefore, my darling, by my love for Him I pledge you true wifely love and fealty and service all the days of my life.

I would that I could tell you in this last letter something more than I have ever told before of what *love* means for me. But there are few places in my heart which I have not opened to you, dearest; I have shown you my heart of hearts. I know because your own words tell me that you have read it and read it aright. You know as well as you *can* know, before the years have brought their proof, how absolutely I am yours; you know the depth and tenderness and fervour of my love,— this "*all-controlling* love"; You know how absolutely I *believe* in you, with what unquestioning confidence. And I believe that you trust me as my love deserves, that you will *rest* in my love ever as I in yours; it is that which makes my joy in your love so great. Darling, my *faith* in you is a part of my *love* for you; the one no less than the other has become the ruling *passion* as well as the controlling principle of my life. Thank God that the man I love is one who will permit me to obey His marriage law. I am to promise next week to *reverence* you. How many of the young men I have known do you suppose it would be *possible* to reverence! But you will be in very truth my head—my being, not only because *I* will it but because *God* wills it, because He made you so to be.

Sweetheart, you never wrote a letter which brought with it sweeter joy than this of yesterday, which tells me that you *can* and *do* love me for "love's sake" alone, simply for its power to bless apart from all else.... When I feel that you give me such love as that, my heart is flooded with a deep peace—a perfect joy in loving and being loved, such as no other thought can give. That *is true love,* the *only* true love, I sometimes think. The other is but a stronger sort of *liking!* Yet I admit that I am *very glad* to be *liked* by you, looked at with *love's eyes* and *so* admired! But it would make me very unhappy to think that I held your heart by no stronger bond than that. I want to *depend* on something else, though all your words of praise are very sweet to me. It would be like trying to work out our own salvation. How little peace or joy we would find in life if that task had been set us. We are heirs of Heaven by *free gift*—and yet love of the Giver urges us to greater effort to please him,—to be what He would have us than any hope of gain. . . .

Your own Eileen

Book II
Marriage

Part 1
The Teacher

On the twenty-fourth of June, in 1885, Ellen Louise Axson and Woodrow Wilson were married. It was an evening wedding in the parlor of the manse, next door to the Independent Presbyterian Church in Savannah. Dr. I. S. K. Axson, the bride's grandfather, and Dr. Joseph R. Wilson, the groom's father, stood side by side and shared the reading of the marriage ceremony. The parlor, with its high ceiling and dignified furnishings, was large but barely large enough to hold all the relatives. Ellen wore the traditional white veil and a simple white dress which she herself had made. The groom wore his dress-suit. They looked so happy that all the women cried. There was only one disturbing incident. The bride's brother, nine-year-old Edward, and the groom's small nephew, Wilson Howe, meeting for the first time, disliked each other at sight. Immediately after the ceremony they staged a knock-down-drag-out battle on the parlor floor. The bride was shocked. The bridegroom enjoyed it.

Arden Park, in the North Carolina hills, was a small summer resort in a pine forest in 1885. Shakespeare-loving Ellen liked the name as well as the fact that it was inexpensive. Woodrow had only five hundred dollars to get married on. There, in a tiny, vine-covered cottage, young Mr. and Mrs. Wilson spent their honeymoon—two idyllic weeks. They walked every day in the "forest of Arden" and Woodrow sang as they walked. They read aloud to each other—poetry, "classic" novels, and the works of Woodrow's "master," Mr. Bagehot. Mr. Hamerton's "Intellectual Life" was not included.

The rest of the summer was spent with relatives and friends, and, in September, the Wilsons settled down happily in a house on the edge of Bryn Mawr's campus. It was one of three small frame houses built by the college authorities and rented for a reasonable price to members of the faculty. There was a cook-housekeeper for each establishment. One, occupied by Dean Martha Thomas, was known as the "Deanery." Another, with a view, was called the "Scenery"; and the third, between these two, was the "Betweenery." Professor and Mrs. Wilson lived in two rooms in the Betweenery. It was rather primitive, but the lovely hills and woods outside their windows and their perfect companionship made kerosene lamps, poor heating, and roads that were ankle deep in slush in the winter seem trivial. And they would soon, they hoped, be able to afford to rent a house and have little Eddie with them.

Woodrow went to work at once with vigor. There was a lot of work; courses to be prepared, lectures to plan, a series of essays he had been asked to write, and frequent, rather trying, consultations with the Dean. "Dean Martha" was not the type of woman that Woodrow Wilson admired. She was, he thought, too modern, too aggressive, and, as he remarked, "ridiculously young." She was twenty-eight and just five days younger than he. She was, besides, a graduate of Zurich University and liked the German method of teaching. Professor Wilson preferred his own method. It was depressing to find that his classes were very small—sometimes consisting of one nervous girl. There were only forty-two students in the brand-new college for women.

But it was not long before he discovered that he liked to teach and that the girls liked him. The professor "was always smiling," they remarked, and his lectures were "fascinating." He was "witty," they said, he had "an infectious gaiety," he was also a "very courteous Southern gentleman." * The only thing they did not like was the long, silky mustache he had grown to make him look older. The second year he shaved it off, remarking that "all the young ladies seemed to set their faces against it." †

He and his Ellen were ecstatically happy. Every evening she sat with him in their small sitting-room while he worked, sometimes helping him according to the plan he had suggested before they were married, often silently busy with her sewing. She had only one worry. "He takes such care of me," she told her cousin, Mary Hoyt, "and I had meant to do so much for him!"

In April, 1886, Ellen went alone to Gainesville, Georgia, to bear their first child. Woodrow had tried to persuade her not to go. Had they not determined never to be separated? How could he let her go through the ordeal of childbirth without him? Why did she want to leave him? She wanted to spare him the expense of a Northern doctor and nurse and the anguish she knew he would suffer if he were present when the baby was born. Mrs. Louisa Hoyt Wade, her mother's sister, had a big house in Gainesville, and servants and a family doctor who would deliver the child for practically nothing. But she kept these reasons to herself, for she knew that Woodrow would not consider them valid excuses for leaving him. She told him firmly that she could not let *her* baby be born "north of the Mason-Dixon Line," and Woodrow gave up. There was no use arguing this point with his incurable Southerner.

* Excerpts from letters written by some of his students.
† Letter to R. Heath Dabney, October 28, 1885.

Two weeks before the child was expected he put her on a train in Philadelphia. Then, because he had promised her to try to distract his mind, he went to Washington to see his former partner, Edward Renick, who had a government job. On the way back to Bryn Mawr, he wrote:

> *On The Train between*
> *Wash. & Phila.*
> *15 April, 1886*

My darling wife,

... I saw Renick and together we went around to see various officials whom he knew to be interested in "Cong. Govt." .... They were all extremely cordial and complimentary.... Altogether I felt quite "set up" to find that I was known in so many offices.... About two I went up to the Capitol and watched the House and the Supreme Court until time to come away to my train (the Senate was in "executive session"). And that's an account of my day.

That, at least is what I *did;* what I have *felt* since last night I dare not say. Oh, my darling, I probably haven't felt the worst of it yet —for I have not yet gone *home* and not found you there!—but I feel enough now to know what it means to be separated from you.... I love you, oh, I love you with a yearning, ever-growing love.... My splendid, brave little wife....

Back in the little apartment in Bryn Mawr Woodrow was overwhelmed by such loneliness as he had never known before. All of his life with Ellen he reacted with the same intensity to every separation from her. The same passionate reassertion of his love appears again and again in his letters, even in the last ones, written in the White House after twenty-seven years of marriage.

> *Bryn Mawr, April 16, 1886*

... You were never loved and yearned over more than you are at this present moment. My heart is full of you *only*. The excitements of going about and talking to all sorts of people, and seeing all sorts of things that demanded my attention kept the dull ache at the *bottom* of my heart yesterday in Washington. The night before, after leaving you, I felt simply dazed and stunned. But to-day my love for you has eclipsed every other energy. I am simply and wholly *yours*—every other part of my identity has apparently disappeared. I am not unhappy, darling: I love you too much for that. I love you too much to pain you by *brooding* over your absence. But I seem to be finding out just how much and how truly you are my wife—*and my life!* I am only half myself away from you, though I still live *for* you as intensely as ever. I can't be *altogether* miserable in your absence because I know that it is only absence of body—that the heart that makes my life so bright and happy—which is my life's *self*—is with me. . . .

In the evening a telegram came from Gainesville. As if to spare her father any further anxiety, Margaret Wilson, named after her maternal grandmother, was born three days ahead of time. Ellen and Woodrow had, like most parents, wanted their first-born to be a boy, but if they were disappointed, no one would guess it from their letters.

Bryn Mawr, April 19, 1886

. . . I've been thinking that, if ever a man was blessed in having a baby —and a baby *daughter*—I am: because a baby—especially a little *girl* —completes *your* life and happiness as no gift of our heavenly Father could—besides elevating my life by a new love and a new responsibility. Oh, my darling, my heart is so full. It will require a life-time with you to give it vent. My precious wife, my precious baby! I love, love, love, love you.

Gainesville, April 21, 1886

I am allowed to write, my darling, just long enough to tell you that I *love*, LOVE, LOVE you, and to tell you how my heart aches to see you, and to have you see the baby. It is a little beauty. Everyone says the prettiest little baby they ever saw & so plump and healthy; so perfectly well. Oh, how good our Heavenly Father is to us—how tenderly he has cared for me!

I am just as well as I can be. . . . Both the baby and I are considered Perfect Phenomenons in the way of "doing well". . . .

Gainesville, May 2, 1886

I am *very* glad that you were not disappointed at little Woodrow's non-appearance! After all I should not be surprised if little Margaret should steal her way into your heart of hearts and find for herself the very tenderest spot of all, from which not even the boy, when he comes, will be able to oust her; though of course he will excite more the paternal *pride* and hope. I confess that I think such a son as *you* would be the *greatest* of God's gifts next to such a husband as you, but a lovely little daughter is the *sweetest* of His gifts. . . .

When the Easter vacation began, Woodrow wanted to go to Gainesville, but Ellen insisted that he must take this opportunity to go to Boston to talk to D. C. Heath & Co., publishers, about the textbook they had asked him to write, and to do some research in Boston's famous libraries. There was also the fact, which she did not confess until later, that she could not bear to have him see her looking pale and tired. He did as he was told.

Boston, Mass., April 22, 1886

My darling wife,

I arrived here safe and sound last night. . . .

The way I feel upon reaching this borough is an involuntary tribute to its fame. I feel that odd sort of excitement which I imagine the literary adventurers of Sam Johnson's time used to feel upon reaching London. After all there *is* more history, political and literary, connected with Boston and her surroundings, Cambridge and the rest, than about any other place in the country. It gives me a queer sense of elation to be here, which, I confess, I did not expect to feel. I am tempted not to make any *visits* at all, but just to go about and spy out the noted buildings and localities. If I did not have the fear of you before my eyes, I believe I should adopt that course. But you sent me here: & I must do your errands. I have not settled upon any program, so that I cannot tell you what I am going to do; but you may be sure that I will tell you each day what I *have* done—whom and what I have seen. . . . I shall carry you and the baby about in my heart to-day as a sort of source and store of smiles and joy. . . .

Ellen's errands kept him very busy during the five days he spent in Boston. He had interviews with various publishers, browsed for hours in libraries, visited historic places, lunched with other authors, had tea with Gamaliel Bradford, and went to see two Gilbert and Sullivan operas. And every morning after breakfast he sent a detailed report of his activities to Ellen, including pen portraits of the men he had met. Mr. Heath was "a very pleasant, open-faced, cordial yet business-like gentleman of about 35 or 40 years"; Mr. Houghton, of Houghton, Mifflin and Co., "tall, somewhat rugged, but genial";* Mr. Mifflin a "brisk, clear-voiced, hearty, well-conditioned, rather young man"; † Mr. Aldrich of the same firm, "Saxon in colouring, briskly executive in manner and interesting in matter." ‡ But half of each letter was devoted to love and longing for his wife and baby. He had been worrying about the baby until Ellen's first letter arrived, because of a dark suspicion that little Margaret might have had the bad luck to look like her father. "And so the baby is a beauty!" he wrote in great relief. "I might have known it—*your* baby couldn't manage to be anything else."

It was hard to have to wait so long to see his first child—so hard that when he returned to the lonely Betweenery, Woodrow sometimes talked aloud to himself.

Bryn Mawr, April 30, 1886

... There was a gentleman in this room this morning, whose performances I wish you could have seen. ... He stood before the calendar there under the mantelpiece and, looking at the date, April 30, exclaimed, "Why, my little daughter's two weeks old to-day! Oh, my little baby!" The words were very simple but the tone in which they were uttered arrested my attention. I couldn't for the life of me look at him, but I am sure there were glad tears in his eyes—his voice was that kind of voice. ... Poor fellow, I am glad he has so much work to do. ...

The "poor fellow" had plenty of work. He and Ellen had decided that he should try for a Ph.D. degree, after all, since it would help him to get a better position in a more important college. So, between class work, studying far into the night, and frequent trips to the Johns Hopkins library, he had few moments of leisure. Yet he was never too tired to write daily love letters to Ellen. At the end of one letter, he remarked:

Bryn Mawr, May 2, 1886

... Well, well! how one's ideas will change! I used to think that when one got married he wouldn't write "love letters," exactly, to his wife:

* April 24, 1886.
† April 25, 1886.
‡ April 24, 1886.

that his epistles to her, though deeply affectionate, would manifest their affection indirectly rather than demonstratively ("My dear wife: etc. etc.—all about family affairs. Your affectionate husband") Whereas, see what I have learned—that eight pages devoted exclusively to that business are by no means sufficient to contain the love—the *courting*— he would put into them! I have discovered that I am *more* irresistibly impelled to make love to my wife than I was to make love to my sweet-heart—and that there will be more romance and delight in going to her in June than there was in going to her *last* June. . . .

Ellen wrote with equal ardor:

Gainesville, May 7, 1886

. . . It would be hard to say that anything could make you dearer to me, —that I could love the father of my child more passionately and entirely than I have loved my husband. Somehow that would seem to be placing the child before the father. I am more sure that the reverse is true, that I love *her* more because she is my Woodrow's child. But most true it is that she is an *added* cause for love between us—a wonderful new bond, closer than any other in some respects. . . .

Bryn Mawr, May 9, 1886

. . . I've been reckoning up, in a tumultuous, heartful sort of way, the value of my little wife to me. I can't *state* the result—there are no terms of value in which it can be stated—but perhaps I can give you some idea of what its proportions would be if it *were* stated. She has taken all real pain out of my life: her wonderful loving sympathy exalts even my occasional moods of despondency into a sort of *hallowed* sadness out of which I come stronger and better. She has given to my ambitions a meaning, an assurance, and a purity which they never had before: with her by my side, ardently devoted to me and to my cause, under-standing all my thoughts and all my aims, I feel that I can make the utmost of every power I possess. She has brought into my life the sun-shine which was needed to keep it from growing stale and morbid: that has steadily been bringing back into my spirits their old gladness and boyhood, their old delight in play and laughter:—that sweetest

sunshine of deep, womanly love, unfailing, gentle patience, even happy
spirits, and spontaneous mirth, that is purest, swiftest tonic to a spirit
prone to fret and apt to flag. She has given me that perfect *rest* of heart
and mind of whose existence I had never so much as dreamed before
she came to me, which springs out of assured oneness of hope and sympathy—and which, for me, means life and success. Above all she has given
me *herself* to live for! Her arms are able to hold me up against the
world: her eyes are able to charm away every care; her words are my
solace and inspiration and all because her love is my life. . . .

I know that I have told you all this before, my darling; but . . . I
have a special right to say it all over again just *now*. During this separation of ours, I have had innumerable opportunities to stand, as it
were, and look at my life as if I were a third person,—and yet with
infinitely deeper insight and more perfect perception than any third
person could have—and I seem to see as I never saw before the deepest
meaning of the happiness that came to me on our marriage day. . . . That
ideal vacation at Arden, the winter of love and work and anticipation
here, all seem to me like an open book of hope assured. I pore over that
dear record of sweet memories constantly with ever increasing joy and
more and more eager purpose to live worthy of the love you have given
me. . . . I would a thousand times rather repay you a tythe of the happiness you have brought me than make my name immortal *without* serving you as the chief mission of my life. Ah, my little wife, do you know
that my whole self has passed over into my allegiance to you? . . .

Gainesville, May 11/86

My darling, my darling, what can I say to you in answer to this *precious*
letter of yesterday! What a mockery it seems, this trying to translate
into words *any* strong emotion, and especially to tell you through such
a medium the *joy* which fills my heart almost to bursting as I read these
wonderful words. Indeed, I doubt if I could express to you in *any* way
all that letter has made me feel,—the exaltation of spirit, the sort of
glorified state in which it has left me. If I were with you perhaps I
could make you understand—ah, if I could but try!—these happy tears
which I cannot keep out of my eyes would tell you somewhat. This letter shall be one of my chief treasures, darling, as long as I live. Time
and again in the old days I picked out some letter of yours as my spe-

cial treasure, but ah how much dearer is this than any of those! For those *promised* that I should be certain things to you, upon which all my heart was set, but this tells me that I *have* been all that and more. *Can* it be that it is all *true*, darling?... Ah, love is verily a wonderful, wonderful thing since by merely *loving* I have acquired such supernatural power,—for I am sure I never came by it in the *ordinary* course of nature.

It is true, as you say, darling, that you have told me all this before, but to *write* it all after a quiet, calm review of all our days together seems different somehow.... I can never tell you with what thoughts and feelings I too have been living over, since we parted, this beautiful blissful year. It is my *deliberate* belief that no one else in the world is as happy as I am and have been since the day I was wed; that scarcely anyone else could be made to believe such happiness was possible. I could not believe it one year ago.... It is like the joys of Heaven which the strongest imagination is unable to reveal to us—until we attain them they are altogether hidden from us. But you, darling, have made an earthly paradise for me....

Childbirth in the South, in those days, was considered a very dangerous undertaking. It was said that a mother, if she was fortunate enough to survive, was apt to be an invalid for the rest of her life. Ellen had been, secretly, a little frightened. Her mother had died in childbirth and she had seen too many women lying all day on sofas for years after their children were born. But now, feeling wonderful a month after her baby's birth, she decided that those pale ladies had been merely spoiled and lazy and that such fears were the result of "old wives' tales." She wanted to go home, but "Aunt Lou" was horrified. Ellen must stay, and be nursed, at least another month. And the windows in her room must still be kept tightly closed at night.

Louisa Wade was a woman with stern religious principles and great determination. She had lived through the grim days of General Sherman's march through Georgia. When the Wade plantation house was burned to the ground, Louisa had calmly collected her children, her servants, a "buckboard" and two horses, and driven off, straight-backed and defiant, through a regiment of Northern soldiers. She was a power in Gainesville. When the town voted for local option and went dry, everyone ascribed it to "Miss Louisa." Farm women from the back country came to her often for advice. "She's a knowin' lady," they said. "She'll tell us what to do." * She was "raising" Ellen's little sister,

* From *My Aunt Louisa and Woodrow Wilson* by Margaret Axson Elliott.

Margaret, with the same love and stern discipline that she gave her own children, and both her nieces loved her dearly, although Margaret sometimes dared to defy her. Ellen never did. She wrote to Woodrow that she would have to do what Aunt Lou ordered, in spite of the fact that it was absurd. She was perfectly well and intended as soon as possible to have another baby—a boy.

When Woodrow, alarmed by the fuss Aunt Lou was making over Ellen's recovery, wrote that he would not let her make such a "sacrifice" again, Ellen was indignant.

Gainesville, May 15, 1886

... If I were too exquisite a creature to be a wife and mother, I would have died in the beauty of young maidenhood and been laid away under the violets, and had ever so much poetry written about me in the local papers, explaining that I was too good and lovely for this world. But you see I missed the chance for that sort of apotheosis;—and I am sure my own husband at least might pay me the compliment of considering me too exquisite a creature to be a "horrid old maid!" ...

Later she calmed down and wrote:

Gainesville, Ga., May 18th, 1886

... I wish there *had* been sacrifices for me to make that I might prove by such means how I prize your love. But there is no sacrifice possible because you give me with yourself everything;—you satisfy every possible need of my nature; my heart and mind are both filled. You have given me someone—the *right* one—to love and trust and believe in perfectly, to look up to and honour entirely. And then, darling, how you satisfy my pride and ambition. You don't know how I *glory* in your splendid gifts, your noble character, that rare charm of manner and "presence." And as for ambitions, mine are destined to be much more fully satisfied than ever yours will be, because, you see, *I* am so fully satisfied with what you do, while you will never be. By the same rule how much greater is my delight in your triumphs than it could ever have been in any little success of my own. Ah, it is a great thing to be the wife of such a man! how much greater to be one with him and follow him in his noble progress than to move on in one's own little narrow

"Mr. Woodrow" and "Miss Ellie"—courting days.

Woodrow Wilson in a professorial pose.

(Above) The young mother in Princeton, circa 1891, and (left to right)
Margaret and Jessie, aged five and four, and Eleanor ("Nellie"), aged
three.

The Fred Yates portrait of Mrs. Wilson painted in England in 1906. It is the most perfect likeness of Ellen ever captured.

Princeton's President Woodrow Wilson with Andrew Carnegie at the commencement exercises of 1906.

In the garden at "Prospect," the University President's house, around 1910.

The President-elect of the United States and his wife leaving Princeton on March 3, 1913, for his inauguration in Washington.

Making the White House more homelike. To Ellen it was "just a bigger Prospect or Sea Girt—with no servant problem."

From left, Mrs. Wilson, Jessie, Margaret and Eleanor on the rear portico of the White House in 1913.

At "Harlakenden" in Cornish, New Hampshire, during Woodrow's and Ellen's last summer together—August, 1913.

orbit! The universe itself seems somehow to grow greater, and life to be infinitely grander and more precious and better worth living. . . .

On the twentieth of May Woodrow began daily journeys to Baltimore to take his examinations for a Ph.D. He reported his progress to Ellen, but briefly and a little absent-mindedly, for he could think of nothing but her and the baby, when he wrote to her.

Balto., May 22, 1886

. . . Of course I am very tired to-day. After writing all yesterday morning and to-day I am entitled to feel a little dull; and one consequence is, of course, that I am not so well satisfied as I was yesterday even with the way I passed the examination paper. But, after all, I guess it's quite safe to say that I got through—and nothing but pride would demand more. . . . How full my thoughts are to-day, darling, of the fact that, God willing, I shall three weeks from to-day be well on my way towards my sweet ones. . . . I can indulge my heart now with a few dreams of what I shall do when I get to Gainesville, how I shall deport myself towards my lovely wife who will be so glad to see me, and towards that little daughter who will not be at all glad to see me, but whom I shall worship—with as little awkwardness as possible. . . .

The last examination was oral, and he was so nervous that when it was over he had a bad case of ''the blues'' and a raging headache. But the next day he wrote in high spirits:

Balto., May 29, 1886

My own precious little wife,

Hurrah—a thousand times hurrah—I'm *through,* I'm THROUGH. The degree is actually secured! Oh, the relief of it! . . .

Back at Bryn Mawr he wrote again to explain why the degree had meant so much to him.

Bryn Mawr, 30 May, 1886

. . . Don't you think, my sweetheart, that it is a perfect proof of the absolute completeness of your reign in my heart that when I am tired or down-hearted there is a perfect cure for me in your love, and that when

I am gayest all my high spirits are transfigured into love for you? Take the present case. The successful conclusion of my examinations in Baltimore, with all that success secures, has lifted a great weight off my mind and raised my spirits just as high as they could conceivably go in your absence. What is the result? I find it impossible to translate my feelings otherwise than that *I love you.* ... You are the centre of my life and no fulness of that life can find expression but in love for you! That's the delight of it all! I won the degree *for you.* I don't care for it for myself ... *I* could live on $1,500 a year very easily: and I hope that my fortunes will grow with my reputation (though that is problematical). But my spur in the struggle of preparation I have just been through was to please *you,* and to make *you* more comfortable. In so far as the degree has a commercial value, it was earned for you; in so far as it has a sentimental value, it was won for you. If there's any triumph, it is *yours.* You see *here's* one key to my happiness in such matters, darling: I know that you would be glad, with the inimitable gladness of love, to live with me on ''nothing a year''—or any pittance that would keep us from starvation; I know that you set no store at all by my *income,* so I have but enough to keep *me* from anxiety and fit for work, and it is that knowledge which makes it so keen and pure a satisfaction to me to be able to do anything to preserve you from the cares and discomforts of too narrow circumstances. Just because you don't require it, I delight to supply fuller means of support. ...

Gainesville, June 2, 1886

I should like to dance, sing, or do something else very startling—for me—to give my spirits vent. Yes, darling, that I am—happy over your success—glad that you have the reward of merit that you so richly deserve. True, I know the degree is but a decoration—a ribband—the merit was all there before and no number of degrees could indicate to the public how transcendent is that merit. I am *always* rejoicing with a joy past telling in all your rare gifts, darling. Oh, I *glory* in you! I never dare tell you in *full* my opinion of you lest so much praise to your face should offend your taste. But my *constant* delight in your powers doesn't prevent my feeling a quick, fresh, thrill of pleasure at every and any fresh recognition of them—at every new honour paid you. Truly I—and all whose sweet privilege it is to love you—have the pleasure of feeling that sort of thrill very often. You seem to be running a race against time to see what you *can* do! You are certainly a rapid young man. Just think of it! in two short years all sorts of University honours—fellow-ship, degree—distinctions of every kind,—then a great book written, published,—a splendid reputation won, with all the various tributes to your powers which follow naturally therefrom! —a list far too numerous to begin upon. Oh, you don't permit your companions on this life journey of yours to lack for pleasurable excitement, especially that companion whom love keeps closest at your side....

Bryn Mawr, June 5, 1886

... Fortunately (or is it *un*fortunately?) I view my own achievements so far as irredeemably commonplace; so that there is little or no danger of this too generous praise of yours turning my head. It all comes to me just as another way of saying the words that are the symbol of the strength and joy of my life—that tell me that I have won your whole heart. Ah, my perfect little wife, you have left out from your enumeration of my titles to admiration the single thing concerning which my pride is without alloy: I won *you!* ... No man ever did more than that —no man ever more completely—surely no man ever *so* completely— made his heart and his mind's—his *spirit's* fortune at a single stroke....

When the Bryn Mawr term ended and, at long last, Aunt Lou decided that it was safe for Ellen to travel, Woodrow went to Gainesville and brought his wife and daughter home.

In the fall he was promoted to a full professorship at $1800 a year and, with the extra three hundred dollars and royalties coming in from *Congressional Government,* the Wilsons were able to realize their hope of having a real home. They found a house on Gulph Road, in a ravine back of the college, and moved in the following spring. The rent was low because it was an old house badly in need of repairs.

When Woodrow and Ellen were married his sisters had mournfully predicted that their brother would not be properly fed because Ellen had never learned to cook. In the South even a parson could afford servants. She was also an artist, and artists were proverbially inefficient. They did not know their sister-in-law very well. Before Margaret was born she had gone twice a week to Philadelphia to take lessons from Mrs.

Rorer, one of the first so-called home economists and author of a famous cookbook, and was well prepared for her new duty. And she was an excellent and economical housekeeper. Sweeping, scrubbing, darning, cooking and taking care of the baby kept her busy all day, and when Woodrow came home in the afternoon she took time off to encourage him while he stoked the furnace, pumped water from the well with a hand pump, and cleaned the yard. Nothing seemed too tiring or too difficult, for they had the privacy they craved.

In July, 1887, Ellen went back, with little Margaret, to Gainesville. Another baby was expected in August. She wrote from there:

Gainesville, July 23, 1887

... Never before, I think, have I felt your love so deeply, have my pulses so thrilled with the exquisite delight of it. But there seems to be no end to the sweet surprises that grow out of being your love—your wife. One would think that two years would have inaugurated the reign of "calm wedded affection" of which we hear so much. And yet you are always doing or saying—not to speak of being—something to throw me into such a rapturous condition as is unparalleled in all the happy days of my most happy courtship and honeymoon. Every joy of that time is mine still, undimmed, and in addition—ah, how much deeper, more wonderful joy—that which springs from the deep confidence and infinite peace which you have taught me to feel in your love.

She had not succeeded in persuading Woodrow to stay at home when the time came for the baby's birth. He lived in a boarding house in Bryn Mawr until the middle of August, when he joined her in Gainesville.

Again "little Woodrow" failed to appear. Instead, Jessie Woodrow, named after her father's mother, arrived on the twenty-eighth of August. And once more her parents assured each other that they were not disappointed.

When the fall term opened at Bryn Mawr, Woodrow went back, leaving Ellen, once more according to Aunt Lou's stern instructions, to rest and recuperate. Alone again in the boarding house, he faced the fact that he was thoroughly bored with Bryn Mawr College:

Bryn Mawr, Oct. 4th, 1887

My own darling,

I have just come from a long and exhausting interview with Miss B——, the new fellow in History. I dread these first interviews and am very glad that this one is over. Miss B. turns out to be a pleasant small person of a mind which it will be very hard, but I trust not impossible, to impress—a mind which has been pressed so often by other things at every point at which you press it that it yields in a *habitual,* acquired way rather than in the way you wish. She seems to herself, evidently, to have heard something of that sort before at the very opening of your remark and so takes it to be what she has heard before to the end, or is only a little confused by something in its course which does not quite exactly tally with what she expected. She seems to talk largely out of her memory; her travels overshadow her reasoning powers; her knowledge of the world makes her ignorant of conclusions which interpret the world, —etc. etc. But she is amiable—''not wilful,'' she says—has some wholesome awe (quite diverting of course to me) of what is expected of her at Bryn Mawr, and can, I confidently expect, be dominated. But, dear me, what a strain and a bore it is to be all the year dominating. Dominating Miss G—— cost me sore, as you know. Miss S—— needed only constant encouragement—but that amounted to carrying her on my shoulders!... I'm *tired* of carrying female Fellows on my shoulders. When I think of you, my little wife, I love this ''College for Women'' because *you* are a woman, but when I think only of myself, I hate the place very cordially....

We shall derive little or no pecuniary (economical) advantage from our connexion with this amiable institution: and that being the case, what sort of advantage *will* we derive? That's the conundrum at present amusing my thoughts. For I *am* beginning to be amused by the whole situation. I've put away worry in the matter: for I have recollected of late that we are under an all-wise Providence in all things, and that it is in a way injurious to worry about the future. Our plain duty is to care dutifully and diligently for the present....

Yet, impious or not, he kept looking about for a way of escape. One, suggested by Edward Renick, brought a brief thrill of hope. Renick wrote him that *Congressional Government* was still attracting much ''favorable'' interest in Washington and urged its author to ''have steps taken'' to have his name presented to the Secretary of State for the vacant office of first Assistant Secretary. Secretary Bayard, it seemed, liked ''gentlemanly, scholarly associates.'' Woodrow Wilson went to Washington and found, soon enough, that, since he did not know a single influential person there, he didn't have a chance.

As always when he was depressed he worked very hard. The college was closed for the summer and he was able to concentrate, without interruption, on his textbook, called *The State*. A "dull fact book," Woodrow called it, but the study and research involved were important to him as a first step in a big project. He planned, as every author does, to write a great book some day—the one great book that every author dreams of. It would be a history of government in all the civilized States in the world, to be entitled *The Philosophy of Politics*. In the family circle this *magnum opus* which was never completed was called, irreverently, P.O.P. When the fall term began, he worked every evening, but never on Sundays. A well-brought-up Presbyterian never worked on that day. Woodrow found comfort and refreshment in church, but one Sunday he did not.

Bryn Mawr, Oct. 9, 1887

I have just done what I never did before—I have allowed myself to be driven from church in disgust. I went to church to enjoy the service of prayer and preaching which we can expect from Dr. Miller; but unhappily he was not present. In his place stood a man about my own age whose whole heart, whether he spoke or read, seemed to be in listening to his own sounding and meaningless phrases and to the sonorous ring of his own voice. He prayed flippantly: not a word, I feel sure went to Heaven. I felt cold and sick—for I longed to hear a prayer: I am sure I would have recognized one had I heard it. Then came the sermon: a vain man's self-satisfied discussion of the Mosaic authorship. At least, so it began: I found I *could* not stay—I felt that I *ought not* to stay to hear it. I was in a back seat and could slip out unobserved by most of the congregation; and so I came away with a sort of sob in my heart. I had gone to God's house to feel its sacred atmosphere of worship and had found only the void of a common lecture hall.... What is one who is above all things sensitive to spiritual influences—to the unspoken meanings of personality and of heart's intent—to do when thrown into the congregation of a fellow like this.... Sweetheart, nothing is so bad but that to think of you offsets my distress. I love you, and ours, *infinitely*.

They decided in October, after Ellen and the babies were safely settled in the house on Gulph Road, that it was high time that young Edward Axson should come to live with them. Eddie had been well cared for by an aunt and uncle, but he had visited his sister when she was in

Gainesville and she had been distressed because his tendency to stammer was much worse. He was a handsome, intelligent, cheerful boy, but he adored his sister and missed her sorely. Ellen thought that this might be the cause of his trouble. Woodrow agreed that they must take him at once and also that Stockton Axson, her elder brother, must spend his boarding-school vacations with them. There was also, Ellen said tentatively, her cousin, Mary Hoyt, who wanted to enter Bryn Mawr, but couldn't afford to pay for room and board as well as tuition. Why not take her in, too? Why not? Woodrow said. So, that year, their house was bursting with people—three grownups, eleven-year-old Eddie, two babies, and "Stock" at Christmas time, Easter, and during the summer. The boys' small incomes from their father's estate helped a little, and the Wilsons managed to hire a cook—a great luxury, although sometimes troublesome. Ellen hired them and Woodrow, when necessary, fired them. "Put the carving knife on the table beside me," he told Ellen, when the necessity arose, "and go upstairs and shut the door."

In the spring of 1888 Woodrow's mother died. It was the first real sorrow of his life and a great shock. Ellen could not leave the babies, so Woodrow went alone to Clarksville, Tennessee, where his father was now teaching at Tennessee University's new Divinity School.

Arlington Hotel
Clarksville, Tenn., April 19, 1888

My own darling,

Oh, what a comfort it is to write to you . . . to write words for my sweet wife's eyes—those blessed, blessed eyes which contain all the heaven of this world's happiness for me. My precious sweetheart, what would become of me *now*, if you were not mine: how could I bear this desolation . . . father's home gone because my precious mother is dead. Oh, the infinite pity and bitterness of it. When I think of dear father and Josie I could almost find it in my heart to upbraid myself that *I* have a sweet home to go to.

As the first shock and acute pain of the great, the irreparable blow passes off, my heart is filling up with tenderest memories of my sweet mother, memories that seem to hallow my whole life—which seem to explain to me how it came about that I was given the sweetest, most satisfying of wives for my daily companion. My mother, with her sweet womanliness, her purity, her intelligence, her strength, prepared me for my wife. I remember how I clung to her (a laughed-at "Mamma's boy") till

I was a great big fellow: but love of the best womanhood came to my heart through those apron-strings. If I had not lived with such a mother I could not have won and seemed to deserve—in part, perhaps, deserved through transmitted virtues—such a wife—the strength, the support, the human source of my life. Oh, darling, without my mother and you what would I have been!...

He was only thirty-one, yet now he felt old, no longer able to capture the boyish high spirits that were a part of his nature, and very despondent about his future. Was there nothing ahead for him but a humble professor's job at Bryn Mawr for the rest of his life? Then, in the summer, came the longed-for change. He was offered a full professorship at Wesleyan College in Middletown, Connecticut, to teach his favorite subjects—history and political economy.

In September, 1888, the Wilsons and Eddie were comfortably settled in an old colonial house on High Street, overlooking the Connecticut River. Ellen and Woodrow always remembered their two years at Wesleyan as among the happiest in their lives. They had imagined, like most Southerners, that New England people were cold and rather grim, and were surprised and pleased by the cordial welcome they received. Woodrow wrote to Robert Bridges in November to tell him that they had "been taken possession of by these good New England folks and are, instead of making, being given our 'Thanksgiving!' " Social life in Middletown was simple, unaffected and gracious, the intellectual companionship stimulating. Woodrow particularly enjoyed the "Conversational Club," a small group formed by members of the faculty for the purpose of "free discussion." It was too informal to need a constitution, which probably disappointed the new member.

Altogether it was a delightful environment with only one disadvantage. They were very far away from their families in the South, and Woodrow knew that his father was miserably lonely. His love and admiration for the man who had so greatly influenced his mind and his character was, next to his love for Ellen, his deepest emotion. In December, he wrote:

106 High St., Middletown, Ct.
16 December, 1888

My precious father,

My thoughts are full of you and dear Dode * all the time. Tennessee seems *so* far away for a chap as hungry as I am for a sight of the two

* Young Joseph's nickname.

men whom I love. As the Christmas recess approaches I realize, as I have so often before, the pain there is in a season of holiday and rejoicing away from you. As you know, one of the chief things about which I feel most warranted in rejoicing is that I am your son. More and more as my talents and experience grow I recognize the strength growing in me as of the nature of your strength: I become more and more conscious of the hereditary wealth I possess, the capital of principle, of literary force and skill, of capacity for first-hand thought; and I feel daily more and more bent toward creating in my own children that combined respect and tender devotion for their father that you gave your children for you. Oh, how happy I should be, if I could make them think of me as I think of you! You have given me a love that grows, that is stronger in me now that I am a man than it was when I was a boy, and which will be stronger in me when I am an old man than it is now—a love, in brief, that is rooted and grounded in *reason,* and not in filial instinct merely—a love resting upon abiding foundations of service, recognizing you as in a certain very real sense the author of all I have to be grateful for. I bless God for my noble, strong and saintly mother and for my incomparable father. Ask Dode if he does not subscribe? And tell him that I love my brother deeply.

... Ellie joins me in unbounded love to you both.

Woodrow's salary at Wesleyan was appreciably larger than at Bryn Mawr, but it was still necessary to augment it. The house, the cook and the food cost more in Middletown, and he had to buy books, as well, now that Philadelphia's and Baltimore's libraries were out of reach. He therefore contracted with Johns Hopkins University to deliver a six-weeks' course of lectures, after persuading the Wesleyan authorities to give him a leave of absence for this purpose. When he left home in February, it was harder than ever to be separated from Ellen. She was going to have another baby and, as usual, he worried about her. In a boarding house in Baltimore, near the one where he had lived during his lonely bachelor days, he wrote:

909 McCulloh St., Baltimore
Feb. 15, 1889

... The active movements and friend-seeing of my journey down here and the excitement of getting launched in my course and settled in my bachelor quarters was all very well: it kept off the blues admirably. But now I've come down to "hard pan," to the *routine* of being without you ... nothing in my room here to make me forget, everything to make me remember. I work, I make calls, I go to the minstrels,—but no use: my darling needs me—I need her....

My love for you gives me the deepest happiness conceivable; but that happiness is not of smiles always. It seems to go deep down where smiles cannot go, where all the serious purposes of life are. There it forms that basis of sober strength which we call peace of mind. It is that sort of happiness that possesses me to-day: a happiness not incompatible with tears—tears of tenderness and longing and hope, meaning that my life is consecrated to you....

Ellen wrote:

Middletown, Conn.
Feb. 18, 1889

... Such a sweet, sweet letter. Oh, how can I be grateful enough for your precious love! When I think of it and of *you*—of all your goodness and tenderness and nobleness my whole nature is caught up in a sort of white passion of almost adoring love and reverence. My darling, my love, my life! ...

She was sure that at last, she was going to present him with a son, but Woodrow tried to prepare her—and himself—for disappointment.

909 McCulloh Street
Balto., Feb'y. 24, 1889

... Ah how I hope that dream may be realized! And yet when I think of our precious, our delightful little daughters, I can't help being as glad at the thought of having another little girl—almost—as at the thought of having a boy. Their sweetness and goodness came over me like a great wave again after my separation from them. They are lights to the house, treasures of amusement, as well as of everything that ought to make a parent's heart glad,—charming in nothing more than in their individuality....

909 *McCulloh St., Balto.*
27th Feb'y., 1889

My precious darling,

No letter from home as yet to-day, and so I must fall back for agreeable thoughts upon the good news from London—since you don't see the papers I shall assume that you have not heard it ... Pigott, the fellow who supplied the *Times* with the Parnell letters upon which that enterprising journal has been basing its charges of crime against the Irish Nationalist party (the charge which the Commission has been trying) has confessed that he forged them (at least the most important and damaging of them) and the *Times* is thoroughly discredited in the whole matter. Parnell is virtually cleared, and what is more, it now looks as if the Nationalist cause has received an important impulse forward. Even the *Standard* (the London N.Y. *Tribune*) concedes these points and advises the *Times* to surrender at discretion rather than make a still worse impression on the public mind. I know that you will agree with me that this is good news. The next election promises to give the Gladstonians a signal triumph. The news has positively excited me. ...

He needed agreeable thoughts and exciting news because he was worried about Ellen and bored with his work. Things were not going well in Middletown. Eddie had the mumps, the cook had departed without notice, and Ellen, who had been advised by the doctor to keep off her feet, had now to be both nurse and cook. His lectures dealt with the same subject as his book, *The State,* which he was still trying to finish. The cold familiar facts of local government were anything but exciting to a man of Woodrow's temperament.

909 *McCulloh St., Balto.*
1 March, 1889

... I can't say that I am *enjoying* my lectures—though I feel sure that most of the class value them as highly as I could wish—for local government, at any rate descriptive local government, is dull matter to lecture on—a mere matter of exact phraseology, no space for the (constructive) imagination to turn in. I have to go so slowly in giving the numerous details of the various systems, that the men may get satisfactory notes, that there's no chance for me to take fire as I go. I'm cold and therefore not comfortable throughout. Next year (I reflect, with satisfaction and hope) I can deliver matter of a different sort—can bring in more discussion, less description—penetrate beyond the forms to the spirit that makes them workable. . . .

In his next letter he told Ellen that he was coming home for the weekend to help her. But she wrote that there was nothing to worry about and begged him not to come, and this brought on a relapse into self-depreciation.

Balto., March 3, 1889

. . . Sometimes, sweetheart—*sometimes*—my knowledge of myself inclines me to think that you are better off away from me than with me, for in my absence you can idealize me, can forget my moods, my occasional discontents and morbid discouragements, and remember only my abiding and controlling love for you; can indulge your fancies as to my "greatness" and "sweetness" and those various other matchless qualities which you so abash and humble me by ascribing to me to my own face. But when I do have such thoughts, I upbraid myself for harbouring them, for my love does not think thus. . . . She waits for me as I wait to go to her as one might wait for returning life after illness, for liberty after long imprisonment, for sight after blindness. I believe in your faith in me as I believe in nothing else except the existence of God and the way of salvation. I only distrust myself—I only know how little I am like what I ought to be to deserve your love. . . .

Some of the students to whom he lectured urged Professor Wilson to go to Washington with them to see President-elect Harrison inaugurated. He had written to Ellen about this and added, "I suppose I ought to see an inauguration, but it will be a very bitter pill to see this one—embodying, as it does, the beginning of the reign of almost every idea and influence with which I do not sympathize." *

On the fourth of March it rained for thirty-six hours. "It's fit enough weather," Woodrow wrote, "to mark the incoming of the Blaine Republicans to the control of the government," † and, using the weather as an excuse, stayed in Baltimore and worked all day on *The State.*

---

* Letter of March 2, 1889.
† Letter to E., March 4, 1889.

Balto., 9 March, 1889

I have completed my revision of the "Local Govt" part of my chapter (and lectures) on England; and now, so far as I can see, there remains nothing . . . to be done for the completion of the volume except a description of the imperial (Roman) forms of govt. and the English Colonial System. Neither of those will take time or labour commensurable with what either Hellas or this English local govt. required—and then I shall be free from this tedious burden—this text-book! What a job it has been! I am thoroughly tired of it and disgusted with it. I hope nothing with reference to it now except that it may some day be off my mind. Catch me undertaking another fact book! Hereafter . . . I mean to be an *author* —never more a book-maker. The discipline has been serviceable, but now that I am coming to the maturity of my powers I can't afford time for any more discipline of *that* kind.

Have I told you that latterly—since I have been here—a distinct *feeling* of maturity—or rather of maturing—has come over me? The *boyish* feeling that I have so long had, and cherished, is giving place to another feeling—I am no longer young (though not old quite!) and I need no longer hesitate (as I have so long and sensitively done) to assert myself and my opinions in the presence of and against the selves and opinions of old men, my "elders." It may be all imagination, but these are the facts of consciousness at the present moment in one Woodrow Wilson—always a slow fellow in mental development—long a child, longer a diffident youth, now at last, perhaps, becoming a self-confident (mayhap a self-assertive) man. I find I look older, my former (Princeton) college friends being the witnesses.

But sweetheart, there's one thing in which my whole nature at one and the same time (my mind and heart) both matures and stays young—and that's *love.* You are, and always will be, to me at once sweetheart, bride, wife, life-companion, my children's mother—everything in one,—remaining your old self and retaining the love I felt for you then, constantly becoming a new self, and winning new love in your new characters, bound to me at every turn and in every character—mine and becoming mine—possessing me and acquiring me—safe in the victory which makes you supreme in my heart and yet daily renewing your conquests. . . .

Ellen also did not like the new administration.

Middletown, Mar. 6th, 1889

My own darling,

I learn ... that, as I supposed, it *did* pour all day at Washington and that everybody, even Harrison, was soaked! I can't restrain some malicious pleasure in imagining the scene!...

When their separation was almost over she wrote:

Middletown, Mar. 17th, 1889

My own darling,

I have just been reading with deep interest and admiration a very fine review of Bryce's book * by one Woodrow Wilson. It strikes me as a particularly fine piece of work!...

Have you read the extraordinarily venomous article on "Irish Secession" in the same magazine? I don't think I ever read an article in which argument was so entirely superseded by abuse—varied occasionally by excited remarks which strongly suggest the exclamation with which "Mr. Puck" makes our protectionists answer the arguments of their opponents, "That's nothing to do with the case." I wonder the "Quarterly" would publish such an article....

What *bliss* there is in the simple thought, He is coming—coming *this week,* only five more days—"and days are short this time of year". ... How true it is that "as the day is so shall thy strength be," for, when at the end of these long separations, I look back over it, it seems almost incredible that it has been borne at all. It seems as though it *could* not have been and could not be. I wonder what would happen to me now if I should suddenly learn that you were to stay six weeks more!...

Balto., March 20, 1889

... Do you know ... that I find it hard to write to you now that the time for seeing you is drawing so near? ... All my energy seems to have gone into my eagerness and impatience to see you. What a wonder it is, dar-

* *American Commonwealth,* in which there was a quotation from Wilson's *Congressional Government.*

ling, this love of ours: how it dominates me at every turn and in every *thing*. I believe, for instance, that if I were not in love with you, sedateness and loss of frolic would go along with the sense of maturity in intellectual matters of which I wrote you the other day. It is *you* who keeps me young, not myself. How *can* I grow middle-aged or old so long as you love me and so command my spirits to laugh and take holiday? Old age of heart will never touch me....

When their third daughter was born, everybody was disappointed. The Reverend Dr. Joseph Wilson, when someone congratulated him upon the arrival of another grandchild, muttered morosely—and inaccurately, "Oh, it's just another of Woodrow's little annuals." Woodrow told Ellen firmly, "No child of ours shall be unwelcome," and Ellen agreed, but seven years later, Eleanor Randolph Wilson overheard a conversation not meant for her ears. Her mother was telling Mary Hoyt how she had cried when the doctor told her that her third baby was a girl. The third girl brooded secretly for years over her misfortune. Her first name was a different version of her mother's, because Ellen preferred it, but she was called Nellie from the start, or Nennie, her own earliest pronunciation.

Woodrow was a great success as a teacher at Wesleyan College and very popular with the undergraduates, as well as the faculty. Political aspirations no longer haunted his dreams. He would never, he said "stand before the Senate," but he could inspire young men to go into politics and become the kind of leader he would have liked to be. He organized the "Wesleyan House of Commons"—modeled after the British House of Commons—to take the place of a dull college debating society, and, of course, wrote its constitution. He became a leader in coaching the football team, and helped to develop one of the greatest teams Wesleyan ever had. Students marched to his house to serenade him after a victory. The college year-book published a verse about him:

> *Prof. W–L–N*
> *A merrier man*
> *Within the limits of becoming mirth*
> *I never spent an hour's talk withal*

At the beginning of his second year at Wesleyan, he was sorely tempted. His classmate, Robert Bridges, wrote that the Board of Trustees of Princeton College was about to offer Woodrow a professorship. He had hoped from the time he decided to make teaching his profession that, some day, he would get an appointment there, but he knew that the Wesleyan Board of Trustees expected him to stay at least two years, and they had "treated him generously and honorably." * He let it be known that he could not accept. At the end of the two years Princeton made him a definite offer—a chair in jurisprudence and political economy, and he accepted it gladly.

The children were never left without at least one parent, so, in the spring of 1890, Woodrow went alone to Princeton to find a house. It was not an easy assignment, for now there were seven in the family, counting Stockton—not to mention Ellen's little sister, Margaret, who, they hoped, would also come to live with them. Woodrow spent almost a week house-hunting before he found what he wanted and succeeded in persuading Ellen, by letter, that the rent was not too high. He was certain, he assured her, that he could earn enough by lecturing and selling articles to magazines to pay for it. And he filled each letter with such ardent "love-making" that she had not the heart to protest. She wrote:

Middletown, Mar. 10, 1890

...Really, dear, I think you have made up your mind to turn my head entirely. Do you suppose, sir, that any feminine head is strong enough to stand such deep draughts of mingled love and praise? Those maddening draughts have such an effect that I am kept in an almost constant state of intoxication. I am fairly "beside myself"; and yet I think I have a remarkably steady head not to show it more than I do. The rest of the family don't seem to suspect that I have "had more than is good for me", anymore than they suspect what an extraordinary woman I am —how very superior to the rest of my sex!...

The house in Princeton was on Library Place, large enough to hold the family comfortably, and attractive, after Ellen had persuaded the owner, a prim professor called "Granny" Hunt by the undergraduates, to let her redecorate it—at his expense. There was a stable in the back yard, which Ellen rented later to two college students. There, in the autumn of 1890, the Wilsons began their life in the quiet, small town which was to be their home for twenty-two years.

Ellen was very proud of her children. Every Sunday morning, while they were too young to go to church, she dressed them in their best—Margaret and Jessie, two little blue-eyed blondes, in "Kate Greenaway" dresses she had made herself, and bonnets tied with wide satin ribbons; and Nellie, with the dark brown curls, in fluffy white, in the baby-carriage—and took them for a walk. She timed it carefully to meet her husband and the congregation as they left the church, and the "ohs"

* W.W.'s letter to Robert Bridges, Jan. 27, 1890.

and "ahs" that greeted the small procession made her eyes dance and her cheeks pink. But that was not enough. If only her grandparents, Aunt Lou, and her cousins and friends in the South could also see her darlings! Woodrow insisted that she must have her wish. He would stay at the Nassau Hotel while she made a "tour" with the children. In addition to his work at Princeton, he had to prepare and deliver a series of lectures at the New York Law School, and would, he assured her, be too busy to feel lonely. So, in March, 1892, Ellen and the children went to Savannah, to Rome, to Gainesville and to visit the Howes in Columbia. Everyone, Ellen reported, "raved" about her babies, but her pleasure was marred:

Savannah, Sunday, Mar. 6, 1892

... Oh me, how my heart aches to think of you there alone! I don't see how I ever made up my mind to leave you. Well, it is the first time and it is going to be the last! *You* will have to do the leaving hereafter....

Woodrow could not help mourning, too:

Nassau Hotel, Princeton, March 6, 1892

... I am calm and as full of quiet, untroubled purpose as ever; but there's no heart in the purpose—nothing seems worth while without you ... I shall do better presently; but for the time I do not *care,* somehow, to feel differently.... It somehow seems appropriate ... while my home life is dead—my dear one gone with her three-fold glory of little children.... My love for you at such a time seems a sort of principle of life —a sort of ideal thing which reminds me in some way constantly of the shortness of life, and of how much there is to do, ere it runs out, if that love is to make itself a name in worthy things done because of it. The strain of such periods would seem to be the strain of growth. Courage must look to itself, purpose must straighten its ways, life must be cleansed and quickened, so that love may be glorified. The pain of separation blesses us in the long run. It teaches us how strong and tender the ties are that bind us to each other, how intimately our lives are connected—united....

They wrote to each other every day. Seven years of marriage had neither dimmed their ardor nor altered their conviction that each had found the perfect companion.

Savannah, March 11, 1892

... Yesterday was prayer-meeting afternoon, and I took the children.
They were *very* good—and very much mystified. But Margaret said she
wanted to go again, she "liked that noise".... People are so delighted
with their friendliness. Even Nellie is "kind" to everyone, tells them
her name.... Everyone in the house sends love,—the children lots of
kisses.... I love you with all my heart and head and life....

Ellen's grandfather had retired and the old parsonage had been re-
painted and modernized. She had tea with the new minister and his wife,
and wrote afterwards to Woodrow:

Savannah [not dated]

... It was both sad and strange to be in the dear old house under such
new circumstances ... I felt especially queer in the parlour though, for
you know the very last time I was there was when I was married. It would
seem at once like something in the far, far past and as if it had been
but the other day—for so many things have happened since, and yet it
all comes back so vividly.

The most striking result of being here again is to make me realize,
more strongly than ever that I am happier—yes, infinitely happier than
I was or ever dreamed of being in all the days of my life before. I wish,
dearest, that I could *show* you the difference, could in some way bid
you "look on this picture and on that" for then you would be so glad
for my sake that you would never again waste a moment's regret on all
the little incidental troubles and sufferings that are the the small price I
pay for it. Ah, my husband, you have been everything to me—you *are*
everything. If I could but tell you how devotedly, absorbedly, passionately I love you in return for all this happiness.

Johns Hopkins University wanted Woodrow to resume his annual
lecture courses and, since he still needed to augment his income, he asked
the Princeton authorities for a six-weeks' leave of absence. This caused
a mild stir in academic circles and even in far-away Georgia. Ellen wrote
in her most practical vein:

Savannah, Monday
[not dated] 1892

... You know people down here are asking me too, if you are going to Baltimore! It seems to be all over the country. Have they been attacking you about it in Princeton? Have you seen Dr. Patton?* How is he? Have you made the strike for the other five hundred as you said you were going to do at this juncture? It is certainly a good time to do it and I hope your courage won't fail you now.... Suppose you tell them to "fix" you by building a house to suit you and giving it you rent free instead of that four or five hundred!...

Asking for a raise in any form was very repugnant to Woodrow, yet for Ellen's sake he did it—in a roundabout way. Dr. Patton was sick, he wrote, and he didn't want to bother him, but he had spoken to the Dean, Dr. Murray. The Dean said that he had approached Dr. Patton on the subject and had received the impression that the president would attend to it, if he didn't forget.

He forgot. Dr. Patton, a Presbyterian minister, was a brilliant preacher, a witty and delightful companion, but absent-minded. "Never do to-day what you can put off until to-morrow" was one of his favorite axioms. But Woodrow finally got his leave of absence.

Princeton, 30th March, 1892

... It seems to me, as I read your letters, that so long as you love me, no sorrow or trial or struggle can ever daunt my heart. So calm and silent and commanding a peace comes into my life. I love all men more, I am juster, more urbane, and tolerant, and hopeful and trustful because my little wife loves me with her pure and perfect heart, watches me with affectionate approval and admiration out of her deep clear eyes —because my spirit has won your spirit to its close companionship....

Rome, Georgia, April 3rd, 1892

... I would like to find the "great heart word"... which would tell with what a *passion* of love and joy and pride in you my heart is swelling. Dearest, it is my deliberate conviction—nay, I do not *believe* it, I *know* —that the combination of qualities found in you is the rarest, finest, noblest, grandest of which human nature is capable. It is a combination

* Dr. Francis L. Patton, president of Princeton.

which, if put in a book in all its truth, would be censured by every critic as impossible—an unwarranted idealism. What! such strength and nobility of character combined with such ineffable tenderness, such unselfishness and thoughtfulness in things great and small, a nature so exquisitely gifted in power of sympathy—of understanding others; ... and the orator's gift—the "personal magnetism" and *all* those gifts which go to make a born leader of men, combined with powers of thought of such a kind that he must undoubtedly rank as a *genius,* no less than Burke himself; and added to all this a strength of purpose and of will and powers of application which result in achievements so great that while yet in his early manhood his rank is among the foremost thinkers of his age!—Well! no wonder the critics scoff and disbelieve! It would be incredible if it were not *true;* for truth is indeed stranger than fiction.

You may smile if you will and call me partial, but you cannot deny, sir, that a wife has excellent opportunities for becoming acquainted with her husband; and the mere *impulse* to make the best of him which we call partiality—"a poor thing, sir, but 'tis mine own!'"—won't carry one through unlimited trials of patience. A wife always finds her husband out sooner or later! On the other hand no one ever knows *how* good a man is except his wife. It is false that we turn our best side toward the world; we keep it only for our nearest and dearest....

Princeton, April 17, 1892

... I can do nothing without you. I wait for my life to begin again. My work goes dully and without inspiration—might be *any*body's work, so much my individuality seems to be merged in you.... I cannot even enjoy myself normally—I cannot enjoy my*self* at all! Last Thursday I stayed in New York all afternoon in order to visit the Metropolitan Museum, but I did not half enjoy it. Every beautiful thing I saw but made me think more longingly of you. I wondered whether it was one of the things *you* had seen there, and what you thought of it. For *that's* the rub: my *mind's* loneliness. All my best and most intimate thoughts I must keep to myself: my mind is a hermit, imprisoned in a dreary silence....

A letter came to Woodrow from the University of Illinois at Urbana. Would Professor Wilson be interested in considering the presidency with a salary of $6000 a year? Woodrow was distracted because Ellen was not there to consult.

Princeton, April 28, 1892

... I need your advice desperately.... It seems a really great opportunity of its kind. I don't want a presidency, as you know, but I *must* increase my resources to provide for you and the children and I am going to New York this afternoon to consult Bridges and several members of the Finance Committee of the [Princeton] Board of Trustees. Then I shall have a definite basis for seeking the advice which will conclude the whole matter—your own!...

Ellen's first reaction was a gleeful prediction that the trustees were now certain to increase Woodrow's salary in order to keep him at Princeton. Then she asked very sensible questions:

Columbia, S.C., April 30, 1892

... Is the salary *just* $6,000 or $6,000 *and* the usual presidents' perquisites, so to speak—a nice house and grounds; the grounds kept up by the college; and his travelling expenses when on college business? How large is the faculty and how many students are there? What is and has been the spirit of the legislature towards it?... Have they nice buildings? What sort of a place is Urbana? How large etc. etc.?... We will want to look over the ground *very* carefully in order to determine if you will have time for original work. It seems to me that that is *the* most important question. All others are dwarfed to insignificance beside it.... I have always thought that there must be something very *distracting* about the duties of a college president....

Woodrow answered these questions when he received the information from Urbana. Then, after much writing back and forth, they decided to refuse the offer, partly because they did not want to leave Princeton, chiefly because they thought it would end or permanently interrupt Woodrow's literary work.

Princeton, May 9, 1892

... I have heard President Angell, of Michigan, speak very fully of the life of a president who has to extract grants from a Legislature and manage a political board of Trustees; and Stock told me the other

day that Canfield, ... now president of the University of Nebraska,
... had said to him that he had once had great plans for original and
literary work; but that since he had taken charge of the Nebraska University ... he had given up all idea of ever returning to books again. ...

Ellen thought it would be a good idea to keep Princeton's Board
of Trustees in suspense for a while, but Woodrow's troublesome conscience rebelled. He wrote, almost apologetically,

Princeton, May 4, 1892

... You know how I am constituted. The question I ask myself is, If
I do not mean to accept the Illinois call in any event, ought I to *"work"*
it in this way? Having done as much as I have already done to stir
things up, would you think me foolish, darling, if I did nothing more
in that direction? ...

He declined the University of Illinois' invitation without further
delay. Princeton's Board of Trustees was, however, sufficiently "stirred
up," since he might, after all, accept some other offer. They voted to give
Professor Wilson $3500 to cover his house rent, and promised him a rise
in salary as soon as possible.

During their engagement Woodrow had wanted Ellen's advice because he loved her. After their marriage he not only wanted it, but needed
it, depended upon it, and never made a vital decision without her approval. For he discovered that, in spite of the fact that she had little
experience of life, outside of the gentle, unworldly atmosphere of a
Southern parsonage, she was extraordinarily wise, even shrewd in her
judgments. Ellen understood people better than Woodrow did, for she
was more detached, less emotional than he. She had also the sort of intuition that comes to every woman who is selflessly devoted to her husband's welfare. Some men might have resented such dependence upon
a woman. Woodrow was humbly grateful.

Princeton, May 1, 1892

... This week, when there were matters of importance to be decided, I
have somehow *realized* my love for you more than ever. I have *needed*
you so much—for counsel and sympathy and sustaining love—and have
been made so vividly conscious of the intimate part you play in my life!
I am so hopelessly incomplete without you. ... I am extravagantly de-

voted to intellectual pleasure such as is afforded by the companionship
of a mind endowed with a great store of broad, sane sense, with quick
powers of sympathetic perception ... and yours is such a mind; that
extraordinary, that almost incredible combination which it exhibits,
of practical wifely sense and helpfulness with the atmosphere of perfect literary perception and an incomparable womanly charm and loveliness, fills me sometimes with an overwhelming sense of delight and
obligation. . . .

Ellen replied:

Columbia, May 3, 1892

... I can never get over the wonder of it, darling, that you can think
and feel so about me. It makes me *so* happy and yet it humbles me so
deeply too; for how can I *help* knowing and feeling how far short I
fall of that description. Ah, how I long to be all that you think me—
all that my darling's wife should be. May God help me to grow into that
likeness. . . .

When a friend became engaged to be married, Woodrow wrote, "I
know what felicity I am wishing you when I wish you success. My own
sweet partner has been the making of my heart not only, but of my mind
too, quickening it where it was sluggish, waking it where it had slept—
supplementing it on all sides. I *must* have wide sympathies with such
a mind as hers, with no necessity of specialization to spoil or narrow it,
—so close neighbor to my own. . . . God speed you, my dear fellow, in
making sure of the same aid and comfort." *
Not long after she and the children came home, Woodrow went to
Columbia to be best man at his brother's wedding, and Ellen, for some
reason, minded this separation more than usual.

Princeton, June 18, 1892

... I have an uneasy conviction that it would not be good for me to
write my soul *too* much now. I am in danger of taking this separation
too tragically. There is something terrible in having so much at stake
in life; it involves sometimes an acute agony. May God help me—make
me a better Christian—more spiritual-minded—there is no other help

* To Charles Kent, Sept. 8, 1893.

possible for one who loves so intensely. How else can she hope to win peace? Joy indeed she has in fullest human measure, but *peace*—security; who save the infinitely Great, the infinitely Merciful can insure that?...

... Every time I am separated from you, my own Eileen, I seem to see one more element of my dependence upon you—my devotion to you. This time I am afraid that it is a *selfish* element I see. Here, where I love everybody and everybody loves me, I seem to miss you ... *more* sorely: for I feel that no one is devoted *particularly* to *me:* and the feeling makes me so forlorn! It is not wholly selfish: it is *you* I miss. It would not satisfy me to have somebody else devoted particularly to me. It is *your* devotion only that can satisfy my infinite longing for love....

Ellen knew that Woodrow's family, while very proud of him, seldom praised him. Her own family were equally reserved, and she as well as Woodrow thought this both wise and proper. "You behaved well today," "You look nice," they told their own children, carefully resisting emotional overstatement lest their offspring become conceited. But between Ellen and Woodrow there was so such rule. Each delighted in praising the other endlessly, sometimes extravagantly, always privately. And because self-depreciation was Woodrow's chief liability, he needed her admiration, as a man needs water in a desert. Ellen's intuition must have told her that this was what he missed now even more than her devotion.

Princeton, June 20, 1892

... To think of you, dear, is a pleasure like that derived from a perfect picture or poem. It is as if a master artist had conceived a grand ideal, "had seen it steadily and seen it whole," and then with truly magic skill had been able to *realize* his vision.... The masterpiece which it is the delight of my life to contemplate has the strength of the strongest without that taint of the *brutal* that sometimes attends it; the *power* of genius and of the born leader with the added fascination of a sympathetic nature, of sensitiveness and of a refined taste. And added to all that again, a beauty of character—a tenderness and charm and lovableness beyond the power of words to describe— Ah, truly such a man is the noblest work of God—grander than a whole material universe. To see such a one and realize what one sees makes one catch one's breath with the wonder of it. . . . Oh, I know you think that my love is the medium through which you loom so large. But why then, sir, does the most casual visitor to the house speak in the same strain? With all of them the wonder is the same—the perfect union in your mind and character and disposition of those elements of strength and beauty usually found dissociated. Truly you are steel of the finest temper—strongest yet keenest and most beautiful of weapons!—And by the way, methought as in a dream I heard that good blade lament because, for sooth, it was not a *hammer!* It may have been the hammer of Thor that it envied, yet that hammer, though it made some noise in the world, *achieved* but little; and Thor himself was but a burly brute:—not exactly the god one would choose to serve. . . .

They vowed, when Woodrow returned, that they would never leave each other again, and for more than a year they kept the vow. Then, in 1893, Woodrow went to Chicago to deliver a lecture, stayed with his friend and classmate, Cyrus McCormick, and visited the World's Fair. When he came home, he insisted that Ellen must go to the Fair while he took care of the children. She went reluctantly, with Mary Hoyt, and every day, along with pages of "love-making," he reported his parental experiences.

Princeton, Sept. 7, 1893

. . . Still we thrive as much as you could wish,—for I'm sure you don't want us not to miss you. That's something beyond praying for. . . . We don't *talk* about you much—that would not be prudent; but we *all* act as if something serious were the matter. . . . I find that I'm getting much more intimately acquainted with the children. Nellie comes to me now, as she would come to you, with all sorts of odd little confidences and singular narratives which delight me. It somehow touches me deeply to be both father and mother to the sweet little chicks. I am really enjoying my maternal functions very keenly—odd as I feel.

Margaret was seven, Jessie six, and Nellie three years old that fall, and, although they certainly missed their mother, they were enchanted to have their father, for the first time, all to themselves. Woodrow Wilson had a delightful way with all children. He listened to their remarks with gravity, never teased or questioned them, and could, at a moment's notice, send them into fits of laughter by twisting his mobile face into fantastic shapes. He found original ways to entertain his small daughters. There was the galloping horse, for instance, produced by slapping his hands on his knees, softly at first, then louder and louder and at last fading gradually away down a road they could almost see. There was a strange bird—Papa's talented right hand—that flapped its wings, flew around their heads, balanced on a glass, drank and stretched its neck to let the water flow down. Their wooden blocks became soaring towers under his fingers, their geography maps exciting when he suggested that cities, states and countries be divided among them and appropriated as personal possessions. This idea, incidentally, brought on a fierce quarrel between his children over who should "own" America. The man who was years later to have something to say on this subject ruled solemnly that no one should have it. The climax of their days came when, after prayers, he sang for them. "Sweet and Low," "The Kerry Dancers," a hymn he loved, "Watchman Tell Us of the Night," and a lullaby with an intriguing chorus—"Peri, meri dictum; peri, meri quartum; peri, meri centum, Domini"—were their favorites. Yet much as he loved his children, his wife came first in Woodrow's heart.

Princeton, Sept. 10, 1893

... You seem to me to contain in your sweet person and your sweet nature, everything that is worth living for in the world,—besides duty. Duty is worth living for, no *man* could think otherwise; but there is often no *joy* in living for it. Everything connected in living for you is full of joy, if only it can be combined with living *with* you. I suppose there is *duty,* too, in living for you; but the duty never comes to the surface, so deep buried is it beneath the gladness that quickens every thought and every act that has you for its object. Nellie told the whole secret to-day. I said, "Nen, *why* do you want mama to come back?" and she said in that sweet, quick way of hers, "To love her!" That's the whole matter. To live *for* you is to love you....

You serve me as a sort of perpetual source of youth. The sort of love I have for you has no age: it is as much a young man's love as a mature man's. It is at once the pledge of youth and of manhood. You are the companion of all my growth, whether of mind or of heart, and I associate you with all my ages. I loved you long before I ever saw you, for you are my ideal. You have been with me, in my desires, ever since I was a boy; you know and keep me close company as a man; you

are all that I *would* be, brought into my life and kept constantly at
hand, to excite my enthusiasm, to kindle my heart into a constant blaze
of joy....

Princeton, Monday, 11 Sept., 1893

... Stock and I sat in the dusk last evening in the most delightful discourse about you. He admires you—your "wonderful critical faculty,
your illuminating sense, your sweet womanliness and sterling strength
of character"—as much as he loves you. I enjoyed what he said more
than fine wine.... And *I* said more than I ever said to anyone else
about you, spoke of you as I never ventured to speak of you to anybody but yourself. You can imagine how I enjoyed the conversation....

They had a rare companionship—these two men who loved Ellen
more than anyone else in the world. They were closer intellectually, in
their tastes and their sense of humor, than they were to their own brothers. Woodrow's was the stronger character. Stockton Axson was very
gentle, unassuming and introspective. He liked everybody and everybody
liked him. He hated to face up to problems—his own or other people's—
and, when they could not be ignored, sank into a morass of melancholy
from which "Brother Woodrow" and Ellen had to rescue him. Woodrow's opinion of his brother-in-law is revealed in the dedication of his
book, *Mere Literature,* published in 1896.

> *To Stockton Axson*
> *By every gift of mind a critic*
> *and lover of letters*
> *By every gift of heart a friend*
> *This little volume is affectionately dedicated.*

Stockton spent most of his summer vacations at Library Place and
lived there for several years after he joined the Princeton faculty.

There was seldom an interval when there were not other relatives,
besides Stock and Eddie, staying with the Wilsons. Woodrow's "Sister
Annie," her husband, two sons and a small daughter. Ellen's cousins,
Mary and Florence Hoyt, and Helen Bones, Woodrow's cousin, came
often for long visits. Margaret Axson made the house her permanent
home when Aunt Lou decided reluctantly that her ward needed a
change of scene. No one, least of all the Wilsons, considered this invasion
an imposition, for they had all been brought up in the Southern tradition
of prolonged hospitality. Kinfolk were always welcome, with or without
an invitation, and expected to stay as long as they wished. And hosts

and guests alike would have felt insulted if anyone had suggested that
a contribution to the household expenses would be helpful.

How Ellen and Woodrow managed financially is a story in itself.
It was done by rigid economy on Ellen's part and by Woodrow's indefatigable industry. Ellen kept a careful budget in which the only ex-
travagance was an annual expenditure for books. She taught a succession of cooks to make tasty dishes out of leftovers and made all of her
own clothes as well as the children's. There was a triumphant occasion
when she proved that she could make a "stunning evening gown"* for
thirty cents. Nellie never had a new dress, only Margaret's and Jessie's
outgrown hand-me-downs, remodeled by her mother. Woodrow went each
year to Baltimore to lecture at Johns Hopkins, wrote articles for magazines and his third book, *Division and Reunion.* So, although there was
seldom anything left for the savings bank, there was never an unpaid bill.

Dr. Joseph Wilson had retired not long after his younger son's marriage. With no home now and no family life, he was restless and despondent, and after a series of visits with friends and relatives went, in 1894,
to live alone in a boarding house in New York. Woodrow wrote to Ellen
from Baltimore after his father had visited him there.

Baltimore, February 4, 1894

... I received a letter from dear father the other day which went beyond the hint contained in an earlier letter about his distaste for the
household on 22nd St. He says that he ... is impatient to get away! ...
I have written urging him to go to you, and establish himself in our
house as we have so often and earnestly urged him to do. You second
the invitation, don't you, sweetheart? My heart bleeds to think of his
desolation and homelessness. He loves you and I believe you love him.
I would do anything in my power to make his last years bright and full
of love and I know you want to help me. ...

I spent the afternoon at the theatre—my first indulgence this week.
For some reason, I have thought of you more intensely the three times
I have been to the theatre, this time, than anywhere else. I wonder why
it is? It is certainly not the sight of the vulgar love-making that goes
on on the stage. ... Neither is it simply that I am in a holiday humour
and can have no *complete* enjoyment or relaxation without you. ... Perhaps it is that when I see an image of life on the stage and look upon
other women's faces there as they seem to be at home or abroad, in
the midst of the world, the meaning of my own relations in life, whether

* Letter from E. to W., 1894.

by contrast or suggestion, is brought vividly home to me,—the meaning of one woman's life to me. I am made somehow conscious of the springs of resolution and action within myself—and go away from the place (no matter how empty, frivolous, or imperfect the play may have been ...) awed and delighted by thoughts of the real life I am myself in the midst of. I remember having felt the same way, to some extent, when at the theatre *with* you:—it is only more vivid when I am alone. It was most powerful the evening I went to that terrible play of Oscar Wilde's * in New York. I was *overwhelmed* with tenderness for you, my pure and perfect little wife. I am always on such occasions fairly *intoxicated* with thoughts of the sweet simplicity of our lives; with your genuineness—with the quiet and love of our home—with the privilege of high thinking and plain living—with the delight of being simply and always your lover and husband and close companion, not a pretense or an artificiality or a breach of privacy in all our life. How unspeakably precious a thing it is, this life that is all our own in which we are sure that we love and trust and help one another.

Ellen replied:

Princeton, Feb. 6th, 1894

I have been sitting here I know not how long dreaming over that precious letter of yours that came to-day.... Indeed, dearest, it is a letter to be laid away forever in my heart of hearts. Ah, how I thank God for the sweet "quiet and love" of this home life of ours—for all its fine simplicity, sincerity and sweet intimacies—how I thank Him for *you,* my darling—noble man, perfect husband that you are—my own *true* love, so absolutely *all* that a woman could desire the man to be to whom she gives her heart and life... Ah, dear heart, you idealize me in a way that often can but frighten me, but one thing at least you cannot over-estimate and that is my great love....

With all my heart I hope that dear Father will do as you beg and come to us "to stay." I need not tell you how glad I should be if he could be content and happy with us—if I could do anything to make him so. Shall I write and beg him to come *now* before your return... ? Can we not find some occupation here for him—a suburban church, or a lecture-

* *Lady Windermere's Fan.*

ship—one hour a week, say—compensation nominal, since they profess great poverty at the Seminary. That would both help to anchor him and to make him happy again. . . .

Old Joseph was proud—too proud to be a "burden." Ellen, he said, had enough to do without having an old man to look after. It was not until a year later that they succeeded in persuading him to live with them.

Ellen had, indeed, enough to do. With a husband who needed constant attention, housekeeping, dressmaking, social obligations and welfare work to keep her busy, she was also a school teacher. There was no school for young children in Princeton at that time, so Ellen had her own school, in the parlor on Library Place. Every weekday morning Margaret, Jessie and Nellie were taught the three R's, geography and history. On Sundays they learned the Presbyterian "Shorter Catechism" by heart, and heard the Bible stories. But that was not all. Homer, Dryden, Shakespeare and many other great poets were their daily fare, for Ellen believed that, when the meaning was obscure, her children would feel the beauty and the music of the words. They did not disappoint her.

Princeton, Feb. 15, 1894

. . . The children and I were reading about the ancient Persians today and I told them how their young men were taught "to ride, to shoot and to speak the truth." That seemed to strike their fancy amazingly; they all three marched about for half an hour chanting at the top of their voices, "to ride, to shoot and to speak the truth!" Once Jessie stopped to enquire, "and *did* they *all* speak the truth?" By way of illustrating the subject I read some verses of Tom Moore's "who has not heard of the vale of Cashmere?" etc; but before I had finished Jessie interrupted me with, "Don't read that—read Shakespeare." How is that for six years old? . . .

Princeton, 1894

I have just escaped with difficulty from three insatiable children clamouring for "more poetry," and again more. . . . "More about the Arabs" is their specific cry to-night, though I had already given them half a dozen poems on the subject, covering that gentleman's views regarding his sweetheart, his horse, his palm tree, & things in general.

That reminds me of the books I ordered for them.... The history—"Montgomery's" is not what I wanted but a U.S. history.... I wonder if they haven't primary general histories in that large bookstore on Baltimore St. that you could examine a little for me.... One wants a book that will give in simple, clear outline a panoramic view of the larger movements of history and also vivid little pictures of the life, character, ideals, general environment of each nation....

Princeton, 1894

... They have been having an imaginary school in which they are teaching a large number of children what Jessie calls "strongery"—viz to leap, to box, to wrestle etc (like the Greeks). Margaret says she is teaching them to be Amazons—Jessie says she has killed *all the Austrians!* She has a long tale as to how she accomplished it. She was the *hero!* After the battle she made a great "oration" to the Swiss. It takes somewhat the form of a *saga* and is chanted with much action....

Princeton, [undated] 1895

... The children are now disputing over the *cardinal virtues,* appropriating them—in name only!—and dividing them up. I am called upon to decide which is best, Temperance or Charity, Justice or Hope, etc. It all came from reading the "Golden Legend."...

Princeton, Feb. 16, 1895

... Jessie has decided that she is *Homer,* or rather "the other man of the same name." She says she lived when Homer did and she and he made up the poems together. You know how busy they keep me trying to define words; now they are constantly setting me a still harder task, viz. to sit in judgment on the relative "greatness" of every character they ever heard of, real or imaginary. Who is the greatest, Shakspere or Homer, Milton or Dante, Themistocles or Miltiades, Zeus or Odin, Aeschylus or Sophocles, Epaminondas or Washington? I think that last "parallel" as coming from them quite interesting, for I had never said a word to associate the two names in their minds....

Woodrow wrote, after receiving one of these letters:

... What charming stories you tell about the children. If all my heart were not absorbed pining for their sweet mother, how I should pine for them! When I am separated from *you*, that pain swallows up all other pains,—and the children seem only part of you. But, if I could separate them from you in my thoughts, I should be very unhappy without them —the sweet little sprites! ...

Neither Ellen nor Woodrow was very socially inclined, but they were well liked in Princeton and constantly invited to the teas, luncheons and dinner parties so prevalent in a university town. When Woodrow was away, Ellen usually went only to women's parties, for she had been raised in the tradition that a woman should not appear in "mixed company" without her husband. But she urged Woodrow to go out often in Baltimore. That year he was, as Ellen remarked, "quite the lion." One day, after Mrs. Edgeworth Bird, a popular and very sociable lady, had taken him to call on some of her friends, he wrote:

Baltimore, February 23, 1894

... After the calls I stayed to tea with Mrs. Bird and spent part of the evening—and I go there next Sunday again! When I spoke to Mrs. Small the other evening about Col. Richard Malcolm Johnston, she said, "Oh you mean Mrs. Bird's Col. Johnston!" I think I shall become known here as "Mrs. Bird's Mr. Wilson!" She takes me around and shows me off. She fairly puts me through my paces ..., making me repeat what I said to her the other day about Andrew Lang etc. etc. I felt quite like a prize horse at a fair! The descriptions she gives of you would lead you, if you could but hear them, to deem my praises dim and colourless by comparison. Her command of superlatives is beyond belief. I feel, after being with her, that I am stepping out of an *aurora borealis* into the common, unprismatic light. ...

Baltimore, Feb'y. 24, 1894

The dinner last night ... passed off most delightfully. ... The feature of the evening, for me, was meeting Mrs. Harry Reid,*—by far the most charming woman I've met here, Miss D—— not excepted. For with all her brilliancy, Miss D—— did not have a tithe of Mrs. Reid's charm—so

_____

* Mrs. Edith Reid, wife of Prof. Harry Fielding Reid of Johns Hopkins University.

bright, so whimsical, so sweet, so pretty! How I should like to see you two together!... She is not at all *intense,* neither is she a bit "advanced," except in the power to think and to see. She engages one's affections at the same time that she captivates his mind. She seemed (I must say, even at the risk of alarming you) to take as much of a fancy to me as I took to her. This morning she sent her husband around with a note begging me to dine with them "any evening I would name." *This* evening is literally the only one left that was not spoken for by somebody else, and so I am going this evening. What would I not give to take you with me,—not for protection, madam, but for your own delight and mine. Your charm, with its deep, and sweet seriousness, without intensity, its unpremeditated art, its constant fine mixture of qualities, as if your whole nature were as deep and sincere as your matchless eyes, —your charm which is so much greater than hers that, while she delights me, you enslave me, is also so different from hers that it would make an excellent foil,—and I believe that, after fifteen minutes' talk, you would love one another for "good and aye"....

I can talk to other women because I know you—and I like to enjoy you through them. I never have such satisfying thoughts of you as while I am talking to them, and realizing your fuller variety, your sweeter naturalness, your more perfect companionableness....

Ellen was too sure of Woodrow's love to be jealous of the women he admired. And, because she felt that she could not provide him with the sort of clever talk and gaiety that amused him, she always urged him to see them often. "I am too grave or too sober," she told Florence Hoyt, and added, quoting Shakespeare's Cassius, "I am not gamesome." Yet, when they met Ellen, Woodrow's women friends became, like Mrs. Reid, her friends too, for in admiring him they had a bond in common with his wife.

The following summer Woodrow went on a long lecture tour, first to New England, which he found "diverting" and "how unlike the United States!" [*] He wrote from Plymouth, Massachusetts, where he delivered a series of lectures:

July 14, 1894

... The lecture audience is most interesting—full of faces that it is a pleasure to dwell upon,—so full are they of the records of character and

[*] W.W.'s letter of July 13, 1894.

thought. . . . I feel sure, as I look at the audience, that the average of intelligence among them is perhaps higher than in any other audience I ever spoke to—at least the sort of *prepared* intelligence needed for such lectures as they have gathered to hear—and of course that is **very** inspiring. . . .

From Colorado Springs, where he saw the Rocky Mountains for the first time, he wrote:

Colorado Springs, July 26, 1894

. . . The second lecture was not quite so successful as the first—though fully twice as many people heard it—because I did not speak with quite so much ease and confidence. The subject—political liberty—was *very* difficult to handle and illustrate. . . . It will be interesting to see how big the audience is next time! . . .

This is the point where the plains, having risen gradually and imperceptibly from the Mississippi to the extraordinary height of six thousand feet, break suddenly into the great peaks and masses of this stupendous range. I want to go *among* the huge structures and feel their terrible grandeur. Oh, my love, how I wish for *you,* my little artist and poet! It almost tortures me to think of the deep wonder and excitement that would spring into your eyes if *you* could see what I am seeing. It makes me feel selfish to see it without you . . . I *must* get you out here by hook or crook, if I have to write half a dozen articles to do it, send Ed with you, and stay home myself with the children. . . .

Ellen wrote from the seaside resort where she and the children had gone to escape the heat in Princeton:

Belmar, July 31, 1894

. . . I am delighted indeed that you are getting so much enjoyment and stimulation from those new and wonderful sights. I *do* enjoy them intensely through your eyes. How sweet it is in you to be so wild for me to see them too! . . . But that particular sort of pleasure—the pleasure of freedom and travel aren't for mothers: and having bartered them for something better, they certainly have no cause for dissatisfaction. It seems to me that one of the greatest sources of mischief in this world is that *dishonesty* in people which makes them unwilling to pay the just price for their happiness. They fail to enjoy the good that God has sent because forever discontentedly striving after other wholly incompatible delights. And if the discontent leads them, as it too often does, to neglect the *duties* which lie at the foundation of all their *joys,* then indeed they have made an unmitigated failure in their art of living. Don't you think that to grasp clearly ''the great & beautiful doctrine of compensations'' would save most people a world of vexation and might have very wide-reaching consequences of many sorts? It might even handicap a ''walking delegate'' or two!—But what a very uncalled for sermon!

I have seen to-day a *paper!*—the first one since I saw you. I feel entirely behind the times,—didn't even know about Cleveland's letter: * wish I had seen it. As far as I can make out it seems to have been a splendid political move,—going far toward shifting the responsibility for the situation from the party at large and himself as its head, and distinctly fastening it where it as distinctly belongs, upon the ''sugar senators,'' etc. Don't you think it may go far towards saving the party in the next election? Is, or is not, a President justified by law and precedent in ''influencing legislation'' in that particular way? For once our legislation, too, seems to have a dramatic element in it. This trial of strength and endurance between House & Senate is positively exciting....

A woman's club in Denver invited Woodrow to deliver ''one or more'' of his lectures there. He accepted, although he was decidedly apprehensive. Club women, especially Colorado women with their franchise to vote, scared him. He wrote when he returned to the Springs:

Colorado Springs, 1 Aug., 1894

... The whole afternoon was consumed in finishing lunch and driving round and about the city. It is a really beautiful place.... It gives one a singular impression, however.... Every style that architects have conceived since 1879 is here to be seen within the compass of a few city blocks. You seem to be in a sort of architectural exhibit....

In the evening came the lecture ''before a small but select audience''

* President Cleveland's letter to William L. Wilson, Chairman of the House of Representatives' Ways and Means Committee. He stated that Democrats in Congress must support the tariff-revision bill, sponsored by Wilson, or be guilty of party dishonor. Tariff on sugar was being strenuously opposed by some Southern Democrats.

(25¢ admission) in Unity Church. Enter to the platform two ladies followed modestly by the lecturer of the evening. He is introduced in a few laboriously chosen words by one of the ladies, a sweet and delicate looking person; he rises and bows to her deferentially; begins his lecture as collectedly as may he under the circumstances; and she and her companion withdraw to the front pew. The lecture is on Political Liberty; it is soon concluded; the lecturer holds a levee at the foot of the pulpit; is then carried off ... by two Princeton men. ... That's the Denver visit.

Colorado Springs, 2 Aug., 1894

... I am rejoiced to say that I not only keep my audience here, but draw new people at every lecture, till now I have quite a "following." One man expressed his enthusiasm by exclaiming, "Why, that fellow is a whole team *and the dog under the wagon!*"

The best of all is that you will be as much rejoiced by it as I am. ... Nothing is quite such an inspiration as your belief in my success and enthusiasm because of it. ... You have yourself produced the conditions of my success. ...

When he returned from his lecture tour, he found that reports of his successes had already reached the ears of the Princeton Board of Trustees, along with a rumor that other universities intended to offer him better-paid and more important positions. They quickly raised his salary, and this, with an increase in royalties from his books, and higher prices offered by magazines for his articles, made the Wilsons feel free at last to dream about building a house of their own. Economizing more fervently than ever, Ellen put every dollar not needed for necessary expenses into a savings account, marked "House."

In 1895 Woodrow went again to lecture at Johns Hopkins.

906 McCulloh St.
Baltimore, 24 Jan'y., 1895

... A flood of recollections has been pouring in upon me ever since I got here last night, sweetheart, for I have been put once more in my old, my first room, third story back ... where my old life and my old anxieties were lived out, till I went south to be happy with you; where part of *Congressional Government* was written; ... the room to which so many times I have been brought back as it were to a sort of centre. It reminds me of so many hopes, fears, achievements, disappointments that it is, for me, almost like the studio round which life circled for the Laird, Taffy and little Billee *—without the tragedy. You may be sure that the *tender* memories of the old place centre about you. I feel both younger (as if reminded of the days when I was making my start, and so made aware how much the same fellow I am,—with all the old sensibilities alive—alive sometimes like the nerve of a tooth!) and older in this room: the memories have *lengthened* so, so much change has come: I seem myself to have become in so many ways another fellow,—more confident, steady, serene, though not less susceptible to all sorts of influences which experience might have been expected to render me indifferent to: enjoying in a certain degree a sense of power,—as if I had gotten some way upon the road I used so to burn to travel,—and yet fairly restless and impatient with ambition, as of old—a boy and yet a man—carrying about with me the marks and records of all the turns and experiences in my life of which this room reminds me. I talk as if I have seen the world, boxed the compass in the vicissitudes of my life, don't I! Well, I *have*,—*inside* of me; quiet and even and uneventful as the outside fortunes of my life have been. Oh, love, love, what a passion it has all bred in my heart for you, my delightful lover, my perfect wife. . . .

By that time the house they wanted to build was more than a dream. They had bought a lot on Library Place adjoining the house in which they lived. Mr. Child, an architect, had drawn plans according to Woodrow's and Ellen's diligently worked out specifications, for an English-type house, the lower part stone, the upper half-timbered stucco. Ellen made a small clay model of it while her children watched, asking innumerable questions, having constantly to be told not to touch it. When it was finished it was placed on a table in the living-room and shown proudly to everyone who came to call. All they needed now was the money to finance it—$9,000. Joseph Wilson, who had, at last, consented to live with them, lent them $2,000, and Woodrow wrote to his classmate, C. C. Cuyler, asking for a loan of $7,000 on which he would, of course, pay interest. When the answer came the serene "other fellow" he had thought himself to be disappeared completely. Mr. Cuyler was

* Characters in *Trilby* by Gerald du Maurier.

glad to oblige—at a much higher rate of interest than Woodrow had expected.

906 McCulloh St., Balto.,
27 January, 1895

My own darling,

I feel as if I were thrusting a knife into you, to enclose this letter of Cuyler's; but of course you must know at once. I have written to Cuyler that my "mistake" as to the rate of interest makes it impossible for me to borrow at all, in all likelihood.... You see how it stands. $7000 at 5½% is $385.... Add taxes and insurance and I see not a cent left with which to make provision for the principal. It would not even be *honest* to count in such a matter on what I *might* make. We must reckon on what I do actually earn as things go now.

Oh, I don't know how I am to stand this.... It is only by force of will that I write this letter to you, blasting all your hopes—(oh, my darling!)—cutting you off from all the plans which have brightened your dear face for so many months past.... May not my love break the force of the blow a little, my poor darling?...

Let Mr. Child go on, of course, dear—he must now; and we shall have the plans complete and payed for, to wait what Providence shall bring. I know that your judgment will confirm mine—that we must simply give our plan for building up altogether for the present.... To play with this ... scheme under which we must borrow at ... 5½%, and trust to the uncertainties of the future, is to play with fire and subject ourselves to an anxiety that would be killing.... Oh, my poor, my sweet, my precious little darling!... Write to me at once, please, as soon as you have had time to think this cruel business over....

He wrote to her again the next day,

906 McCulloh St., Baltimore
28 January, 1895

...Somehow disappointments come almost without pain to me. I've never been sanguine. Things hoped for have never been real enough to me to build upon with confidence. Since I married my only dread has been lest disappointments should touch you to the quick. I know you, how staunch and brave you are. . . . But it has shaken me almost beyond endurance to think what the pain would be that was sure to strike to your heart. . . .

In his great distress he had forgotten how sensible Ellen was. She was shaken only by his emotionalism.

Princeton, N.J., Jan. 28, 1895

Ah, my darling, it seems to me I could literally fly in my eagerness and impatience to be with you *now*—at this moment—to reassure you as to my feelings in this matter of the house and so comfort you; for how plainly it appears in every word of your dear, heart-breakingly sweet letters that all your thought, all your distress is for *me*. I have been such a little goose over the house—so absorbed in plans about it—that no wonder you thought that disappointment in regard to it would cut me to the quick and that I would show neither sense nor self-possession when it came to the decisive point. But I *gladly* agree with you that the only thing to be done is to give it up, and I am as far as possible from having to force myself to say that. Let me whisper a secret,—I am rather relieved to have it over with! I believe it is providential; for ever since it became apparent that it must cost $9,000 instead of $7,000, I have been tormented with misgivings. The misgivings, as you must divine, were wholly regarding the effect of the undertaking upon you. I could not but fear that the debt and the responsibility would burden and harass your spirit, that your precious time might be frittered away in attempts to relieve the strain by extra earnings. I feel my spirits rising by leaps and bounds at the thought that now we are not to incur such risks and if I could only send this letter to you through a pneumatic tube, so as not to suffer from the thought that for twenty-four hours more you will be agonizing over *my* disappointment, I should be perfectly happy. It is too bad about the hundred and fifty to Mr. Child, is it not? But perhaps we may use the plans some day yet. . . . And now, my darling, you must believe that from the bottom of my heart I mean every word I say—that I am *perfectly happy* with you in *any* house,—that no disappointment can hurt for more than a few moments as long as I have *you*. How do I know but that we were making a mistake . . . that might have gone far to prevent your achieving the work for which God meant you,—and *I* should have been responsible! the very thought makes me tremble. . . .

906 *McCulloh St., Balto.,*
29 January, 1895

My own Eileen,

Never, surely, did any man have such a wife, such a lover as I have,—so sweet, so spirited, so brave, so wise. I *knew*, darling, as I said yesterday, how like a perfect woman you would come out of the disappointment: what I feared was its first great pain, the woful upsetting of all cherished plans. You are the wisest, most Christian little woman I ever knew; but you are *so sanguine:*—so sanguine that it frightens me to see how confidently you can hope,—and I have no means of knowing how a sanguine person would be affected at the first shock of being snatched back at the very threshold of realizing everything that had been hoped for. . . . Was ever such a letter written before, I wonder? There's enough love in it to keep a man's heart full for a lifetime. I've been on my knees since beginning this letter to relieve my heart of its great burden of thanksgiving. We are closer together than ever, now, darling, incredible as that may seem. . . .

He referred to the ''cruel business'' once more to make her a promise —and received a gentle reprimand in reply.

906 *McCulloh St., Balto., 2 Feb'y., 1895*

. . . This whole affair is a *love* affair with me, Eileen! I want the house as *your* house,—your framework and possession,—your setting, and I shall work for it unremittingly from this time out. The history itself may be made to pay for it! I know what you will say; but I also know what my love for you demands! . . .

Ellen replied:

Princeton, Feb. 4, 1895

. . . Won't you . . . so to speak, come out finally from under the shadow of this house? You will break my heart if you continue to grieve about

it, and especially if you talk, or think about ''working for it unremittingly''.... If you were only here, you could *see* then, in a moment, ...
that I am not in the least a heroine, but am really and *absolutely* light-
hearted about it. It amuses me to plan and scheme, but my heart is
never so set on carrying out my plans as you suppose....

In reply to a letter from Ellen telling him about one of Bliss Perry's * lectures, Woodrow wrote:

Baltimore, 18 February, 1895

... What you say about Perry's lecture on Hawthorne interests me very
much. Your praise is certainly very high and, knowing you, I know it
must be deserved. I am the more impatient to hear him,—and the more
content that you cannot hear me.... I cannot sufficiently rejoice at anything that brings you diversion: and *this* is the sort of enjoyment to
which you most respond, my ... sweet little born critic! Dear me, how
I fear and stand in awe of you, Eileen! How abashed I am to do my
work under your constant scrutiny,—to keep my mind constantly under
your eye, with its insight. It is beyond measure healthful and stimulating,
but, ah, me, embarrassing too! For you are not simply my critic and
mentor: you are also my wife. I am madly in love with you.... I would
die if I could not win and hold your admiration: the homage of your
mind as well as of your heart! And to think of the critical business! To
think how slender my title is! My defence is that you are a woman and
loyal beyond all words!...

Yet fear of his wife's critical faculties had not prevented Woodrow
from trying again to express his love in verse. Two of the twelve stanzas
read:

Baltimore, 16 February, 1895

> You were the song I waited for.
> I found in you the vision sweet,
> The grace, the strain of noble sounds,
> The form, the mien, the mind, the heart,

* Professor of aesthetic criticism at Princeton. Later editor of *The Atlantic
Monthly*.

That I had lacked and thought to find
Within some spring within my mind,
Like one awaked from dreaming
To the blessed confidence of sight.

. . . .

Shall I not tell what you have wrought
What you have done to make me free?
Shall I not sing my song aloud
That thou has taught me by thy love?
I am thine own, thine instrument;
Thou playest upon me as thou wilt
As one by love transmitting
The lovely beauties of thy soul.

But when Ellen read this poem she was in no mood to criticize.

Princeton, [undated] 1895

... You see, you are a poet after all; you prove it in two ways, first by writing a *poem*, and second by showing yourself such an *idealist* as only a poet could be.... Had you written such things when we were first married I should have been in a fine panic, expecting soon to become a lost illusion; feeling sure that, "however fain, you could not see me always as befell your dreams to see me." But ten happy years have given me a still happier confidence in the immortal *strength* as well as immortal *beauty* of love like yours. It is such love as yours,—as *ours*, for in this matter of loving I am your equal,—that the poet-painter * dreamed of when he painted his "Love and Life"—a love that is lord of life itself. That life may have been but a "poor, pale, miserable, despicable Actual," but when she has yielded to his guiding hand she finds him *strong* to make her what he will—to transform her into an *Ideal.* ...

Woodrow protested:

Baltimore, 19 February, 1895

No, sweet, I am no poet ... and those lines written the other day are no poem. The night I wrote them I thought they were. A hot fire was in my

* George Frederick Watts.

brain: my imagination was thronged with every sweet image of love; and, while I wrote, I thought I was writing poetry.... That I am an idealist, with the heart of a poet, I do not hesitate to avow: but that fact is not reassuring. On the contrary, it is tragical. My heart fairly breaks to utter itself like a poet,—and cannot. It longs for the metrical form: its air is suffused with colour; prose seems intolerable to it. It will *die* of prose yet, I sometimes think—so galling, so intolerable are the fetters,— the mean fetters, so humiliating to an idealist. Ah, how I *hate* prose—that *any*body can write,—because I *must* write it: I cannot write anything else. I suppose I shall continue to be fool enough to hate my own limitations, and shall continue, at long intervals, to attempt poetry as long as I shall live. If I could only write prose that was delicate, imaginative, full at once of grace, force, and distinction, that would be something: my thoughts would at least go clad like aristocrats. But alas! I shall but wear myself out trying. Why should a passion such as I feel for you be born dumb, I wonder, and tormented with the dumb devil all its life: quivering with a poetry that it can never utter. *Why* did you not marry a poet? Certainly you were meant to: you who provoke poetry every moment of your life. *What* poetry a man could write if he were a poet and had you, as I have you, in his heart.... I'm like Svengali! It's all in my head,—at my brain: the exquisite harmonies, the noble images, the unspeakable strains of perfect verse....

Toward the end of his stay in Baltimore, Woodrow Wilson made his first public appearance in the nation's capital. He delivered two lectures, and wrote concerning the second:

Baltimore, 22 February, 1895

... I believe I can say that I made a hit in Washington. I did not hit very many people,—about a hundred and fifty, I reckoned,—but the few who heard me seemed smitten rather hard and it became, during the course of the performance, a pleasure to speak to them. Being questioned by cranks and dull people afterwards, which was part of the programme, was a rather painful and stupid experience. But I played the "queer" ones off successfully enough, and seemed to satisfy the serious dull ones reasonably well.

He had been married for ten years, yet when all but two of his twenty-one lectures were delivered and the day of his homecoming drew near, Woodrow wrote that he had been "not half so much excited on the eve of our marriage." "A young lover," he explained, "knows nothing of the real, deep ecstasy of tried and accepted and hallowed love." * And in his final letter, he wrote,

Baltimore, 27 Feb'y., 1895

... I've been a different man since this week set in that is to take me to you. My friends have noticed the difference, the access of spirits. It comes so much easier to talk, and to talk enthusiastically, imaginatively. ...

I can find no substitute,—no *partial* substitute, even—for you. There are charming women here ... but they are in no degree *like* you. ... I delight to compare you with the most charming women I meet,—the comparison is so much to my advantage. No wonder you are not jealous when I express even an enthusiastic admiration for other women; for you must have some consciousness of your power,—some knowledge of how complete your dominion over me is! Is is not so? Do you not feel infinitely safe in your possession of me? Do you not know how you can keep and turn and govern me at your own sweet will? ...

Ellen was excited too. She could not, she wrote, find any words to tell him how she felt, and again she let a poet speak for her.

Princeton, N.J. [undated]

... So I shall see him in two days
And just two nights, but nights are short,
See how I come, unchanged, unworn!
Feel, where my life broke off from thine,
How fresh the splinters keep and fine
Only a touch and we combine!

Toward the end of 1895 they were able at last to begin to build their house. Royalties from Woodrow's biography, *George Washington*, published that year, $4,000 earned by lecturing, together with his father's loan, made it possible; and Ellen saw to it that everything down to the last doorknob was good material bought at the lowest possible

* Feb. 25, 1895.

price. Almost every letter she wrote to Woodrow during his stay in Baltimore in 1896 was filled with the practical business of turning a dream into reality.

On a memorable day in 1896 the Wilsons moved into their own home. By evening, everything was in place—carpets, furniture, curtains, kitchen utensils, even pictures. Ellen had decided that it was quicker and as economical to hire ten helpers for one day as one helper for ten days. That night a very happy family knelt together while old Joseph prayed for a blessing on the house.

There were seven bedrooms, three for the family, four for visiting relatives. Woodrow's "study" was separated from the rest of the house by a hallway, and Ellen made it plain to all and sundry that, when he closed the door, no one must disturb him and everyone must speak softly. The study was lined with books, and over the bookcases hung five crayon enlargements, by Ellen, of photographs of the men he most admired, Daniel Webster, Gladstone, Bagehot, Edmund Burke and the Reverend Joseph R. Wilson. The largest piece of furniture was a roll-top desk which Woodrow always closed when he stopped working. His children listened for the sound of that closing and the soft whistling that followed, for it meant that he was coming out to play with them. It was the high moment of their day.

But there was, besides money, a price to be paid for the house. Ellen had not been able to prevent Woodrow from "working unremittingly" to enlarge the account in the savings bank and, one day in May, he found that his right hand, which had become increasingly painful, was now almost useless. "Writer's cramp," the doctor called it, and insisted upon a long vacation. There was a neighbor, a rich old lady, who doted on Ellen and admired Woodrow. Would they accept a small gift, Mrs. Brown wanted to know?—a trip to England at her expense? Woodrow said "No thank you"; Ellen said "Yes," but Woodrow must go alone. She would not leave the children and it would cost Mrs. Brown less that way. So it was settled in spite of his protests and periods of gloom when he thought of going so far away from his family. He went to New York for a physical check-up, and wrote that he could not make himself go to the steamship office to engage his passage. Ellen would have none of such weakness.

Princeton [undated] 1896

. . . I am not so foolish, as to try and tell you how hard I find it to have you away when you are unwell,—not to be able to watch you and see for myself, hour by hour, how you are,—and to have you *so far* away! But this is only a temporary weakness; my permanent feeling will be one of deep disappointment if you give it up. For of course, *if you will only go in the proper frame of mind,* it will do you infinitely more good than to bury yourself in the country here. I am counting so much on the sea voyage, and after that on the mental refreshment, the *rest* without ennui, the complete change from all the trains of thought that have been making such exhausting demands upon you for so long. I simply *can't* have you give it up, darling. Let us be very brave about it, and remember, what *I* am too apt to forget, that bravery implies something more than *merely* bearing things in any sort of dismal fashion because we *must.* The best courage shows always an undaunted front, and a calm cheerfulness or a gay smile,—according to temperament,—in the face of the danger or the pain. . . .

In June, Woodrow Wilson left his native land for the first time. He took his bicycle with him, and spent two and a half months pedaling along the highways and by-ways of England and Scotland. Part of the time two new, ship-board friends, Mr. and Mrs. C. A. Woods from Marion, North Carolina, accompanied him. In a letter to Ellen, Woodrow described them as "people whose kindness, simplicity and quiet way of being cultured delight me." Mr. Woods was a lawyer and, although others have claimed this distinction, the first "Wilson for President" man. Woodrow promised, laughingly, that if Mr. Woods' prediction came true he would make him a judge. In 1913 he kept this promise.

Most of his tour was a sort of pious pilgrimage. He visited Adam Smith's tomb, Edmund Burke's grave, George Washington's family home, Coleridge's birthplace, and Bagehot's, and Anne Hathaway's house. He spent weeks in the English Lake Country, carrying a small one-shilling edition of Wordsworth's poetry in his pocket. He sent Ellen a flower plucked from a wall at the poet's cottage at Rydal Mount, but he felt guilty all the time. Letters to Ellen were as necessary to him as food, so he learned to write with his left hand—short notes, almost illegible at first, but soon a reasonable facsimile of his fine script.

The Clarendon Hotel, Edinburgh
Scotland, June 14, 1896

. . . Oh, why was I ever so selfish as to come without you,—how shall I endure to see all these things with your absence all the while at my heart? . . .

The Grand Hotel, Charing Cross,
Glasgow, Scotland, 21 June, 1896

... Today is Sunday (observed by Scots almost with Princetonian rigour)....

I am feeling, and, I believe, looking very well. My arm ... is a most promising patient. But there is danger in thus sitting still, with nothing to do,—the danger of thinking too much about you (as you are thinking too much about me),—the danger of heartsickness.... Yours is the *strain* of this separation, my brave darling (mine the sharp pang at sight of every new thing I know you would delight in seeing).... Ah me! I wish I could think of you less,—or write to you more. It takes me half an hour to one of these pages....

Yet in spite of these pangs, Woodrow's first visit to the British Isles was a stimulating experience. He had always admired the British people, not only because of their solid common sense and reliability, but because his thorough knowledge of their governmental system had convinced him that it was the best in the world, next to that of his own country. Now, riding slowly through the lovely hills and valleys of Scotland and England, staying overnight at village inns, he watched them at work and at play, listened to their quiet, deliberate talk and acquired a lasting affection for them.

He visited Oxford and Cambridge and was so enchanted by their beautiful colleges that years later, when he became president of Princeton, he insisted that every new building should be designed in the same Gothic style of architecture. After his first sight of Oxford he wrote:

Wilberforce Hotel, Oxford, England
9 July, 1896

... We reached here about lunch time to-day and have only the afternoon to look about us, but, dear me, a mere glance at Oxford is enough to take one's heart by storm. It's true we went at once to Magdalen, the most beautiful of the colleges, but we saw within the quads of others too, and it is what nature as well as art has done for the incomparable place that has taken us captive. I have seen as much that made me feel alien as that made me feel at home since I came to England, and have been made on the whole to love America more rather than less ... but Oxford!

Well, I am afraid that, if there were a place for me here, America would see me again only to sell the house and fetch you and the children. . . .

In Princeton, Ellen took charge of his mail, forwarding only such letters as would please him and answering the rest herself. One of these came from the president of Johns Hopkins University concerning another course of lectures.

"I am requested to say," he wrote, "that the trustees would esteem it a favour if you will continue your services here another year at the compensation hitherto offered."

For once Ellen was glad that Woodrow was not at home. He hated to argue about money and was incapable of pointing out his own worth. Ellen with no such inhibitions, especially about the latter, handled the matter skillfully, and told him about it afterwards.

Princeton, June 15, 1896

. . . I was certainly embarrassed as to what I should do with such a letter as that, but finally decided it would be best to write to Dr. Gilman explaining that you were abroad, could write no letters so did not wish them forwarded, and had left me to attend to your affairs. I told him that I did not understand the letter; that yours was a three years course; that I noted that the trustees "would esteem it a favour if you would continue your services for *another* year" at the old rate; that if they meant to imply that at the end of the one year they hoped to offer you compensation more fairly proportioned to the length of the course and your own reputation, I could answer for you that you would gladly accede to their request; for the Hopkins had no more loyal son nor one more willing to make sacrifices to help her in an hour of need. On that understanding I could speak as with authority from you in saying they might consider you engaged for next year; otherwise the matter could of course not be settled without further consultation with you. For it went without the saying that you would not wish to give the first year of such a course without some definite understanding as to the other two; and it was your misfortune—having builded an house—that you simply could not afford to lecture indefinitely at so low a rate. And I reminded him delicately of how much more you could make by giving those weeks to popular lecturing—a fact which your necessities and not your will made a temptation. I put it all very circumspectly and unobjectionally, I think. Hope he will answer soon. . . .

Dr. Gilman's reply was noncommittal, "as was to be expected from him," * Ellen wrote in disgust. She advised Woodrow to accept an offer from the "University Extension" to deliver a course of lectures in Philadelphia. This, she pointed out, would net him $750 for six weeks, in comparison to $400 netted at Johns Hopkins.

After receiving an ecstatic account of the Lake Country, she wrote:

Princeton, July 8, 1896

... That it should all be so lovely, even beyond your expectation, and that you should be evidently enjoying it so enthusiastically,—so deeply, gives me the most perfect and intense satisfaction conceivable. You dear, dear thing! I wish you could stay a year. ...

Maitland Alexander † has refused the call to the church. Dr. D—— is entirely crushed and the rest of the people are knocked all of a heap ... they were wild to get him because he is rich and can support himself! It seems they are not going to offer anyone more than a thousand. In that case, say I, they don't need us to help pay for it. I shouldn't like to commit myself to listening "ez a constantcy" to a thousand dollar man,—at least not until we found a Presbyterian order of begging friars to serve our churches. ...

Woodrow wrote from London:

The Covent Garden Hotel
Southampton Street, London, W.C.
20 July, 1896

My own darling,

Now I feel guilty indeed: I have been long in the National Gallery, and all the while the feeling was strong upon me to sadness that the Rembrandts, Rubenses, Reynoldses, Gainsboroughs, Turners, Titians and the rest *belonged to you,* and that I was a selfish thief to take sight of them without you. The feeling isn't temporary with me; it is all the while in my heart. I do not know that I try to throw it off, tho it saddens me. It is just the uppermost part of the love upon which I live, that supreme love for you which has brought everything that [is] bright and ennobling into my life. ...

* Letter of June 16, 1896.
† Pastor of Long Branch, N.J., Presbyterian Church. Later pastor of First Presbyterian Church, Pittsburgh, Pa.

You know how poor a hand I am at systematic sight-seeing,—how I hate it and how it tires me. But I have gotten a very vivid impression of London, externally, have realized it, and felt its singular charm....

Three weeks before his return Ellen wrote:

Princeton, Aug. 13, 1896

... My thoughts are beginning to be very unruly now, and perhaps it is safe to let them have their way, so short grows the time. Indeed I am sure that the pleasure *far* outweighs the pain; so far indeed that I wonder anyone can be pessimist enough to doubt whether life is a good thing when *anticipation* alone can give such exquisite happiness. And then how often, in spite of what they say, it is far exceeded by the reality.

Ah, my darling what a wealth of delight you shower upon me daily, hourly, a very infinitude of happiness! And how unutterably, overwhelmingly *I love you!* May God bless you and keep you, dear love....

Clydesdale Hotel
Lanark, N.B.
24 Aug., 1896

This is the little note that is to go to-morrow to my sweet, sweet love, as the harbinger of my home-coming....

I rode the whole length of the Yarrow yesterday morning with the poets in my heart and spent the afternoon and night beside St. Mary's lake.... This is only to tell you that my heart has travelled not a step from your side all summer,—has drawn closer, rather,... I know now, too, how much I love our precious children, God bless them....

He came home in good health and with his hand almost well, but now to ward off further trouble, he typed his manuscripts although he preferred a pen.

In October of that year Princeton had its one hundred and fiftieth birthday and was also re-christened. It became Princeton University instead of the College of New Jersey, the original name which had been almost forgotten. The sesquicentennial celebration lasted three days. There was a torchlight procession on Nassau Street in which alumni, undergraduates and the faculty marched exuberantly together. Professor Wilson carried a torch, striding behind the band like a happy boy. He loved parades. On the second day he made the principal address of the occasion. Alexander Hall was jammed to the doors. When Woodrow appeared his classmates of 1879, seated together, stood up and cheered. Ellen sat just below the platform, spellbound with pride. A few days later she described the scene ecstatically in a letter to Mary Hoyt.

Princeton, October 27th, 1896

... It was the most brilliant,—*dazzling*—success from first to last. And *such* an ovation as Woodrow received! I never imagined anything like it. And think of *so* delighting *such* an audience, the most distinguished, everyone says, that was ever assembled in America;—famous men from all parts of Europe.... As for the Princeton men some of them simply fell on his neck and wept for joy. They say that those who could not get at Woodrow were shaking each other's hands and congratulating each other in a perfect frenzy of delight that Princeton had so covered herself with glory before the visitors. And that of course is what makes it such a sweet triumph; it was not a selfish success, it all redounded to the honour of Princeton before the assembled academic world. How I wish you could have heard it; of course you can read it later, but then he delivered it superbly....

The speech was called "Princeton in the Nation's Service," its theme: that education must not only develop the individual intellectually but also train him to serve the state. Ellen's account of her husband's success, although far from impartial, was confirmed by the fact that many people outside of Princeton were also impressed. Newspapers quoted extracts from the speech, national magazines published it in full, there was a lot of complimentary editorial comment, and his articles, as well as his lectures, now under the auspices of the University Extension, were considered newsworthy. Ellen had some advice to give on this development—very wise advice, proving how well she understood her over-sensitive husband:

Princeton, Feb. 25, 1897

... The article on your Cleveland paper I enclose simply to point a moral I want to draw. I intended before this to try and extract from you a promise to take particular pains *not* to read any press comments on that sub-

ject. When papers show such bitterness, as some of them have done, over
your treatment of dead issues, or abstract questions, we can imagine how
rabid they will become over a live subject like Cleveland. Of course
neither of us were unmindful of that when you agreed to write it; it
did not cause you to hesitate,—and I would not have had it do so; because the writing of it was a good and worthy thing to do, and it would
be utterly beneath you to swerve from your course because of such
clamours,—past, present or to come. But it is one thing to *act* in proud
and brave disregard of such things and quite another to *feel* indifferent
when the missiles are actually striking us in the face, one by one. I think
it is only an act of self-preservation to turn one's back to them. They are
not *worth* noticing; —there is nothing to be gained by it. As you know,
I should like to extend this to the press notices of *all* your work and persuade you to read absolutely *none* of them. It is part of the general policy
of "conservation of force" which I would have you adopt. To resist
those little poisoned slings and arrows involves as much wear and tear
of nerve and will as the doing of any other task that doesn't pay and
leaves just so much less life power for the things that do pay— But I
did not mean to harangue you at such length!...

In another letter she had advised him to read "nothing except serious, thoughtful, unprejudiced monthlies and weeklies." *

When he went to Washington to deliver a lecture and wrote that
he wanted to talk to some government officials, but hesitated to seek in-
troductions, she replied:

Princeton, Feb. 8, 1898

... I hope, dear, that you *will* see some of the men you speak of, if for
nothing else than because it will be of service to you in your work to
know such people as the Speaker of the House, and get informal inside
views of "present history." I sympathise with you entirely in the feelings you confess in these matters; it is so exactly my disposition too
that it is difficult for me to press such a point! But I can see that we are
not "wise in our generation." Perhaps it might be better for you if I
were to some mild degree a woman of the world with "social ambitions"(!) ...

* March 1, 1897.

If failure to capitalize on favorable publicity is foolish, then Woodrow was indeed not "wise in his generation." For two years he rarely accepted a speaking engagement, and stayed quietly at home, sticking faithfully to his professorial duties, and work on his new book, *A History of the American People*. But the house on Library Place now had frequent callers from the outside world. Distinguished men from other countries, as well as the United States, asked, when they came to Princeton to lecture, to meet this professor with the liberal and original ideas. There were long evenings in the sitting-room when the conversation covered almost every aspect of the world—its history, its problems, its literature and its future. Margaret, Jessie and Nellie were advised to listen until their bedtime, as long as they did not speak. Curiously enough, since they were very young, they enjoyed it. Although they could seldom understand the meaning of what was said, they were fascinated by the easy flow of words, the lively, intelligent faces, the excitement of an argument. And their father, they thought, was always the central figure in the room, the one to whom everyone listened as they listened to no one else. They were intensely proud of him and believed that there was no problem in the world that he could not solve.

This pride got them into trouble. Ellen, looking very serious, lined them up in front of her one day. "Your father," she said, "has been told that you are boasting about him. Is that true?" Nellie was seven and not sure what boasting meant, but she promptly denied it. Jessie hung her head. Margaret said boldly, "Well, I do—I tell them a few things." Ellen looked at them a moment, with love, before she said, "I understand how you feel, but it embarrasses your father. So after this we'll have a lovely time talking about him when we're alone, but not to other people."

Sometimes, in the evenings, when there were no guests, Woodrow entertained the family with impersonations. He was quite an actor and gifted in the imitation of brogues, dialects and affectations. There was the American vaudeville conception of a "heavy" Englishman, an insufferably superior fellow, deftly managing an imaginary monocle. There was a dour Scot with a fierce burr, an Irishman, fighting mad and laughing as he fought, and the drunken man, who was the children's favorite, perhaps because he was so weirdly unlike the impersonator. With an utterly vacuous expression and incoherent mumblings, he staggered helplessly among the chairs and tables, while the children shouted with laughter and Ellen, rather shocked, murmured, "Oh, Woodrow!" Life was very pleasant in those days—a time to look back to with longing in the years to come. In 1911, harassed by the problems of his first political office, Woodrow remembered that carefree acting with nostalgia. "Let's run away," he said to his youngest daughter, "and go on the vaudeville stage. We'd make a fine father-and-daughter act." And Nellie, a ham actress herself, believed for one thrilling moment that he meant it.

In February, 1898, the *U.S.S. Maine* sank in Havana harbor. If Woodrow commented on this event, his letter is missing, but Ellen had something to say which he may have remembered in 1915 when the *Lusitania* was torpedoed. He was lecturing in Philadelphia when she wrote:

Princeton, Feb. 17th, 1898

... I suppose you hear nothing but the "Maine." Its happening then and there is certainly an extraordinary coincidence, for surely it is nothing more. That it was an accident, due to some unknown chemical cause, seems much easier to believe than anything else,—when one considers the variety and enormous quantity of explosives aboard. Don't you think the people as a whole are behaving well?—showing sense and self-possession? I can't express my contempt for people who talk—as some of the senators have done—*trying* to cause a still worse explosion!—the very ones who *should* set the example of self-control to the nation. ...

In 1899, because she thought he seemed worn out, Ellen again persuaded Woodrow to go abroad, taking Stockton with him. This time he needed no kind Mrs. Brown to finance the journey. They sailed in June, with their bicycles, landed in Glasgow and pedaled the next day to Edinburgh, Woodrow's favorite city in the British Isles. One Sunday he attended the "military" service at St. Giles, the church on the great rock that towers above the city, and sat near a regiment of Gordon Highlanders in full regalia. There was a lump in his throat as he listened to them roaring the hymns his Scottish mother had taught him. He described the scene to Ellen, and added:

The Imperial Hotel, Edinburgh
2 July, 1899

... It moved me so to hear the old hymns sung to the old tunes in such surroundings, that I had no voice to sing with. Assuredly my mother's blood is strong in me, and is strangely stirred in this land which gave her her breeding. ...

Ellen's first letter, written the day after his departure, contained news which she knew he would think important. Although he was later to shock many Princeton alumni by insisting that education, rather than sport, was the primary function of a university, Professor Wilson seldom missed a football or baseball game. He was as melancholy as any undergraduate when Princeton was defeated, as elated over a victory—pounding his cane on the floor of the bleachers and shouting *yay, yay, yay* in rhythmical accompaniment. Ellen, try as she would, was never able to understand what it was all about, and was always both puzzled and amused by his excitement. But she wrote:

Princeton, June 19th, 1899

...But now comes something *really* important, viz. the result of the game. It was eleven to four in *Princeton's* favour!—sis! boom! ah! Our men batted splendidly ... a freshman—I forget the name—made a home run and brought in two other men. If the news-boy's uncle had not died, I could have told you more, or even sent you the printed story. Thus mysteriously are human destinies linked together!...

Woodrow and Stock stayed two weeks in Edinburgh; then, putting their bicycles in the luggage car, travelled by train to England. This time, with no writer's cramp to hinder him, Woodrow kept a sort of diary for Ellen's benefit. Each evening he set down the experiences and impressions of the day and twice a week sent a bulky envelope to Princeton.

Dumfries, 7 July, 1899

Here we are in another part of the "Burns country", still hero-worshipping.... We went to the depths of a narrow court to the Globe Inn, the quaint little Tavern which Burns frequented here, and in a delightful little low-ceilinged room, just such as one's imagination would have promised, with the original wainscoting and fireplace, saw the table about which the poet and his cronies used to gather, and the chair in which he used to sit and hold forth for their delectation. One Axson could at first hardly be induced to sit in the chair, but sat gazing at it with eyes big with deepest reverence,—such delectable things am I seeing! But at last he was persuaded, and sat there for a moment or two, with a face full as a child's of wondering emotion.... We saw the outside of the house Burns lived in ... and we saw his tomb in St. Michaels churchyard.... Here his customary ill luck has followed him and his grave is covered with a Greek mausoleum—this least Greek of our poets!...

Keswick, 12 July, 1899

... This little inn is very humble and unpretentious, but very comfortable indeed. Landlady and servants alike are friendly ... indeed that's the way in every homelike, unfashionable inn we go to. These are surely the most friendly people in the world. The roughest of them knows how to be kind, and the busiest will stop to be courteous. It's always the same story : stiff and ungracious in manner when first approached, but kindly, helpful, interested, communicative, when once your need or question is stated,—even the railway porters and the stage drivers! The only persons we avoid are the *too* communicative and companionable tipsy men, who slap us demonstratively on the knee and tell us incoherent details about their own affairs, with an air of camaraderie about them that it were more wholesome not to smell. ...

"White Lion," Ambleside
13 July, 1899

... I wish I knew how to think of you, and how to end my letters without cutting myself to the quick. It brings tears into my eyes to come too near you in my thought and try to turn my yearnings into words. Dove cottage * was almost too much for me to-day. It is such a little *home,* has so much of the old home furniture in it, was actually so sweet a covert of love in all its deepest and most sacred kinds, so works upon the imagination of every man who knows what it stands for that it quite overcame me,—overcame me with thoughts of you,—very sacred thoughts that hurt, but did me good, being holy and elevating. ...

Durham, The Three Tuns
16 July, 1899

... It's good to be in a cathedral town on Sunday, if you like your worship richly done. ... And this morning we had a little extra picturesqueness thrown in, not on the usual programme. Her Majesty's judges (two of them) are holding assizes here (this is the criminal court for the trial of the more heinous offences called) and they attended service in wig and gown, coming in and going out again with the procession of the clergy and the choir ... and accompanied by an officer of the royal navy

* Wordsworth's house,

in full regimentals. What is more, they came to the Cathedral and left it in a state coach, attended by tip-staves and constables and footmen in stunning costume. They were preceded as they went by the tuneful blare of trumpets. . . . Truly, I never before saw such going to church ! . . .

This is Stock's first cathedral and he is enjoying its impressive beauty after his own chastened style. . . .

You don't know, my sweet one (or *do* you know ?) how you profit by the assessment my heart makes of you these long days. I have so much time to think ;—every avenue of thought leads to you ;—every scene seems to remind me of how much sweeter you are, and more interesting than any other thing or person I know or see *into*. Other men marry ''such things'' :—I, no better than they, was permitted to marry you, and crown my life with the sweetest love, the most satisfying communion the world affords,—and so the song goes on ! It has this unselfish characteristic : it is not in a single thought *egotistical*. I did not *win* this lady,—she was *given* to me, a wonderful gratuity. I can think of her in all her real beauty of mind and person and never for a moment incur the self-suspicion of admiring myself. It is the purest pleasure I shall ever know,— and probably the only blameless self-indulgence !

17 July, 1899, Monday

Here we are, still in Durham this evening, my love. We had intended to go to York to-night . . . but since Assizes were being held we wished to have a glimpse of them ;—one glimpse was not enough : we became absorbed in a murder trial, held before Judge Grantham, one of the most honourably noted of the English Assize justices,—and we stayed to see it go through all its processes to an acquittal. Stock was as deeply interested as I was. We were both struck by the dignity and yet efficient speediness of the trial; by the power of the judge to be a veritable trier of the case,—his privilege to tell the jury frankly what he thought the just inferences from the several items of evidence, direct and circumstantial,—and what he thought *they* ought to conclude from it all. Of course the judges came to court with the same impressive show of state as that which accompanied them yesterday to church—the Lord High Sheriff coming with them in full and splendid uniform; trumpeters and stave bearers going before them; their carriage like a thing taken out of an old picture, swung on its long springs; and the judges looked stern and formidable indeed as they walked solemnly in to their seats, sober and impassive under their wigs and gowns. But all the acid went out of Lord Grantham's face when he began his summing up to the jury. He is reputed the severest criminal judge in the kingdom; but to-day he believed the accused innocent, and his face grew infinitely sweet as he spoke. It was an intellectual treat to hear him put the case—with shrewd insight, briefly, incisively, always finding the word he wanted, always wanting the right word; firm, transparently fair, courteous with the perfect courtesy that is inbred and instinctive. We were charmed—I think we were a little awed. . . .

Princeton, July 20, 1899

Ah, my darling, I love you *infinitely,* and it is indescribably sweet to be so loved in return,—even though I *know* that I do not deserve it,—know how out of measure your thoughts of me are. Surely, surely, you are in a land of magic and the glamour of it all has covered even me in far-away Princeton. But I am perfectly sure that whether or no I deserve such love I am the happiest woman in the world in possessing it. It seems a very miracle that such a man as *you* should so love *me.* How, I ask myself a hundred times, can he help seeing and feeling all that he is and all that I am *not:* how can he help being simply bored with me? This is a great mystery. . . .

On a day when his brother-in-law had gone off on some sight-seeing project of his own, Woodrow wrote:

4 August, 1899, The Covent
Garden Hotel, Southampton St.,
London, W.C.

. . . It is when I am alone that I most keenly realize the part, the supreme part, that love plays and must ever play in my life,—my capacity for loving, my need for being loved,—the almost feminine sensibility I have with regard to the feeling others may have for me,—an insatiable desire to be loved,—an infinite passion of love in me, longing to be spent: and spending itself, with what unspeakable delight upon you, my incomparable sweetheart! It is a source of keenest suffering to me, when I am with you and when I am away from you, that I cannot find *words* for the deepest and most beautiful thing in me. What's the use of cultivating style and seeking literary power if your *life* be inexpressible?...

He went back to Oxford and one evening met a Miss Weld, Tennyson's niece.

> *The King's Arms, Oxford*
> *6 August, 1899*

... She was a great deal with Tennyson and he "spoiled her greatly," she says. Like everybody who knows, she represents him as most open, approachable, affectionate, lovable at home; and says that his apparent boorishness upon occasion, in the presence of strangers, was due wholly to shyness. He did not like to be approached with flattery or praise of what he had written. He liked everyone, rather, to give him what was *in them,*—particularly good accounts of new scientific knowledge or achievement, or some authentic experience. ... I am to take tea with Miss Weld this afternoon. ...

> (Later, as the papers say)

I have been to the tea, met several well-known persons whose names I did not catch or have forgotten, and one person of celebrity, Prof. Sayce, the distinguished Oriental scholar, who called (it *was* he, wasn't it?) who called Herodotus a liar. He is one of the Oxford monks,—a Fellow under the old arrangement that preceded the legislation of 1872, —the old plan under which a man had to take orders to get a fellowship, and remain unmarried to keep it, but could keep it all his life if he remained a celebate. Prof. Sayce keeps his fellowship, and faith, he looks it,—tall, thin, high-vested, a narrow face, like some crane-like bird, thrust forward beyond the line of his slender, bending body. And his timid manner and rapid, thin utterance, suit with his appearance. ... He is perfect with his shovel hat on. ...

Woodrow had booked his passage home from Belfast, for he wanted to have at least a glimpse of Ireland.

Drogheda, Co. Louth, 20 Aug., 1899
"The White Horse"

... I am not sure whether I am pleased with my Irish venture or not. Certainly the Dublin part of it proved a great fiasco. In the first place, the steamer from Plymouth was late, crowded and most uncomfortable.... Its accommodations were like those of an ill-kept sleeping car. The crowds on board were going to the Dublin Horse Show, "the greatest horse show in the world," I am told.... By the same token Dublin was packed; hotel rooms not to be had,—had been engaged, all of them, weeks ago ... and the only thing I could do was to take the first stage of my journey northward at once, and by rail, asking chance acquaintances where I should go, and therefore I am in Drogheda. I don't clearly know yet exactly where Drogheda is!... I know only that it is some thirty or forty miles north of Dublin and somehow on the way to Belfast.

I did not come out of Dublin without looking at it. After I had had my breakfast, I rode about the city on my wheel and saw a great deal of it,—the Castle, the old Parliament houses, and all that I could think of as worth seeing, but most particularly, of course, Trinity College.... I wandered through its quads for quite half an hour with my thoughts full of Burke.... The magnitude of the college struck me, quad within quad, and round about two sides spacious gardens. I should say the circumference of the whole was nearly a mile,—and that in the very heart of the city. At the front of the buildings ... stand striking statues of Burke and Goldsmith; and in the open space which the college faces ... there is an uncommonly fine statue of Grattan *....

This is the last letter before I come myself.... Ah, how my heart leaps at the thoughts that crowd upon that fact! The joy of the expectation of coming to you, my *darling*, is almost too acute to give leave to.... My delight in you is so complete, my loneliness without you so irremediable, all satisfying companionship so impossible! I literally never know what it is to have either heart or mind satisfied, or even at rest, away from you. The explanation is plain, to me.... My love for you released my real personality, and I can never express it perfectly either in act or word away from you or your immediate inspiration. And so, without you, I feel *pent*, unnatural, cheated of full life.... Love unlocks everything within me that is a pleasure to me to use. I never used my

* Irish statesman and orator.

mind, even, with satisfaction till I had you,—and it seems to me I never used my heart at all. My reserve was a veritable jailer before that,—and it can play, does play, the jailer yet when I am long away from you. I seem shut away from the sun and morbid. And so I feel now like a man about to be freed!...

Ellen was equally happy over his homecoming, but first she must tell him about the literary progress of their daughters. Nellie's was a little disappointing.

Princeton, Aug. 14, 1899

... The children spend their time embroidering, playing games and reading Scott's novels. Jessie has read twenty and Margaret sixteen. Nellie found all of them, after "Ivanhoe" and the "Talisman" too hard for her and has betaken herself to "Lorna Doone." I am impressed every day with the *value* of these novels as educational works, with the innumerable pictures of English life and impressions of English history with which they furnish the children's minds. In our reading together it seems to me very few things ever come up that they don't already know *something* about from reading some novel of Scott's.

Our literary researches go on famously; we have gone all the way from Caedman to Burns now....

It seems almost too good to be true, my darling, that the time grows so short.... My heart leaps up almost to suffocation at the thought.... Ah, dearest, can you imagine how I love you,—how constantly my thoughts are occupied with you?...

In 1900 Woodrow decided that Ellen, too, must have a complete change. Her unselfishness was being carried too far for his, or her, good. The house, as usual, was crowded with people. Stockton Axson had moved into his brother's room when Eddie, now a Princeton undergraduate, moved out to live in a dormitory. Woodrow's sister Annie and little Annie had been practically permanent guests since Dr. Howe's death. There was also a governess, Fräulein Clara Böhm, who had been engaged to teach the children French and German. And last, but by no means least, there was old Joseph Wilson, regarded by his grandchildren with fearful respect. Ellen's insistence that Margaret, Jessie and Nellie needed her fell flat before this army of guardians, and in February she agreed to visit the Smiths in New Orleans.

Miss Lucy and Miss Mary Smith, strict Southern Presbyterians, charming personalities, loyal and devoted friends to everyone they liked, loved by everyone who ever met them, lived in a rambling frame house on Henry Clay Avenue. Ellen and Woodrow had met them in 1897 while the Wilson family was spending the summer vacation in Virginia. A warm friendship began then which lasted all their lives. And, because Lucy and Mary were descendants of John Randolph of Roanoke and one of Ellen's ancestors was Nathaniel Fitz-Randolph, a northern relation of that famous clan, they called each other "cousin" from then on.

Ellen was fascinated by New Orleans and enjoyed herself at first, after she had recovered from the wrench of leaving her family and had convinced herself that her children could get along well enough without her. They did. It was their "Uncle Stock" who spoiled her visit. Stockton had a sudden attack of appendicitis and an emergency operation in his room at Library Place. Woodrow told Ellen about it, after the operation was successfully over, in a letter beginning, "I have good news for you." But Ellen was horrified.

New Orleans
Feb. 12th, 1900

... Oh, my darling, my darling, to think what you have all been through, and I here utterly unconscious! It is easy to understand why you and Stockton,—being what you are, were glad that I was not there on Thursday; that I was spared that awful suspense. But why should you be glad now? Surely I *ought* to be there now and you will let me come,—will you not? I won't distress you, since you put your desire so strongly, by coming at once without your consent,—but it is almost more than I can bear to think of Sister Annie and you having all that care and I here.... *Please* telegraph me to come....

Lucy and I decided that we would go over to the Palmers in spite of the rain. I took your letter and read it;—they were all *lovely*, and Dr. Palmer * was so sweet and tender that I shall never forget it. He made the most beautiful prayer too for Stockton and all of us.... I am feeling much more like myself.... And oh how I *love* you all, my precious ones! Won't you let me come back to them?

Princeton, 15 February, 1900

... Of course you do not want me to say, Come *now*, when the seventh day is over and the storm and stress all past. The nurse needs little or

* Pastor of a Presbyterian church in New Orleans.

no assistance. We are carrying no burden, even of anxiety. It would be absurd to cut your trip short now, when you have every reason for going on to have a good time, with a light heart about the dear boy.... *Please,* darling, accept the infinite blessing God in his mercy has brought us and be *glad,* not anxious....

How sweet the scene is to my imagination at Dr. Palmer's, as you paint it,—when you went to him for comfort,—and how I rejoice and praise God that you had such a comforter to go to! Bless them all! How I love them for loving my darling. You don't know what private glee there has been in this your own household that you were out of it. We love you for your *own* sake, we would have you understand, and when we get you where we can indulge our taste in that line to our heart's contents, we don't mean to surrender our advantage....

Ellen agreed to stay on in New Orleans and, to please Woodrow, tried to enjoy the constant round of entertainment. But her heart was not in it, which may account for a letter in which she broke a life-long rule—never to ridicule anyone:

New Orleans
February 20, 1900

... I met yesterday, at luncheon, a lady whom I supposed from her conversation was married to *all* the trustees of Tulane University! She insisted strenuously and at length upon your coming as President and assured me upon her personal responsibility that it should not interfere in the least with your literary career. She said Tulane had a wonderful future, and Louisiana was a glorious field for an historian; that she herself was a whole historical association and could put inexhaustible material into your hands. It seems she is Miss Kate Winter who was at the head of the Louisiana historical exhibit at the world's fair; ever since *which* she has not known the difference between herself and Louisiana....

Woodrow Wilson needed the understanding, affection and support of friends more than most men, and gave as much, if not more, in return. To him love and loyalty were interdependent and nothing saddened him more than a friend's defection. By the same token he was deeply grateful for any proof of sympathy.

In Philadelphia, after delivering a lecture, Woodrow wrote:

Hotel Lafayette, Philadelphia,
22 Feb., 1900

... Everything goes perfectly well at home. You have no idea what help-ful friendliness has cheered us all through Stock's illness and from all sides. Of course the Hibbens * have been chief among all. They were on hand all the time, before and during the operation and were of infinite use and comfort. And after all the *work* was done, they came twice daily to see how we fared. They have won our loyal love and admiration all over again as of the true stuff from the heart out.... But others have been scarcely less kind and faithful—the Magies,† Harry Fine,‡ the Daniels,§ Mrs. Cleveland ¶—even Dr. Patton. I saw people come up the walk those first few days of greatest anxiety whom I had never before seen on the premises. It's good to know how kind and attentive people can be....

Lucy Smith was trying to decide whether or not to marry a man whose environment did not appeal to her and Ellen, believing that Lucy loved him, was shocked.

New Orleans,
Feb. 25, 1900

... Today is *perfect;* with every breath I draw of this delicious air I think, ''ah, if *he* were only here to breathe it with me, how indescribably happy I should be!'' Oh, my darling, *you* are the breath of life to me; it seems to me that I *literally* could not live without you.... Just imagine for a moment trying to construct a life out of such elements as have filled my days since I came here, with love left out,—or even with most sorts of love left in! There is only *one* sort however that is soul-satisfy-ing,—and that, thank God, is mine in full measure, pressed down and running over.... I am, beyond a doubt, the happiest and most fortunate of women....

Knowing what we do of the worth of love, isn't it strange that any-

* Professor and Mrs. John Grier Hibben. Hibben was Woodrow's closest friend in Princeton.
† Professor William Magie.
‡ Professor Henry Fine.
§ Professor and Mrs. Winthrop Daniels.
¶ Mrs. Grover Cleveland.

one could ever weigh it in the balance with anything else whatever except duty? It seems inconceivable to me that a woman could care enough
for a man to even dream of *marrying* him and yet stop to consider where
he lived, for instance, whether in the city or the country, and what sort
of "society" the neighborhood afforded. Certainly I took no such thought
for the morrow. But indeed I never even seriously considered whether
or not you could "make me happy." I *loved* you and was more than willing to let happiness, like everything else, take care of itself. . . .

Miss Kate Winter had apparently not exaggerated her influence with
Tulane's Board of Trustees, for Woodrow received an invitation to make
the Commencement Address there in June. He had to refuse, however,
because, as he wrote Ellen,

Princeton, 25 Feb'y, 1900

. . . I shall by that time be in the toils of my agreement to supply *Harpers Magazine* with not less than ten thousand words per month *. . . .
The portion of my work that lies immediately ahead is in a sense the most
difficult of all. The story of the Revolution, so far as it is a history of
opinion and of political action, needs retelling, recolouring, reassessing
from end to end. As at present it is false and partial, not deliberately
false, but essentially sophisticated and misconceived. Of course *I* can
reconstruct it and make it true! Ah, there's the *deep* work! Not to write
a decent style and keep the narrative clear and coherent, but both to see
the truth and to tell it,—to be artist enough to get the picture drawn,
—to believe in myself steadily enough to apply the strokes with certainty and confidence,—to be sure what to say and what not to say! See
an essay entitled *The Truth of the Matter,*† and add to the difficulties
of which it discourses what you know of the failings and weaknesses of
the particular author whose case is now under consideration, and you
will know the anxieties of the present situation, and the chances that
Harpers Magazine will next year contain a work of genius, in which
American history will be for the first time adequately narrated. . . . Ah,
how I should like to make you glad by making it, both in truth and exe-

* *Harper's Magazine* had bought the serial rights to Wilson's *A History of the
American People.*
† Essay by W.W. published in 1896 by Houghton, Mifflin & Co. in book entitled
Mere Literature.

cution, a *really* great work. There *ought* to be a genuinely first class narrative in me somewhere.... At any rate thoughts of you will animate me through every page. I shall write for you as I used to talk to you in the days of our first taste of each other,—as I still talk to you, with the conscious and passionate desire to win your admiration and approval. We must be partners in this, as in everything,—else I shall grow cold to the marrow and write without blood or life....

Years later, in a public speech, Woodrow Wilson said, "I wrote the history of the United States in order to learn it.... I lived in the United States and my interest in learning their history was, not to remember what happened, but to find out which way we were going."

The *History* was inscribed: "To E.A.W. In loving acknowledgment of gentle benefits which can neither be measured nor repaid."

On her way home Ellen stopped for brief visits in Georgia and North Carolina. Woodrow wrote to her at Savannah.

Princeton, 4 March, 1900

...What a singular impression I have of a *spell* being broken! You were *so* far away in New Orleans.... You seemed lost to me for the time being, because absorbed by the life of a city I had never seen, whose aspect I could not imagine,—appropriated by people I did not know, ... constantly engrossed and wrapt away, in the midst of scenes where not even my mind could follow you, in a bewildered quest.... Rub my eyes as I might, I could not *see* you,—it was almost as if you were lost! In Savannah it is different. There and in Rome and in Asheville I can *realize* you. I have seen and loved you in all those places....

Ellen wrote on her way to Asheville:

Hotel Imperial, Knoxville,
Tenn., Friday 10 P.M.
March 16, 1900

...I reached here at nine, found supper over and nothing to eat in the house; was told that I could get something at a café in the neighborhood, but took fright at the very idea and resigned myself to a fast. See how inconvenient it is to be a woman! I wonder if those who are more accustomed to the role of unprotected female would have gone to that café! However the porter came to offer me a cup of tea from the said café, so at the cost of 20 cts. for the food and something more for the porter I have had quite a dainty supper and feel almost as if I were in an English Inn. . . .

My darling, you feel very, very near to me here where all the other voices are still and my heart can commune with you alone. I am very busy with memories of that other night I spent in this house, sixteen years ago last September just after I had given you my "promise true." How happy I was that night,—and how much more happy now! . . .

President Patton had asked Woodrow to find someone for the Chair of Politics, recently vacated. He wrote to various knowledgeable people, including Theodore Roosevelt, for suggestions, and later wrote to Ellen:

Princeton, 15 March, 1900

. . . I am getting some interesting letters (actually containing practicable suggestions, some of them) in answer to my requests. I enclose a note from Mr. Roosevelt, because I think it will interest you as showing a side,—a very sane, *academic* side of him,—not known by everybody so much as to exist, but constituting his hope of real and lasting eminence. . . .

Ever since 1896, when President Patton had approved a plan for a residential graduate college at Princeton and then done nothing to put it into effect, the younger and more progressive members of the Princeton faculty had become increasingly dissatisfied with his administration. Very little was being done to make Princeton a university in the real meaning of the term, and it was, therefore, very difficult to attract men above the average to the faculty. Woodrow had been offered the presidency of several universities since the Illinois invitation, and had more than once, because of his own feeling of frustration, been on the point of accepting. By 1901, the spirit of unrest came close to revolt. A movement was started by Professor William Magie to investigate Princeton's scholastic standards and to recommend reform. After long-drawn-out debate at faculty meetings, the Board of Trustees decided to take a hand in the matter. They proposed, in March 1902, that an executive committee, composed of two trustees and three members of the faculty, be appointed to control the university. But in June, while this was still being considered, Dr. Patton resigned and suggested Woodrow Wilson as his successor. They had differed on many subjects, but Dr. Patton ad-

mired the man who had done much to augment Princeton's reputation.
The vote in the Board of Trustees on the first ballot was unanimous for
Wilson in spite of the fact that this broke a tradition, as old as the university itself—that its presidents should be ordained ministers. Woodrow and Ellen were not taken entirely by surprise. There had been rumors floating around. A week before Dr. Patton resigned Woodrow had
written to Ellen:

Princeton, 1 June, 1902

My own darling,

Harry * had nothing new to tell me,—I don't know what Pyne † can
have been alluding to,—but after the luncheon at the Inn to-day
(Bayard Henry ‡ had a numerous club of Philadelphia lawyers up here,
and I lunched with them) C. C.,§ who was also there, gave me this
intimation: "It looks now, Tommy, as if you were going to have a great
deal of responsibility." That was all,—in the midst of a crowd no explanation could be entered into,—but it was said in a very significant
way and carries an obvious implication.

When I came home after the lunch I found the new number of the
Alumni Weekly on my desk. You may imagine how startled I was to
find on the cover, in bold type, "Woodrow Wilson, '79, for President."
My first thought was that some fool was taking a hand in college politics
from the outside! But it turned out entirely harmless. Somebody has
written to the Indianapolis News to suggest that the Democrats nominate
me for the presidency of the United States,—that's all!...

* Professor Fine.
† Moses Taylor Pyne, trustee.
‡ Trustee.
§ C. C. Cuyler, W.'s classmate at Princeton, also a trustee.

Part 2
The Administrator

There was rejoicing in Princeton on the ninth of June, and a happy family in the house on Library Place. Dr. Patton and three members of the Board came to notify the new president. Before he left with them to receive the congratulations of the trustees and make a speech to cheering students and alumni on the steps of Nassau Hall, Woodrow went, with Ellen, to tell his father. Old Joseph was sick in bed, but he rose, paced his room in great excitement and, when Woodrow left, shouted for his equally excited granddaughters. "Never forget what I tell you," he said. "Your father is the greatest man I have ever known." Margaret said, "Oh, we know that, Grandfather." He frowned. "You're too young to know," he told her, "*I* know what I'm talking about. This is only the beginning of a great career."

Woodrow had an exhilarating sense of release. For seventeen years he had tried to convince himself that he was entirely satisfied to be an author and a teacher. He had never succeeded. Writing, he had told his family, was "just a talking profession." Here at last was the opportunity to act, to build, to lead. Ellen's eyes were bright with pride, although there was a shadow of dread in her heart. She did not, of course, know that her sensitive husband would be involved in battles that almost wrecked his health. She knew only that this was the end of their simple, ideal life, the privacy they valued. And to leave the house they had built with such joy and move into "that great, stately troublesome 'Prospect'"* would be a terrible wrench.

"Prospect," the president's house on the campus, is built of yellow stone. There are more than twenty rooms, most of them large and high-ceilinged. The entrance hall is paved with marble under a large rotunda. There was gloomy stained glass at the top of an impressive stairway. It was not Ellen's idea of a home, yet, characteristically, she began at once to plan ways to make it so.

By dint of persuasion and gentle insistence she succeeded in getting the college authorities to consent to thorough redecoration, and to allocate funds to pay for it. Then, after a brief vacation with her old friends, the Tedcastles, living now in Massachusetts, she went to work with

* Letter to Florence Hoyt, June 28, 1902.

speed and efficiency. Woodrow was consulted on every detail, but Ellen would not let him do anything, except once in a while look up a bargain in furniture when he was in New York. He must devote himself entirely, she said, to having a real rest and to writing his inaugural speech.

He wrote while she was in Massachusetts:

Princeton, 18 July, 1902

... The address advanced by a little more than its daily stint.... My old hack mind is a most reliable beast, and can apparently be counted on to do its task whenever bidden! I am in the thick of its thesis now.

I find that the trouble with me when you are away is that I *think* too much,—even after I go to bed. There are none of those delightful periods in my day when I can go to you as a tired boy would go to his mother to be loved and petted. The close, unargued sympathy of those dear intervals is unspeakably soothing and refreshing to me....

Princeton, 19 July, 1902

... This morning I got, I believe, to the mid-point in my address. The task grows harder as the argument thickens, but with the modest stint [650 words a day] to which I confine myself I get through, copying and all, by half past eleven or twelve, and have time enough before lunch to grind off the business letters of the day,—so that I feel quite like a gentleman of leisure, and realize that it is vacation.

Fortunately I never worked out the argument on liberal studies, which is the theme of my inaugural, never before having treated myself as a professional "educator" and so the matter is not stale but fresh and interesting. I am quite straightening out my ideas!—and that amuses me. I feel like a new prime minister getting ready to address his constituents. I trust I shall seem less like a philosophical dreamer than Mr. Balfour does....

Princeton, 20 July, 1902

My own darling,

A passage in a letter which I received yesterday will interest you: "I remember you distinctly as an infant of a few months old, very plump and fat and remarkably quiet," Dr. Woodrow * said to me once: "that

* Dr. James Woodrow.

baby is dignified enough to be Moderator of the General Assembly.'' What do you think of that as an example of a remarkably early case of ''feeling one's oats?''...

...I often marvel at the circumstances of my life, there has been so much sweetness and unmarred good fortune in it, so much love and deep content, so much quiet delight. I thank God from the bottom of my heart! I have been so trusted and loved and honoured. It is marvellous. What deep ingratitude it would be should I repine or fret at anything. And you, my darling, are the centre of it all,—all the greatest delights, all the deepest content, centre in you....

Ellen had consented to take her vacation on condition that he, too, would take one after she returned. He tried now to persuade her to let him stay at home because he ''hated going away more than ever, now that everybody is so durn polite to me as a great personage!'' * But she packed him off, to the Tedcastles, a few days after she came home.

Clifton, Mass., 6 Aug., 1902

...I think a good deal about college affairs these quiet hours.... The right to *plan* is so novel, the element of vexation, the sense of helplessness we had for so long is so entirely removed, that it is a pleasure to think out the work that is to be done. If it did not have the incalculable money element in it, there would be no touch of worry about any of it. There is something, too, in doing the thinking where there are no Princeton people!... How fine it is that nobody here knows or cares about universities and their presidents!...

The ''money element'' always bored and embarrassed Woodrow Wilson, even where his private affairs were concerned. But asking for donations for Princeton was an essential part of his job as president and could not be shirked. He took the first plunge manfully.

Clifton, Mass., 9 Aug., '02

My precious darling,

I am going into town to-day, to make inquiries about a Princeton millionaire who lives in these parts, upon whom I wish to call, if he is accessible, and invite him to my inauguration. He is an old gentleman of

* Letter of July 24, 1902.

the class of '48, without heirs, and ought to be thinking of his duty to his alma mater. This is to be just a preliminary skirmish, to get acquainted. I hope he is not off somewhere where I cannot get at him. . . .

. . . All that I am, all that has come to me in my life, I owe to you. . . . If there is anything that commends me to the admiration of other men it is a certain poise and elevation of spirit,—that I know from what they say to me—and that I get from my deep content and happiness with you. It is not natural to me. Deep perturbations are natural to me, deep disturbances of spirit. I could not make the impression I do, I could not be what I am, if I did not take such serene happiness from my union with you. You are my spring of content; and so long as I have you, and you too are happy, nothing but good and power can come to me. Ah, my incomparable little wife, may God bless and keep you!

Clifton, Mass., 10 Aug., 1902

I spent an idle, pleasant day in Boston yesterday. Mr. Wyman I did not find (the alumnus of '48) and, after making a few small purchases . . . I went to Keith's theatre and sat for almost three hours and a half enjoying music, song, dances, horse-play and gymnastics. It was all of the most respectable kind, and a look around at the audience made me feel quite at home. . . . They were the most solid, genteel, cultivated looking set I ever saw in such a place: old gentlemen who looked like clergymen, bank presidents, railway directors; old dowagers who looked like patrons of society. . . . Nothing like being far away from home to get a chance to indulge my old bohemian instincts! . . .

I find, now that I get a certain remove, that my election to the presidency has done a very helpful thing for me. It has settled the future for me and given me a sense of *position* and of definite, tangible tasks which takes the flutter of restlessness from my spirits. . . .

Ellen was as absorbed in the refurnishing and redecorating of Prospect as she had been when she carried out her plans for the house on Library Place, although not with as much delight in the work. All of her letters were filled with what she had accomplished and how much she had spent or must still spend. The widow of one of Princeton's former Trustees, who considered herself, for some reason, a sort of custodian of the president's house, insisted upon being consulted. Ellen dealt with her firmly. One day in the drawing-room, the lady announced, ''We shall

take the rug for the key-note and build up the furnishings from that."
The rug was hideous. Ellen said sweetly, "I shan't use the rug at all.
And I shall take out the mantelpiece." Mrs. B. couldn't believe her ears.
"But Mrs. Wilson, *I* chose that mantel myself the last time the house
was done over." "Did you?" Ellen sighed, "I never knew who chose it."
After several frustrating days the widow capitulated. The rug, the man-
tel and other atrocities were removed. Even the stained-glass window was
replaced—by Tiffany. In her gentle way, Ellen was a general.

Princeton, Aug. 25, 1902

... I am not going to be so full of business now for a time because everything is under weigh. Plumbing, heating, lighting, painting, papering,
carpets, shades, bedding, hangings, upholstering, refinishing are all
settled in *detail* and contracted for and everything begun and I can
rather rest on my oars.... If you could see me you would certainly not be
anxious about me, for I never felt better in my life, or less tired as a
rule....

From Clifton, Woodrow went to North East Harbor in Maine to
visit friends and from there to Gorham, New Hampshire, to join the Hibbens at a summer resort hotel. He spent the days walking through the
lovely hills and the evenings in good talk, but he was homesick.

Gorham, N. Hampshire
25 Aug., 1902

My precious darling,

It is Monday morning! *Next* Monday morning, if you will let me, I shall
start for home.... How it makes my blood leap to think of it,—I shall
dream of it all the week through.... The summer days of idleness are,
with me, always days of self examination and self-distrust,—days of
weakness when I do not feel equal to the tasks set for me the rest of the
year,—and all that is intensified when I am alone, and too much with
myself. What a source of steadying and of strength it is to me in such
seasons of too intimate self-questioning to have one fixed point of confidence and certainty,—the even, unbroken, excellent perfection of my
little wife, with her poise, her easy capacity in action, her unfailing
courage, her quick efficient thought,—and the charm that goes with it
all, the sweetness, the feminine grace,—none of the usual *penalties* of

efficiency,—no hardness, no incisive sharpness, no air of command or of unyielding opinion. Most women who are efficient are such terrors. . . .

In September the Wilson family moved into a rejuvenated Prospect. Ellen had brought light and color and comfort into the old house. Woodrow's study, facing the front lawn with its beautiful old trees, was, like his study on Library Place, lined with books. And his intellectual and spiritual mentors, Webster, Bagehot, Joseph Wilson and the rest still kept him company. The old roll-top desk was there, too, in the best light. A bronze bust of George Washington, presented to Woodrow by his Princeton classmates, Apollo Belvedere, the Marble Faun, the Winged Victory and a rose-colored carpet improved the echoing entrance hall. And, in a quiet corner of the house, a small family sitting-room was furnished with comfortable, well-worn chairs, sofas and tables from Library Place and adorned by Ellen's paintings. Only the outside still looked grim. She changed that too, eventually, with tall shrubs against the walls, hedges, and a garden that became a show place.

On the twenty-fifth of October Woodrow Wilson was inaugurated as the thirteenth president of Princeton. His inaugural speech made headlines in many newspapers.

Ellen and her daughters, feeling very elegant in the first "store bought" dresses they had ever had, were not in the least surprised by the thunder of applause when he finished. They expected it. He was the most wonderful man in the world. Old Joseph was supremely happy. He was very ill, but neither pain nor weakness could keep him away from the ceremony. That night he had a sharp attack of angina pectoris and never again left the big, sunny bedroom facing the garden which Ellen had furnished as he directed. Every evening, in spite of the exacting duties of a new office, his son read aloud to him or sang him to sleep with the old hymns he loved. Three months after the inauguration he died, and for weeks it took all of Ellen's love and wisdom to comfort Woodrow.

For two years there were no more long separations. They were good years. Trustees, faculty, students and most of the alumni were enthusiastic about President Wilson's new and revolutionary plans for Princeton. Woodrow was happy, absorbed in his work, full of energy. Invitations to speak still poured in, but he accepted very few. He was in St. Louis, to deliver an address on "The Expansion and Character of the United States," when Ellen had a change of mind—so unusual an event that it upset him.

George Howe, "Sister Annie's" son, had graduated, with honors, from Princeton, and the classical department suggested that he should be asked to fill a possible vacancy there. Woodrow and Ellen had talked it over. Was it right to appoint a relative? They had finally agreed that it was, since George was well qualified, but after Woodrow had left Princeton Ellen consulted a clever friend, Miss Henrietta Ricketts, and wrote,

Princeton, April 26, 1903

... She was much excited about it and I must say I was greatly impressed by what she said, and feel as if I did not want you to let George come after all. She said she could not bear for people to have any such opportunity to question your motives however unjustly. She said she knew better than we could how people feel about you now,—their enthusiasm, their reverence for your "almost romantic disinterestedness," —even people that were of an opposite character themselves. Of course a reputation like that is a great power for good and should not be risked except at a very obvious call of duty; it is very different from mere popularity. Can't something more be done to find that boy a place elsewhere? ... You see I do not need to confess, dear, that my mind has completely changed on this matter. I even feel thankful for having told Miss Ricketts about it,—as if it might be the means of escaping a pitfall. Of course I *knew* all this before, but I seem to have got a different perspective,—to feel that you were to have been in a sense sacrificed to George. ...

Woodrow replied:

51 Vandeventer Place
St. Louis, Mo.
29 April, 1903

My own darling,

I find myself a good deal upset by your complete change of mind about George's appointment. I had allowed the Latin men to make their arrangements on the assumption that they were to have him. ... No doubt you are right: but we must not be too selfishly careful of my reputation. There is deep selfishness in that. ...

Ellen, however, remained unconvinced and George did not get the appointment.

The president of the World's Fair, then in progress at St. Louis, invited the president of Princeton to be his guest at a "dedicatory exercise.'' Woodrow accepted, without enthusiasm, and escaped almost before the program began. The man who was later unable to escape innumerable exercises, ceremonies, parades and spectacles wrote from the house of the friend with whom he was staying:

51 Vandeventer Place, St. Louis, Mo.,
30 April, 1903

My own darling,

Here I am after all, a prudent man, sitting quietly in the house instead of spending the day, as I was expected to do, at the Fair Grounds. It has blown off piercingly chill, and after trying the reviewing stand (without a seat) for about an hour, I took flight. The program would have been tremendous and alarming enough in any weather. We (the official guests) were expected to ride out to the grounds in carriages; sit behind the President for an hour and a half to see a review of troops (some 12,000) go by; take a cold, standing lunch in a windy tent; hear some two hours' speaking and ''dedicating'' in the Liberal Arts building, and sit out a long formal dinner! I was glad of an excuse (namely anxious thought for my health!) to run from April-turned-November and celebration-run-mad and come back to the empty town and deserted house. I was not made for ''functions'', but for equable work that tells and long, refreshing chats with those whom I love. How I hate show and the crush of spectacles! How I love the quiet enjoyments that strike deep and leave the heart at ease! What a chap to be put to playing public character! . . .

What a luxury it is to love you, my Eileen. . . . Never for a moment lose hold of me, my precious love,—never for a moment lose consciousness of possessing me, of being the medium of my life, by the genius and the power of love. . . .

51 Vandeventer Place
St. Louis, Mo.
1 May, 1903

. . . As I sat here alone last night waiting for dinner to be far enough away from bed-time, I read, in *Littell*, my sweet one, of a delightful woman, the mother of Anatole de France, who had ''the heavenly patience and joyful simplicity which belong to those who have no business in the world but love,''—and it set me musing upon the wonderful little lady who has given her life to me. . . . Some of the sweetest and most attractive women have *only* the power of love and it is no marvel that they make it their business; but *you* have every power and *yet* make love your business. And so love is enhanced, adorned, made transcendent by the service of a mind and nature with wealth and resources for any enterprise. . . .

That year Margaret, Jessie and Nellie were respectively, seventeen, sixteen and thirteen—old enough at last to be safely left without either parent. They spent the summer with the Howes in North Carolina while Ellen and Woodrow went abroad for the first time together. Except for a few days in Paris, devoted almost exclusively to the Louvre and the Luxembourg, they traveled only in England, where Woodrow showed Ellen the places he loved best. She, too, fell in love with the Lake Country. They decided to buy a house there to retire to when they grew old.

In 1904 Woodrow sent Ellen to Italy. She had dreamed of seeing Italy ever since, as a young girl, she had decided to make painting her vocation. It was not only the great museums, the churches, the fabulous scenery that drew her. Robert and Elizabeth Browning had lived there, had written poems she loved about this land. And Garibaldi was, next to her husband, Ellen's hero. But because Woodrow could not leave his work at Princeton to go with her, she went reluctantly with Jessie, Mary Hoyt, and Lucy and Mary Smith. Woodrow, Margaret and Nellie went to New York to see them off, and, afterwards, Woodrow spoke at a teachers' convention. Back in Princeton again, he wrote:

Princeton University
Princeton, N.J.   21 *March, 1904*
President's Room

My Eileen, my own darling,

There's nae luck aboot the house noo ye are awa! And to think that as I sit here and write in this quiet room, at the old desk, my sweet one is out, hundreds of miles, upon the broad seas! Ah, weel, it's ma ain do'in; and I'm no repinin'. I'm but lettin' ma heart gae its ain gait the moment!

The address to the schoolmasters, and mistresses, was a grand affair. Standing on my little platform there in the tenth story of the building of the University of the City of New York, on Washington

Square, I looked straight out on the stream of the river itself, and expected to see the nose of the white steamer thrust itself into sight any moment. And what poetical, impossible counsels of perfection I did give those poor wondering souls who sat puzzled and gaping before me, not knowing what stirred the fancy within me. I showed them an idyl of how American history should be taught and filled them with a glow that could not possibly help them to do anything I can think of, except make love! Oratory is surely an imaginative art, but who shall explore its sources? . . .

. . . Nell and I [went] to the circus. We found Mr. Hibben and Beth *
without any trouble; and the extraordinary show,—*truly* extraordinary and full of wonders,—proved the best tonic I could have taken. It took me quite out of myself and for the time being made children of us all. . . .

Yesterday . . . afternoon, and in the evening again, the dear Hibbens came to keep us from seeing too suddenly the smallness of our tiny circle. (Do three make a circle?) To-day lecturing, letters, and the routine of office hours have brought me to the steady, and steadying, round of familiar duties again,—and so we are off for the voyage, my heart and you. Fortunately *it* need not stay at home! . . .

The travellers spent ten days in southern Italy, then went to Rome. On Sunday they found a Presbyterian church and heard a "splendid" sermon by a Scotsman, a professor of church history at Aberdeen University. Puritan Ellen wrote:

Rome, Italy
April 10, 1904

. . . I enjoyed it exceedingly; it seemed especially good to hear a strong, intellectual address after our ten days of rioting in sensuous beauty; it had a sort of tonic effect.

They stayed at a little "pension" which, Ellen wrote, was shabby but comfortable, and spent every day in the art galleries and churches.

Rome, April 15, 1904

. . . We have had a truly *wonderful* week! Every day has been an epoch in my life! It is impossible to say how I have enjoyed the Michael

* Hibben's daughter.

Angelos and the Raphaels,—what revelations they have been of glorious
beauty and majesty. Of course the photographs give a fairly good idea
of the separate figures in the Sistine Chapel; but I really don't think they
prepare one at all for Raphael's great compositions because the composition has everything to do with it. It is the largeness of the whole conception, the harmony of line and mass, the sense of air and space, the
wonderful grouping of all those glorious, majestic, god-like figures who
are holding high converse together. "Such harmony is in immortal
souls." It is hard to keep away from them and do one's duty to all the
lesser lights. And yet the rest are enchanting. I saw, for instance, this
morning at the Corsini gallery, a Fra Angelico that was perfectly
adorable and some six other masterpieces that I will never forget, mixed
up with an acre or two of trash. I should think people who did not know
what they were looking for would have a dismal time in the private
galleries here. . . .

Revelling in beauty, the artist for once transcended the ever-anxious
wife and mother—until Woodrow's letter, written two weeks after the
day at the circus, reached her. Nellie had the measles. Ellen was still
brooding over this misfortune when another letter arrived.

Princeton, 12 April, 1904

My own darling,

The plot thickens! Margaret has the measles, on schedule time! . . . Isn't
it a rum go? And yet I must say that the amusing side of it appeals to me
strongly. Happily, measles is a disease which we *cannot* take tragically.
And in one way it brings me real relief. I shall of course give up my
southern trip. . . .

Margaret and Nellie enjoyed the measles. Margaret was studying for
her college entrance examinations and, since she was forbidden to use
her eyes, Woodrow came every evening to read the required subjects
aloud, and discuss them with her. After that he played Parchesi,
dominoes, or double solitaire with Nellie.

Ellen tried to take the "rum go" calmly.

Rome, April 17, 1904

. . . I *will* not worry. Surely with a good trained nurse and strong healthy
children there can't be any danger. I am so sorry my darling should

have the extra care and mental burden. Something always happens when I leave home. I'll never do it again. My conscience has hurt me from the first about this journey, and more now than ever....

Woodrow laughed at her conscience, and comforted her with good news.

He had told her in a previous letter about the progress of one of his projects:

Princeton, N.J., April 14, 1904

... To-day our committee on the Course of Study completed its labours, and next week our report, with which we are all really delighted, ... will be laid before the Faculty in a series of meetings. Fine * will take the chair of the Faculty, and I, as chairman of the Committee, will take charge of the measure on the floor in debate. It is all most interesting, a bit exciting, and most encouraging....

Now he wrote:

Princeton, 26 April, 1904

My precious darling,

Nothing but good news this morning. The dear patients are both *perfectly* well.... The other piece of good news,—and it is *very* good,— is that the course of study was last night finally, and unanimously, adopted by the University Faculty. It took only four meetings to put it through all its stages.... Everyone seemed to accept the *principle* of the report and all the main features of the scheme at once and without cavil; and the final adoption was characterized by real cordiality. All of which makes me very happy. It is not, as it stands now, exactly the scheme I at the outset proposed, but it is much better....

Another cable has come this morning to make my heart sing. And your letters, my darling, what perfectly delightful reading they are,—for all of us, but particularly for the one who loves you best.... How sweet it is to know that just the joy has come to you that I planned and expected. I dream all day of that dear look of deep wonder and delight that must be always in your eyes now,—the look I have seen in them in

* Now Dean of the Faculty.

the Louvre and at the English Lakes,—and sometimes when you have looked at me, when my heart leaped within me. . . .

From Rome, Ellen, Jessie and Mary went to Assisi, a place of enchantment, especially for Jessie, who knew and loved the story of Saint Francis and his birds. But the day after they arrived, she was very ill. After three terrifying days, Ellen wrote:

Hotel Leone, Assisi, May 1, 1904

My own darling,

I will begin this letter as you did yours on a certain memorable occasion by telling you that I have some good news for you. Of course it won't strike you so at first, but if you were here you would be quick to agree that we have the profoundest cause for gratitude. Jessie has had diphtheria, but her throat is already perfectly clear and has been since yesterday morning. It was a short, sharp attack. Of course she is not to raise her head from the pillow for a week or more, to guard against heart trouble, and every possible precaution is being taken, but the disease is already conquered. . . .

Ellen handled the crisis with her usual swift efficiency. She wired to the American Embassy in Rome, asked them to recommend the best English-speaking doctor there, then wired Dr. Bull, the man they suggested, to come to Assisi. In the meanwhile a local doctor had given Jessie anti-toxin.

Woodrow wrote in great distress:

Princeton, 12 May, 1904

. . . It has given us a dreadful shock and has filled our hearts with unspeakable things. The shock to you, my darling, must have been awful, and the wait of anxiety intolerable, away from home and me and every familiar aid and comfort,—and my dear, precious Jessie! . . . May God keep you both, my sweet, sweet darling. This must *never* happen again. We must never have the sea between us again. We need each other too much. . . . It seems as if my heart would snap under the strain and tragedy of it. Ah, the anguish of not being on hand to help! . . .

Ellen wrote pathetically:

Hotel Leone, Assisi, May 4, 1904

... That *all* the children should be ill during practically the whole of my absence from home is strange indeed.

I am certainly being bitterly punished for my selfishness in leaving home. Well, I hope I have my lesson by heart at last. . . .

She wanted to go home as soon as Jessie was able to travel, but Jessie insisted, with tears, that she would feel guilty all her life if her mother did not see Florence and its great art galleries. And Ellen, haunted by the memory of Ruth Cleveland's death in Princeton after diphtheria, gave in. Jessie's heart might also fail, if she were unhappy. There was a letter from Woodrow waiting for Ellen when they arrived in Florence.

Princeton, 23 May, 1904

... My heart burns with love ... a love for my darling Jessie more tender, more deep, more full of admiration and joy that we should have so lovely a daughter than I know how to say (she must be wholly compounded of you!) and a love for my Eileen that seems the very breath of my life. Dr. Bull is *right*,—you *did* save your sweet child's life "in acting immediately in the right time and in the right way." You are the most wonderful combination of sweetness and strength, charm and capacity I ever knew of, and I shall not breathe right until I have clasped you in my arms again. . . .

I have only one complaint to make against you,—your repeated explanations of the *expense* you have been put to, and your words of half apology *as if I would care*. Why, darling, the money has come from the *History:* There is plenty, and I send it to you with joy! Don't be a goose! Don't I know that you manage better than I could? Don't you know that the sweetest thing in the world is to be *able* to send you what you want? It is a positive luxury to have some way in which I can help a little,—something to do besides *words* merely to express my devotion to you. . . .

Ellen and Jessie never forgot their visit to Florence. It was as though the ordeal they had been through had raised their love of beauty to an almost unendurable pitch. Ellen wrote:

Villa Trollope, Florence,
Italy, May 25, 1904

... I have been to the three great galleries, the Uffizi, the Pitti and the Bella Arti, but as for really *seeing* any of them yet!—they are simply inexhaustible! I am left gasping—overwhelmed—almost dismayed at the feast spread before me. Everywhere I turn there is some masterpiece that I have longed to see all my life, and I rush from one to another and am so overcome with rapture and excitement that I end by holding my head with both hands in a sort of despair....

She was both shocked and amused by two of the guests of the pension.

Florence, May 29, 1904

... Those poor creatures came here for four days and planned to spend half of one going to see Egyptian *mummies!* Isn't that pitiful!—in a place more full than any other in the world of things eternally *alive* and young and beautiful. One of them took me aback to-night by asking me—at table d'hote—if I ''knew the story of Leda and the *goose!*'' But I managed to hide my embarrassment and simply say that it was supposed to be Jupiter in the shape of a *swan.* But the other at once explained to her friend in a loud voice that it was a ''very improper story and she ought not to ask about it.'' Wasn't it dreadful? ...

Princeton, 27 May, 1904

My own precious darling,

To write the last letter that can reach you before you sail seems like saying good-bye to you for two, no, four long weeks.... But these letters will be coming to you till the last, till you sail.... I want them to make you realize—every moment of your journey—how my thoughts hover about you, night and day, with a tenderness, a pride, a joy, and yet a longing, which I have spent twenty years in the vain attempt to put into words and which, God willing, I shall spend all my life trying to put into acts of love and devotion....

Before they left Florence, Ellen, Jessie and Mary Hoyt made a pilgrimage to the Protestant cemetery, with lilies for Elizabeth Browning's grave. And before they sailed they went to Venice and "did it thoroughly," as Ellen put it,—the Bridge of Sighs, St. Mark's, galleries, gondolas and all—in two days.

Florence, June 5, 1904

...Your dear letter of the 23rd reached me to-day. I wonder if it will be the last! I fear it will, but something sweeter than even your letters is soon to follow. I hardly dare let myself dwell on it much, but try to live in the present. Oh, how I pray that never again we may have the ocean between us! I don't have to pray that *I* may never again be on the wrong side of it without you!—How constantly I shall think of you on the steamer, and of all you are about, and of the baccalaureate, and oh! how I shall groan in spirit that I shall be missing it. May God, in His mercy, bless us all and give us a happy home-coming.

Young Edward Axson had married in 1901 and was living in the South. Not long after Ellen and Jessie returned from Italy, he and his wife and baby were drowned when runaway horses swept their carriage off a bridge into a river. It was the only great tragedy in Ellen's life. Eddie had been like her own child—the son she had never had. For weeks she moved in a daze, seldom speaking, doing her household tasks with desperate concentration, as if her life depended upon keeping her mind closed against memories. Woodrow and the girls, accustomed to go to her for comfort, advice and never-failing cheerfulness, were utterly desolate. Then, one day, perhaps because she remembered her own desolation when her father had given in to grief, she was suddenly herself again. It seemed to her family as if the house itself breathed a long sigh of relief.

Woodrow's plans for Princeton's regeneration were going well. The faculty had been reorganized and strengthened—dead wood swept out to be replaced by men with brains and energy. Students who had come to Princeton only for social background, or athletic fame, had been sent home when they failed to meet the higher scholastic requirements. Money for new buildings was pouring in. And when the fall term began the new course of study went into effect. The president reported to the trustees that it was being "cordially received even by that arch conservative the undergraduate himself." There were, of course, some loud groans. The more frivolous among the alumni complained that Wilson was spoiling the best country club in America, but Woodrow considered that a great compliment, and continued his efforts to spoil it. When several hundred students who had failed to pass their examinations departed, a cartoon in the *Princeton Tiger* depicted Woodrow Wilson sitting alone on the cobweb-draped steps of Nassau Hall. And the caption, borrowed from the advertising slogan of a famous whiskey, read, *Wilson! That's All!* In the fall of 1905 he launched his "preceptorial system," which was so successful that Harvard, Yale and other universities were later to adopt it.

All of this, with the ordinary tasks of college administration, would have been enough work for a man without Woodrow Wilson's particular brand of conscience. He had said repeatedly that it was the duty of educated men to seize every opportunity to serve the nation, and, because he seldom failed to practice what he preached, he continued to make public speeches, besides those he often made to college and alumni audiences. Most of these were about the nation's problems—political, economic and moral—and throughout the country many who heard or read them became ardent "Wilson for President" advocates.

Ellen worried about him. He was risking his health, she thought, and she was right. One morning in May, 1906, he awoke to find that he could not see with his left eye. A doctor in Philadelphia told him that a blood vessel in the eye had ruptured, that he had arterio-sclerosis and should retire and live quietly for the rest of his life. The doctor was later proved to be wrong in this diagnosis, but it seemed for a while to be a major catastrophe. Two things happened then to comfort Ellen and Woodrow. They discovered that they had more friends than they imagined, and that their faith was strong enough to meet even this test. If God willed that Woodrow's career was over, it could not be a catastrophe.

The Board of Trustees passed a resolution expressing their solicitude and insisting that President Wilson take a vacation until he recovered his health, and Ellen and Woodrow thought at once of their beloved Rydal in the English Lake Country. They took their daughters with them, arrived there in June, rented a cottage and returned to the simple, quiet life they loved.

One day Woodrow went for a walk and on a lonely road met a tall Englishman with a handsome rugged face and thick, tousled hair. "Are you Woodrow Wilson?" the man asked, with un-English abruptness, and when Woodrow said "yes," introduced himself.

"My name is Yates. We live near here. Come to see us. We're poor but, thank God, not respectable."

It was a case of friendship at first sight, although they were unlike in many respects. Fred Yates was an artist, delightfully uninhibited, careless of his appearance, unversed in world affairs. Yet the painter and the college president had also much in common. They both loved poetry, humanity, all forms of beauty, and laughter. Each had a devoted artist wife. Both were idealists.

Yates gave Ellen painting lessons and made portraits of all five Wilsons. He had difficulty catching the particular expression in Ellen's eyes that he wanted until, one day, Woodrow read Browning's "Saul" to them while she posed and Yates suddenly shouted, "I've got it!" And he had. No portrait or photograph of Ellen is so perfect a likeness.

While Ellen sketched, Woodrow and his daughters explored the lovely valleys and mountains on foot or in slow-moving ancient charabancs, coming back to the cottage in time for high tea by the fire. In the evenings Woodrow taught the girls to play whist. Every Sunday they walked together to church. There was only one mishap to mar an idyllic summer. Nellie had the German measles.

In August Ellen took Jessie and Nellie to London and the cathedral towns, leaving Margaret to keep house for her father. Woodrow reported every detail of their days to Ellen.

> *Rydal, Monday afternoon,*
> *27 August, 1906*

...I sat for Mr. Yates again to-day. The portrait lacks something of being fine, but every touch now brings it nearer to what it ought to be, and I feel sure that, especially after he has acted upon your suggestions concerning it, you will like it thoroughly,—since you have an inexplicable weakness for the original....

You are making me very happy by this expedition. How perfectly delightful the opening of our dear Nellie's eyes and heart to noble things must be. I envy you the sight of it!

It did not exactly clear up yesterday afternoon but at least *held* up, and dear Margaret and I walked over to service at Grasmere. They had the evening service in all its simplicity, and it was very sweet and soothing. The somewhat simple young man who conducted the service preached on Elijah!... Our walk home in the waning twilight, with the mountains very solemn about us gave the proper final touch to our spirits. We had supper, counted the clothes for the laundry, and went to bed with peaceful, quiet minds.... Above all things else, I love, love my darling.

Woodrow's health improved with unexpected speed. While Ellen was away he went to Edinburgh to consult two famous doctors, and reported to her afterwards:

> *Rydal, 2 September, 1906*

...Now that I am back at my type-writer, I can give you a more particular account of what the doctors said. I went first to Dr. Berry, the eye specialist, a very quiet but very satisfactory person. He said that he found the eye in excellent condition, perfectly healed, and that it would be quite safe for me to read, indeed he seemed to think that it would be best for me to use it in that way, with moderation. Altogether he was very encouraging, and did not hesitate to say that I could go back to work without risk. ...

After looking me over very carefully and thoughtfully Dr. Boyd,* said that he thought it would probably be better for a man of my temperament to go back to work than to lead an aimless and perhaps anxious year on this side the water; and he said that with the proper moderation in work, I could return with perfect safety. "If," he said, "we should lay off from work every man whose blood tension is slightly off the normal, a great many very useful and important men would be idle." Yesterday morning, by his direction, I went to the Royal Infirmary and had the tension of my blood tested. ... It was not much off normal. ... And so you see, my darling, I have practically no doubt about our sailing, a very happy family, on the sixth of October. My spirits have gone up delightfully since the consultations. Both doctors seemed so simple and so sincere that I knew just how to read what they said and was very much reassured. ...

When they sailed for home, Woodrow was in fine shape, although the vision of his left eye was permanently impaired. He took up his work at Princeton with more enthusiasm than ever, but Ellen exacted a promise. He must take a short vacation every winter, as well as a long summer vacation. In the winter of 1907 he spent two peaceful weeks in Bermuda.

Bermuda, 14 January, 1907

... Nations and all big affairs of whatever kind seem here remote and theoretical. What have *we* to do with such things on this little island far out at sea?

A Princeton man stopped me on the street just now: I dare say there will be a number of them turning up. I ought to have raised a beard, before starting! This lantern jaw of mine is unmistakable.

Ah, my precious one, how unspeakably I long for you. There is, really no offsetting by any means I have yet discovered the loneliness of being separated from you. I can amuse myself and fill my days with this

* Specialist in blood pressure.

diversion or that and keep my spirits alive and in a way have a good
time, but there is always the pain that you are not here, that I am cut
off from those sweet influences of love and tenderness which are as necessary to my heart as air is to my lungs. . . . However foolish and selfish
and exacting I am, I nevertheless live by means of what my darling
gives me and could know neither health nor peace nor joy if she did not
give them. . . .

He needed that vacation. The honeymoon at Princeton was over.
Two plans which he had presented to the Board of Trustees had met with
strong opposition. One was to develop and enlarge Princeton's embryo
Graduate College and erect a building to house it. Woodrow insisted
that the college should be on the campus and remain an integral part
of the university. Andrew West, Dean of the college, wanted it to be
segregated, both geographically and academically. The other project was
a plan to abolish Princeton's exclusive upper-class clubs and divide the
university into colleges, where all the students, as well as unmarried
professors, would live. It was, in some respects, like the Oxford and Cambridge plan—units built around quadrangles and called colleges—and,
therefore, came eventually to be known as Wilson's "Quad system."
Most of the undergraduates were not averse to the idea, but to a large
majority of the alumni, who during their college years and at Commencement enjoyed the privileges and social advantages of the luxurious
club houses, it was dynamite. Reform in the educational system, higher
scholastic standards, strict discipline, were all very well. To change the
social life and habits of the majority of Princetonians was sacrilege. To
Woodrow Wilson it was a matter of principle. A university divided into
clubs and cliques where men were chosen for social background, charm,
wealth, or athletic prowess, while others were left out in the cold, was a
crime against democracy.

Fierce controversies over both of these plans were raging when he
sailed for Bermuda. When he returned he took up the gage of battle
with renewed vigor, but in October he met with his first defeat. He had
convinced most of the faculty and a majority of the Board of Trustees
that social reformation was needed, but when rich alumni threatened to
withdraw their financial support if the clubs were abolished, the Board
voted against the plan. It is interesting to note that, while Princeton
still rejects the Quad system, both Yale and Harvard later adopted it.

The following January Woodrow went back to Bermuda with a
heavy heart. The fact that his closest friend, "Jack" Hibben, had joined
the opposition was a terrible blow—much harder to bear than his defeat. But Ellen had begged him not to brood about it and he did his best.

Bermuda, 26 January, 1908

... I feel very sedate and middle-aged at this remove from my field of battle, and look upon myself with a sort of half-sad amusement. Are there any rumbles of Democratic Party Politics? I am entirely cut off here from news. ... I love you, I love you! My heart sings it all the time. ...

Every morning he worked in his room at the hotel, preparing some lectures which he had agreed to deliver. For the rest of each day he was unusually sociable. Bermuda was a gay, friendly place and most of the people he had met the previous winter loved to give parties and invited him to all of them. Among these was Mrs. Mary Allen Peck, a vivacious and charming woman, who knew "everybody," kept open house and collected celebrities. Woodrow wrote:

Bermuda, 4 February, 1908

... I am all right and enjoying my stay. My work prospers. One of the two lectures is finished and the other is on the stocks, to be launched, I confidently expect, before I write you again. I find that, though, as usual, it is drawing blood as all my writing does, I am enjoying it and getting real mental strength and spiritual relief out of it. Bermuda is certainly the best place in the world in which to forget Princeton, at least Princeton as an organization and a problem; it would in any case afford me the most soothing rest; but a bit of work is tonic added. It keeps the blood moving aggressively. ...

My social duties have begun. I did not realize how many people I had met here last year until the calling began and the calls had to be returned. And now there are luncheons and dinners. Mark Twain has been down here between boats and I have seen a good deal of him. He seems to like being with me. Yesterday Mrs. Peck gave him a lunch at her house and gathered a most interesting little group of garrison people to meet him. He was in great form and delighted everybody. ... There is quite a household [at Mrs. Peck's,] all of whom I enjoy: her mother, a fine old lady with the breeziness of the West about her, a step-daughter ... a perfectly charming young person of twenty-two ... her son by a first marriage, for the sake of whose throat and lungs she stays down here, his tutor, who is preparing him for college ... and another youngster who is her son's most intimate friend. ... It is a lively and most engaging household, in the midst of which your husband is as young and gay as the youngest member, never, unless expressly challenged to it, saying a serious word. They are nearly out of the woods: they have heard nearly all my stories! I brought two pictures of you with me...and Mrs. Peck is so charmed with them that she insists upon keeping one of them on the mantel-piece in her drawing room, so that it sometimes seems almost as if my darling were there. You can imagine how delightful it is for me to have such a jolly circle to resort to. They are a thoroughly wholesome lot.

The man I like best is the Chief Justice * ... [He is] full of what one may call the vivacity of knowledge and of thoughtfulness....

Tomorrow evening I dine at the officers' mess at the barracks.... And all the while my thoughts follow my darling.... Ah, how intensely, how passionately, how constantly I love you.... If you were not there to think of and to return to, how flat and empty everything I enjoy would be!...

He returned to Princeton to find that the Graduate College controversy was growing daily more difficult to handle. Dean West's contention that the college should not only be built some distance away from the university campus, but also controlled by him, rather than by the university authorities, was now approved and strongly backed by a former President of the United States. Grover Cleveland had been living in Princeton ever since the end of his second term and was on the Board of Trustees. He was, apparently, one of Woodrow's admirers, had been instrumental in giving the new president sweeping powers, and had voted for the Quad system. But he knew little of educational matters, and what information he had concerning the graduate school project was acquired from Dean West, his closest friend at Princeton. Ellen and Woodrow always believed that his rapidly failing health had much to do with his attitude, for it seemed otherwise incredible that the man who would never have tolerated decentralization when he was President should now approve of it for Princeton.

At the end of the term Woodrow developed a severe case of neuritis. Ellen decided that he needed to be very far away from Princeton—and from her, because she could not hide her anxiety—so she sent him off to the British Isles, went with her daughters to Old Lyme, Connecticut, and calmed her own nerves by studying landscape painting.

On the ship Woodrow devoted his time to disciplining both his mind and his body. Every day he ran for an hour on an upper deck. He slept

* Gollan—Chief Justice of Bermuda.

fourteen hours out of every twenty-four. He forced himself to do what he called "turning off his mind," and thus instantly fall asleep. He read nothing but poetry.

Before he sailed he had heard that George Harvey, editor of *Harper's Weekly,* and other political writers, as well as friends and admirers, were suggesting that he should be nominated as Vice-President of the United States at the Democratic Convention in June. They had been advocating him for the Presidency, but since it was obvious that William Jennings Bryan would receive that nomination, they were willing to settle for second place. All this was without Woodrow's knowledge or approval. He thought it most unlikely that his name would even be considered but, just in case, left instructions with Stockton Axson to keep close watch and, if any such move were made, to decline it categorically in his behalf. The battle of Princeton was exhausting and disillusioning, but not bad enough to make him want to be Vice-President.

SS California, 26 June, 1908

...I do not know when I have so longed for you, so tenderly and passionately, or with so keen a consciousness of my utter dependence upon you, as I have since I left you on Saturday. You are my heart's home and its very life....

For once I am impatient to land and to have the distraction of a strange country—not as strange to me now as it once was, but still strange enough to be fascinating. What with going to see Mr. Carnegie and lingering somewhere while the Democratic convention sits, in order that Stock may be able to reach me directly by cable, it will probably be the twelfth of July before I am on the road and headed for the Lakes, but I shall try to find some means of diversion, and every day my love for my darling will be my chief thought, my chief joy, my chief disturbance!...

Glasgow, 29 June

We reached our dock here about midnight last night, my darling, and by 7:30 this morning I was at my hotel. Like the creature of habit I am I have come to the Grand Hotel, the hotel I came to twelve years ago when I first came over alone for a bicycle trip, and here I sit in the writing room where I then laboriously wrote my first letter to you with my left hand! The moment I entered the room the whole thing came

over me again with startling vividness, and with that every detail of
the trip—I remember how we parted in New York, and how you went
to the 23rd St. car with me and there left me ... how I watched your
dear figure as long as I could see it, with an intolerable lump in my
throat. I remember the dress you had on as if I had seen it yesterday.... I love you more now than I did then,—with a deeper, tenderer
knowledge of what you are and all that you mean to me....

Of course the news of Mr. Cleveland's death met us at Moville, the
Irish landing port. I was greatly shocked and astonished. When I saw
Mrs. Cleveland the previous Friday she was unusually cheerful about
him ... I do not think my knowledge of how he failed and disappointed
us during the past few years, and particularly since he allowed himself
to be made West's tool, will long obscure my admiration for his great
qualities and his singularly fine career....

Give my dearest love to our precious girls and to dear Madge.* God
bless you, my own darling.

Edinburgh, 10 July, 1908

... I have taken to serious reading! I saw a review in one of the papers
of a volume, just published, of lectures on English Constitutional
History which Professor Maitland † delivered in 1888, and I at once
made for a bookshop to buy it. I was somehow suddenly hungry for
just that—something solid and suggestive in my own neglected garden.
Maitland is never dull, but I could have relished even a dull book, if
not written by a fool! I tried a novel, but it was no go. My *mind* was
hungry.... I find that I *must* keep my attention on something all the
while, to keep Princeton discouragements out, and to prevent myself
from examining old wounds so curiously as to open them again. I hope
it will not be so all summer! I find I am a little dreading the Lake District,—dreading its loneliness—its emptiness of what made it so sweet
to me two years ago—its association with my darling and my home....

Last Sunday ... I had gone, as I supposed, to the church where, the
morning paper announced, Dr. Twitchell of Hartford, was to preach;
but I had got into the wrong building and heard a dear Scotchman preach

* Margaret Axson.
† Frederic William Maitland, who had died two years previously. He was professor of English law at Cambridge, and the author of a number of books on the legal
and social history of England.

... one of the best sermons I have ever heard. I constructed my next baccalaureate on the spot. I have not the least idea what the man's name was,
but he put the very meat of life into the unlikely text, "If a man compel thee to go with him a mile, go with him twain." My text is to be
"We are unprofitable servants; we have done that which was our duty
to do." I think I need not tell you what my theme will become in showing that the text is no paradox. I would like to begin it at once....

From Edinburgh Woodrow went to Carlisle, part way by train
and the rest on his bicycle. If those who imagined that the president of
Princeton was dignified and unapproachable had seen him that day they
would have been startled. Over a blue shirt and knee-length shorts, a
long waterproof cape flapped in the breeze. His glasses gleamed beneath
the long, peaked visor of an ancient golf cap. His pockets bulged with his
few necessities—a toothbrush, a comb, a change of underwear and the
Oxford Book of English Verse. It rained incessantly and by the time he
reached a little town called Ecclefechan, birthplace of Thomas Carlyle,
he was a sorry sight. He wrote when he finally arrived at his destination:

Carlisle, 13 July, 1908

... I wish you could have seen me when I alighted at the door of the
Bush Hotel in bleak little Ecclefechan! My *cape* was all right, oh yes;
but what had taken place *under* it! My bicycle has no mud-guards over
the wheels, as the English bicycles have, and all the wetness of the road
was thrown up on me and on the bicycle at every revolution of the suc-
culent things.... The very seat under me was streaked with mud. What
a time I did have cleaning the machine the next morning before church!
I ... had to make shift with some unspeakable garments lent me by mine
host till mine should be dried and brushed. The rain kept on and I
stayed all night.... I must say the host and hostess of this little inn
were most kind and attentive. Like so many Scottish people of their
class they had not a little education and some tincture of letters. Mine
host took me to the sitting-room and put in my hands the latest volumes
of Carlyle's letters (edited by Alexander Carlyle), which I noticed had
been sent to him by the publisher, Mr. John Lane, and I spent a very
cheerful evening over them—for Carlyle is a much more cheery and
agreeable companion in these letters than in Froude,* for example. I

* James Anthony Froude, English historian—1818–1894.

dwelt on the earlier letters chiefly,—with my natural inability to *skip*,
—and found them charming, every page irradiated with some flash of
his singular genius for *perceiving,* either a person or a thing.

On Sunday morning (yesterday) I went to church. It was communion Sunday and the church was full—a congregation of solid self-
respecting folk amongst whom I, with my blue shirt, blue tie and cycling
shorts, felt vulgar and common. (They did not give me a seat among the
communicants nor utter any invitation from the pulpit.) The service
was ... very touching and solemn. The seven elders (an eighth lay dying and was prayed for in very beautiful phrases) sat on the dais in
front of the pulpit with the preacher and were a most impressive body
of men, the very incarnation of plain, handsome trustworthiness, men
you could tie to, and who believed and looked what they professed. The
church was fuller of men than I have seen in any mixed congregation
in America. ... I was put on one side, and felt like a little boy or some
uninitiated yokel looking on. ...

It was pitiful to see Carlyle's grave, untended, by its grim, brown
headstone ... in the midst of as bleak, unkempt a churchyard as you will
anywhere see, apparently unused now. ...

I think that this time I have at least found the locality of the house,
under the castle walls, in which dear mother was born. The town must
have changed a great deal in these eighty (?) years and I have little to
go by, but I feel pretty sure of the general locality. There are only two
places where houses *could* stand with their gardens running behind them
to the castle wall, as she used to tell me theirs did. Uncle James, she remembered, used to play handball against the wall of the castle itself, at
the back of their garden. ...

Grasmere, 3 Aug., 1908

... It makes me *so* happy to get your dear letters. They are so full of
love and sweet thoughts and content and good news of health and enjoyment. I am so glad that you all went to Lyme, and to "Miss Florence's" *. ... I want you to know that I especially rejoice in your present vocation, your chance to make a step forward in your art, your days
of interesting occupation and diversion, as different as possible from the
occupation and the *absence* of diversion of your winters. ... My days are
spent, in thought and feeling, with you. My very loneliness during the

* Miss Florence Griswold—owner of a house where many famous artists boarded.

first week of our separation I knew to be a loneliness, not for company, but *for you.* It always comes when I am away from you. I am naturally a lonely spirit. It was the spirit of isolation and loneliness in me that was exorcised by the blessing of my marriage to you, the most loyal, the most truly womanly darling in the world. Whenever I am away from you for any length of time it comes back upon me. When I am actually *with* other persons whom I enjoy, the consciousness of it often leaves me; to come back again when I am alone. But, thank God, it no longer rules, or can rule, my life. If ever a woman's love and union with her husband was tried and proved, yours is. God has been singularly good to me, and you, my incomparable darling, have been generous beyond words! You have blessed me with the deepest, truest love that ever a woman gave a man. Ah, how I love you and how unutterably I long for you! If only I could just for a moment every morning look into your eyes and hear your voice and touch your lips, I should find the days so much brighter and sweeter. . . .

I have everything here *except* you to make me content. The weather is uncommonly fine; friends multiply and are very kind and thoughtful; I am comfortable in my lodgings; I am conscious of growing every day more normal both in nerve and muscle, and, consequently, in mind also. My vacation is giving me solid profit and each added day there is usury from it. . . .

The letters the dear girls are writing me are a source of great comfort and delight to me. Their love for me touches and surprises me as much as it delights me, and their assurances of it will be one of the brightest memories of this summer. . . .

Andrew Carnegie, having learned that Princeton's famous president was coming to England, had invited him to spend a weekend at his "castle" in Skibo, Scotland. Woodrow had accepted in the hope that he could so interest Mr. Carnegie in Princeton University that he would contribute financial support.

Edinburgh, 16 Aug., 1908

My precious darling,

Here I am in Edinburgh again, on my way back from Skibo to Grasmere,—and very eager I am to get back! I do not know that it is worth while to attempt in a letter to describe the visit,—it can be so much better done with the little touches of conversation. They have a perfect stream of visitors at Skibo: I should think that a season of it would utterly wear poor Mrs. Carnegie out. The Castle is like a luxurious hotel. Some twenty or twenty-five persons sit down to every meal. Guests are received, for the most part (if—say—of less than Cabinet rank) by the servants; shown to their rooms; and received by the host and hostess when all assemble for the next meal. The list of guests while I was there was, so far as I can recall it: Lord Morley (i.e. Mr. John Morley translated to the House of Lords, and an old goose for accepting the translation!); Ambassador and Mrs. Whitelaw Reid; the Baroness von Suttner, (a very fat Austrian lady whom Mr. Carnegie introduced as having won the Nobel prize for the best book written in promotion of international peace, and whom I had to escort as far as Perth yesterday—with the incidental inconvenience that she rode first class and I third!); a Mr. Moschelles, a portrait painter etc, etc, once a familiar friend of Du Maurier's and one of those persons born to have and to write Reminiscences; Mr. Shaw, the present Lord Advocate for Scotland in the Cabinet,—a jolly good fellow and my favorite in the list,—and Mrs. Shaw, a sweet Scottish lady with no conversation to speak of; a young Englishman named Hernden, who was generally out shooting (for I reached Skibo the very day the shooting season opened) and whose identity I could not establish, even by inquiry; Mr. "Tom" Miller, a lifelong chum of Mr. Carnegie's and a most docile creature; Mr. Reid's son, Ogden, a Yale man just through with his bar examinations; and a Mr. Sam'l Dennis, his wife (very pretty and entertaining) and their young son and daughter,—the son a junior in Princeton. Mr. Dennis is the son of an old friend of Mr. Carnegie's.

There was everything to do that you can think of: hunting, fishing, golfing, sailing, swimming (in the most beautiful swimming pool I ever saw, the water tempered to about 70°), driving, motoring, billiards, tennis, croquet; and there was perfect freedom to do as you pleased. Wednesday afternoon I managed the boat for Mr. Miller and Mr. Carnegie while they fished; Thursday morning and afternoon I was with a party on a small steam yacht; Friday morning I followed the players over the golf course; Friday afternoon I went with a big party in a motor carryall to inspect the kitchen gardens of the tenants on the estate who had been competing for a prize; Saturday I came away. The estate is some twenty miles long and, on an average, about six miles broad, and includes a whole town in its sweep,—or, rather, a large village. The evenings were spent in dining, talking, playing whist or billiards (I naturally chose the latter), or reading,—by those who had nerves steady enough for it.

It was an interesting experience, of which I shall have many things to tell you not suitable to be written down. My opinion of my host, in particular, had better be reserved for the modulations of the voice, rather than of the pen. Mrs. Carnegie is *very* sweet and true, and sent you every cordial message. I like and admire her extremely. I was of course, very glad to see Mr. Morley (as I will take the liberty of calling him still) and enjoyed what I heard of his talk very much. ... What he said had that flavour of sincerity and simplicity which I so love in the best English men, and was expressed as you would imagine he would express it,—with an elegance natural to a real man of letters and a deliberation (such as I greatly admire, but have not) characteristic of a man who thinks both before and while he speaks. I was a good deal shocked to find him old and bent and a bit feeble. ... He is over seventy and is Secretary of State for India,—a post of the heaviest labour and, just now, in particular, of the gravest anxiety. To be Secretary of State for India is like being all the ministers at once for that vast and restless and, in large part, incomprehensible empire, and it is telling on him seriously. I imagine, too, that the whole Liberal ministry is just now, besides, on the anxious bench. Opinion here is not on the whole, I should say, sustaining them. The Lord Advocate does not seem to take it very hard. He is as jolly, as genuine, as humorous a Scotsman as I would care to meet. We took a great fancy to one another, and I sincerely hope that I shall run across him again,—though I do not care to have to converse with his wife again throughout a whole dinner! I am glad to be away and free again, and am eager to get back to the little Rothay Hotel and the more simple friends at the dear Lakes. I am tired and in a humour to be entirely my own master again. ...

Grasmere, 27 Aug., 1908

... As the sweet days approach when I shall see you again, ... it seems to me as if my love for you was all that I am conscious of. I can think of nothing else for long at a time,—can desire nothing else,—grow uneasy and impatient, and would start to-morrow if I could! My darling, my darling, God keep you and recompense you for all you have been to me and to all who love you. . . .

I am quite well and hope that I shall come back to you in a condition which will render me "fit" for anything. . . .

He needed to be fit for anything. The time that lay ahead was the most difficult and, finally, the most heart-breaking he had ever known. For a while after he came home the situation seemed to have improved. Mr. Cleveland's death had deprived Dean West of his most influential ally and the tide was turning against him. He was, however, a stubborn and resourceful fighter. Managing, somehow, to persuade the trustees to postpone a decision, he searched for, and found, a new ally, William Cooper Proctor, of Proctor and Gamble, a Princeton alumnus. And, in the spring of 1909, Mr. Proctor offered to give Princeton University $500,000 toward the building of the Graduate College, if an equal sum was raised and Dean West's plans carried out.

Princetonians, even some of those who had disapproved of West's plan, were thrilled. In those days $500,000 was a fortune, and the very thought of refusing such a gift was inconceivable to all but those who still believed that no university could thrive under separate and divergent leadership. Woodrow, well aware that the scales now weighed heavily against him, fought harder than ever. Speaking at St. Paul's School in June, he reminded his audience of his struggle to abolish Princeton's upper-class clubs, explained the Graduate College issue and added, "A danger surrounding our modern education is the danger of wealth. . . . So far as the colleges go, the side-shows have swallowed up the circus, and we don't know what is going on in the main tent: and I don't want to continue as ringmaster under those conditions. I don't want you to think that I contemplate going out of business. I shall not, until I have made as many of my fellow-countrymen as uncomfortable as possible."

He was in this mood when he went with his family to spend the summer in Old Lyme and wrote a number of articles designed to reach the general public. One, published by the *Delineator,* was called, "The Ideal University"; another, "What is a College For," by *Scribner's Magazine.* When he went back into action in the fall, his name was a by-word in academic circles. And people outside those circles, even those who never quite understood what the struggle was all about, applauded him as a courageous advocate of what he thought was right. In February, 1910, at a meeting of the Board of Trustees, a motion was made to decline Mr. Proctor's offer, and he, anticipating its adoption, withdrew it.

Woodrow had won, or so it seemed, until various Princeton alumni woke up to the fact that their Alma Mater had lost half a million dollars. Then the storm broke over his head. Angry protests, vitriolic abuse, demands that the president resign and that Mr. Proctor be informed that his terms would be accepted, if he would renew his offer, arrived daily at the president's office. Most of the undergraduates were on Woodrow's side, but the faculty and the townspeople were torn apart by dissension between "the West party" and "the Wilson party." The public press found dramatic material in the situation. Stories appeared in newspapers all over the country featuring the man who had twice challenged the power of wealth, meeting the first time with defeat, the second time with victory. An editorial in *The New York Times* rebuked the "stolid groups of wealth and fashion" who "through gifts were interfering with sound academic principles."

Woodrow and Ellen were encouraged by this support from the outside world, but the little world of Princeton, seething with anger and resentment, was closer—much too close to be ignored. It was Woodrow's first experience with unpopularity, and it hurt. He was also so tired that Ellen insisted upon another trip to Bermuda.

Bermuda, 14 Feb'y, 1910

My precious darling,

I am more lonely than I dare say, away off here by myself—but it is only the first shock of being separated from all I love and depend on. I am ashamed to find myself very deeply affected (in my nerves) by the abuse that has recently been heaped on me. I am intensely self-conscious and shy of my fellow-beings. But that will wear off when I get acclimated and the old charm of the place begins to take effect. . . . The boat returns at once, and I am getting this off on her—to carry some broken syllables of the infinite love I have for my darling. . . .

This time he welcomed what he called the "round of entertainment" not only as a distraction but also as an antidote to the social ostracism he and Ellen had experienced in some quarters at Princeton. Mark Twain was in Bermuda again, looking much older since his daughter's death, but still a delightful companion.

Bermuda, 17 Feb'y, 1910

. . . Mark Twain . . . says that he does not see why he should ever leave Bermuda again. What he particularly rejoices in having got rid of is (for some reason) trolley cars and (quite reasonably) newspapers and newspaper reporters. . . . He is certainly one of the most human of men.

Yesterday I started in to work, and spent half the morning making a working abstract of my article for Scribners (I wonder if they will want to publish it now?) which I shall call "The Colleges and the Country"....

And so the days go, and my mind begins to be at ease. I did not realize until I got here how hard hit my nerves had been by the happenings of the past month. Almost at once the *days* began to afford me relief, but the nights distressed me. The trouble latent in my mind came out in my dreams. Not till last night did the distress—the struggle all night with college foes, the sessions of hostile trustees, the confused war of argument and insinuation—cease. But now the calm has come and I am very peaceful,—very, very lonely without my love to sustain me with her sympathy and understanding, but myself again....

Ellen was lonely too—more so than she had ever been. There were, as usual, relatives to keep her company, but all of her daughters were away from home. Margaret and Jessie were at The Woman's College of Baltimore *—having persuaded their mother that "higher education" would not, necessarily, make them unfeminine. Nellie had not been persuaded. Nellie was the frivolous one, who was bored with Sir Walter Scott and Thackeray and Anthony Trollope; who loved clothes and dancing and going to football and baseball games with her father or a beau. She said she didn't want to go to college and detected a gleam of sympathy in her mother's eyes. But, because her father thought that she was too dependent on the family and her mother worried because she talked like a Yankee, Nellie was sent, unwillingly, to St. Mary's College in North Carolina. Ellen found distraction in intensified activity.

Princeton, Feb. 17th, 1910

... There is quite a little file of "nice" letters from alumni, but, after much hesitation I have decided not to send them unless you write for them; so if you want them, say so.... I *hope* you had a good voyage, my darling, and have found real Bermuda weather; and that the peace of it all is sinking in and through you. How I love to think of you there!

Tuesday I went, according to schedule, to Camden to the convention of Associated Charities.

Yesterday afternoon I heard a lecture by Miss Ida Tarbell—on "American Women" and it reminded me of what a flighty person at

* Now Goucher College.

the convention told me of one of the speeches there, "Oh! it was *perfectly splendid!—so* depressing!" Miss Tarbell's was all the more depressing because in my opinion it was perfectly true. You can hardly imagine anything more conservative, it might have been one's grandmother talking. Indeed it was largely a demonstration of the fact that the grandmothers were incomparably superior to us. We are like Kipling's ship which had not found itself. We are consumed with restlessness and self-consciousness, and like a certain Sally, "always want to be where we aint." We are without steadiness of purpose or deep sense of obligation, things which our grandmothers had intensely. Therefore they had true dignity and the real secret of living, for they respected themselves and their work in the order of society, and did it efficiently and serenely. . . .

The girls send love beyond expression. We miss you more than we can say,—and are happier than we can say that you are away! As for me, you know, dearest, that it is quite impossible to express my love. It is greater than ever and I had thought that, too, was impossible!

> *Bermuda, Sunday morning*
> *20 Feb'y., 1910*

My precious darling,

How I wish you were here beside me this morning! How sweet it would be to sit by you and hold your hand and talk! There is so much to talk about, with the clouds thickening and lowering more and more at Princeton. . . .

Did I tell you that I found some beautiful carnations from Miss Dickson * at the steamer when I came away? It touched and pleased me very deeply. She is very sweet and thoughtful. It is peculiarly delightful to have such tokens of thoughtful affection when I am so widely hated and attacked. . . .

> *Monday, Feb'y 21st*

. . . This is the sweetest day I have had here. It has brought me letters from you so sweet, so tender, the best tonic my heart ever had! . . . Ah! my sweet one, what would become of me if you did not love me and stand by me and make it all so sweet and give my heart *such* times of peace and reassurance! I feel like another man. I have been fighting a

* A Princeton friend.

hard fight here with myself and have not succeeded in getting myself in hand as well as I should. But it will be all right now, I feel sure. The morning's work always steadies me and does me good, notwithstanding the fact that it concerns the everlasting college problem around which all the hate and ugliness centre. There is something calming in the large aspects, the unpartisan importance of any great subject. The accidents of its discussion seem submerged and relatively unimportant. But, above all, *you* are a blessing.

I went to church yesterday and heard a quiet young Scotsman preach, who did me good with his confident and simple versions of belief; and then, in the afternoon I went up to Government House and had tea with the Governor, brother to *the* General Kitchener,—a plain straightforward soldier out of whom one could no doubt make a companion and friend,—if he were not in a position which renders him more or less inaccessible ... I might become a very conversable person if I remained long in Bermuda....

It makes me feel deeply selfish to think of having left you there in all that horrid weather ... and in the midst of all the talk that must be distressing you, or the silence that may be puzzling you. We would probably dwell on it all too much if you were here, or I were there, but the bliss of being together would be compensation enough. How sweet it is to think of you, to count on you, to know what you are. We have no compromises to look back on, the record of our consciences is clear in this whole trying business. We can be happy, therefore, no matter what may come of it all. It would be rather jolly after all, to start out on life anew together, to make a new career, would it not? Experience deepens with us, my precious darling, and with experience love, and I thank God with all my heart....

At Princeton the senior class, indignant over the attacks on the president, passed resolutions commending him for his stand, and the college paper, *Princetonian,* published them with an approving editorial. Ellen wrote, triumphantly:

Princeton, Feb. 21st, 1910

... Of course I do not want to fill my letter with "facts and fancies" on the usual subject. But I am sure it will do you good to know about the position taken by the undergraduates, so I am enclosing their resolutions and the editorial,—resolutions passed by the senior class. Paul van Dyke * went to Ivy † in a fury about the resolutions, "banged on the table" and told the boys they were insulting to Mr. Pyne ‡, etc., etc. But the fellows stood their ground perfectly and took back nothing. Think of *that!*—at *Ivy!* . . .

Mr. Kirk preached yesterday. . . . He is a tremendous partisan of yours, and such a cheerful, manly, straight-forward person;—and so interesting, too, a real personality. His sermons were *fine*—just like him. In the morning it was on one's life choice—"And when Moses was *grown* he went unto his brethren and looked on their burdens." But you should have heard him at night! It was on Jeremiah, the Jewish leader, his struggles with all sorts of difficulties, the various tests he was put to and how he met them, ending with the time when his life was in danger and he was urged to take refuge in the temple, and he said, "Should such a man as I flee?" It was prepared after five o'clock that afternoon,—avowedly suggested by the situation here;—yet he was wise enough to make its *direct* appeal to the seminary students. The analogies were startling enough even with that precaution. . . . He is tremendously in earnest and has enormous force and vitality. If we could only have preachers like that on the board! [of Trustees]. . . .

Princeton, Feb. 24, 1910

. . . Nell and I went into New York yesterday to see several small picture shows and the Ben Greet Players in "She Stoops to Conquer". . . . It was given at the Garden Theatre—just opposite Mrs. Peck's. So, as we reached the theatre at one sharp, we decided to run in and "say howdy" to her. . . . [She] begged us to come in for tea after the play. We did so and had a delightful little visit with her,—were there almost an hour.

. . . We are all happier than we can say, dearest, at the thought of you in that lovely place, among congenial friends and at *peace!* . . .

Recurring newspaper stories about Princeton's fighting president had increased the already numerous suggestions that he should run for

* Princeton professor, brother of Henry van Dyke.
† Ivy Club, one of the most exclusive upper-class clubs.
‡ M. Taylor Pyne, trustee, opposed to Wilson's plans.

the Presidency of the United States. Why, people asked, should he continue to try to reform Princeton, where he was not appreciated? Why not enter politics and reform the nation? Colonel George Harvey, the shrewd editor of *Harper's Weekly,* had a bright idea. A strong progressive movement was spreading throughout the country. In New Jersey the reactionary Democratic organization, headed by ex-Senator James Smith, was searching desperately for a candidate who could win the gubernatorial election in 1910. Their only chance, George Harvey pointed out to Smith, was to nominate a progressive Democrat. And Woodrow Wilson was not only a progressive, but also a strong personality and a fine orator—just the man they needed. Smith was shocked. Who in hell, he demanded, would vote for a professor! And the organization —"the boys"—wouldn't like "that Presbyterian priest." Yet Harvey had finally persuaded him to go along with the plan and urged Woodrow to agree to try for the nomination. He would be elected, Harvey predicted, and that was a long step toward the White House. Woodrow had refused to consider it. He was needed at Princeton, and could not possibly leave in the middle of a crisis. He also did not relish the thought of being sponsored by "Jim" Smith.

When he told Ellen about this conversation she did not altogether approve of his decision. She was so outraged by the attacks being made upon him that she thought Princeton deserved to lose him. And she had not forgotten how he had longed for a statesman's career.

During Woodrow's absence in Bermuda the question arose at a meeting of the Board of Trustees as to whether or not Dean West should be asked to resign. Ellen kept the news of their decision from Woodrow and was indignant when one of his friends wrote to him about it.

Princeton, Feb. 28, 1910

... Everything is going very quietly here,—the most exciting thing that has happened was the *preacher* yesterday,—Mr. Fosdick.* He really was *splendid*—such fire and force, such evident sincerity and such splendid command of language! "Exciting" was the only word for it. His text was Gallio's protest "If it be a question of words and names look ye to it,—for I will be no judge of such matters;" and it *was* a "protest,"— against all forms of hair-splitting etc. which tended to make of religion a petty thing, when it was really so inexpressibly great. He is a young man and very simple and unaffected in manner. He is an elder brother

* Harry Emerson Fosdick, at that time pastor of the First Baptist Church in Montclair, N.J.

of Raymond Fosdick who was, you remember, a good debater, etc....

How I hope your lovely weather lasted all the week, dear, and that you enjoyed it, through and through and had a cheerful, peaceful week among your English friends, for I sadly fear that Mr. Fine has spoiled your last week for you! I was inexpressibly vexed with him when I heard that he had written you. Who could have supposed that he would be so inconsiderate,—so *cruel*,—as not to wait until you came home to tell you that they wanted to keep West on as Dean after all. He said he wanted to give you time to think it over before your return! And you only *had* two weeks there,—and now he has *ruined* one of them. Oh!—but words fail. You told me to "mark your words,"—that they never would make a clean cut issue and push it straight through to the bitter end. You seem to be a true prophet. They really seem to want both sides to be able to claim the victory. Of course there *is* something in what they say,—that West being really defeated,—his scheme swept away,—it would only give him an advantage to be made a martyr of, and that if we keep him on as Dean—and "ignore him in practice"—the other side will have no issue on which to make a fight. They actually think, after last year's experience, that they *can* ignore him and organize things to suit themselves.

There is one point in the plan which *does* appeal to me, viz. that it sets you free again to leave if you wish,—that is to accept the nomination for governor and go into politics. If they had turned West out you would, of course, be obliged to stay no matter how outrageous the Alumni were. If I were you I should accept their proposition coolly, rather indifferently,—saying that of course if the trustees won't vote to turn him out, he *can't be* turned out,—and there is nothing more to be said about it; then keep my own counsel, stay in for the present and next year run for governor. This thing has strengthened you *immensely* throughout the whole country, it is said that there have been hundreds upon hundreds of editorials and all *wholly* on your side. Moreover, though your enemies talk themselves blue in the face they cannot convince the country that you have not won,—the West college having vanished in thin air and the trustees report being what it is. Your position is so commanding that we can really afford to laugh at the howling of the Alumni, "mongrel, puppy, whelp and hound, and curs of low

degree''! But no more of this. Of course I would not have mentioned the
subject but for Mr. Fine's letter;—after that it is useless for me to ignore it. . . .

All send love inexpressible to our dear one. I am with you constantly
in thought and in feeling. I would give my life, ah, how freely, to make
life happier for you. I love you with all my heart and soul and strength
and mind.

Woodrow found, when he returned to Princeton, that Ellen had
been too optimistic. West's college had not ''vanished in thin air.'' The
wild lament of alumni over the loss of half a million dollars had weakened
the resolution of several of his supporters on the Board of Trustees and
it now appeared that Mr. Proctor might be asked to renew his offer on
his own terms.

Woodrow decided to ''appeal to the country,'' as he was to do
many times in the years to come. He made a tour, speaking to alumni
audiences in the West as well as in the East. It was so successful that
once more the tide turned toward him. Then, one morning in May, his
youngest daughter, coming down late for breakfast, heard him laughing.
There must be good news, she thought, and ran to ask what it was. Her
father had a letter in his hand. An old man named Isaac Wyman, of
Salem, Massachusetts, had died, he told her, and left Princeton over two
million dollars to be used to build the Graduate College. Andrew West
had been named as trustee to administer the fund at his discretion.
''We've beaten the living,'' Woodrow said, ''but we can't fight the dead.
The game's up.'' Nellie, not understanding the grim humor that had
made him laugh, looked at her mother. Ellen's smile was a little forced.

Woodrow was right. The game was up. The Board of Trustees did
not dare to refuse two million dollars.

Part 3
The Politician

In June the state Democratic Committee called at Prospect and were ushered into the book-lined study. When Woodrow came in, Jim Smith, a large impressive figure with a silk hat in his hand and a stunned look on his face, asked, "Do you read *all* these books, Professor?" "Not every day," the professor assured him, and laughter broke the strain of the encounter.

When the interview was over, Woodrow went at once to Ellen, waiting patiently in their bedroom. Mr. Smith and the others, he told her, had said that he could be nominated for Governor, if he would make a statement that he would accept. Smith had promised, at Woodrow's insistence, that no one would ask him for any pledges or commitments of any sort. Woodrow had said that he would think it over. What, he asked Ellen, did she want him to do? The main question to decide, these two devotees of duty, agreed, was how he could serve his country best—at Princeton, or in the political arena. And, since his authority, and therefore his usefulness, at Princeton had been seriously undermined, it seemed clear to them, finally, that he must choose politics.

In July, he announced that he would accept the nomination, if it was offered, and in September the Democratic state convention, meeting in Trenton, nominated him on the first ballot.

The curious, even amusing, aspect of this event lay in the fact that all the early part of Woodrow's life he had longed to enter politics and yet, when the opportunity came, he was reluctant to grasp it. He had renounced his political aspirations, believing that there was no possibility that he could ever attain them, and had thrown all his energy and enthusiasm into the work that he believed Providence had directed him to do. He loved Princeton, and felt that he was serving his country as well, if not better there than in the political arena, by training young men for leadership in the never-ending struggle to improve and purify the Republic. And then, with no effort on his part, he was pushed—and pulled—into public life. Pushed by the Board of Trustees, by their refusal to support him, pulled by New Jersey Democrats into allowing himself to be nominated for the Governorship. It is still said in Princeton that Wilson's enemies "kicked him upstairs into the White House."

As a political campaigner Woodrow Wilson surprised everybody—except Ellen. The professor discarded, apparently with ease, the academic phrases of the classroom and spoke in language anybody could understand. He had a fund of amusing stories with which to illustrate his points, using his gift of mimicry with great effect, and he had the real orator's ability to fire the imagination and yet never rant or shout. A newspaper columnist wrote that Wilson was the only orator he had ever heard who could be confidential with a crowd. And after one of his speeches a farmer remarked that he couldn't "see why a smart guy like that had been hanging around a college all his life." Only his family knew that he was, at first, very unsure of himself, so unsure that he would not let them hear him speak. They rebelled only once. They went secretly to Trenton, and hid behind the curtains in a box at the Opera House, trembling with fear that he would discover them and break down.

He had resigned as president of Princeton after his nomination, and had refused to use any campaign funds for his own expenses, but the trustees had urged him to stay at Prospect until the election, which helped to ease a precarious financial strain.

On election day he was the only calm person in the house. To Ellen this was very strange and wonderful. She knew better than anyone else how painfully sensitive he was, and she had been afraid that he would be deeply hurt if he were defeated. Yet here he was unconcerned, relaxed, and she realized with joy that, although he suffered over a lost cause or unjust criticism, he still had faith, as he had told her years ago, "in the right ordering of Providence." Her faith was not, in this respect, as strong as his. She was as excited as her daughters and the usual quota of visiting relatives when, in the evening, the returns began to come in. Woodrow teased them. When he answered the telephone, which rang every few minutes, he gave no sign to indicate whether the news was good or bad, merely saying "Yes" and "Thank you," while he watched their frenzied faces with amusement. Then he told them that the news was good, but cautioned them not to be too optimistic. By ten o'clock it was certain that he had carried the state by the largest majority, with one exception, ever given to a gubernatorial candidate in New Jersey.

Immediately after his inauguration in January, 1911, Governor Wilson dismayed Jim Smith and his henchmen by launching his plan to reform New Jersey. Once more there was a struggle, but this time Woodrow thoroughly enjoyed it. This was not like the Princeton battles where old friends had turned against him and academic subtleties often obscured the real issues. This was a battle everyone could understand, a recurring war that had been lost—or won—time and again in many parts of the nation; a war against political machines, against undercover manipulation of the people's rights, a war for clean government and good laws. And now that Woodrow had arrived at last at the goal he had aspired to in his youth, self-distrust, over-sensitiveness, dark moods disappeared. Ellen, watching him sail serenely over stormy seas, was enormously relieved. As for Jim Smith, the ''Big Boss'' who had secretly hoped to boss the new Governor, was once heard to mutter under his breath, ''My God, why didn't we notice his jaw!''

New Jersey had been labeled the ''Mother of Trusts.'' In three months she was well on the way toward becoming one of the most advanced states in the union in reform legislation. Four bills that Woodrow had set his heart on were passed by the legislature—a primary and election law, a corrupt practices act, a workingmen's compensation act, and a bill giving control over public utilities to a state commission. The Democratic machine was broken to bits and the bosses cast into outer darkness. There was an editorial in one of the more exuberant newspapers which was the Wilson family's delight:

''His garments odorus with the vapours of Parnassus, his lips wet with the waters of Helicon—this long-haired book-worm of a professor, who had just laid his spectacles on his dictionary, came down to the Trenton State House and licked the gang to a frazzle.''

Even less picturesque writers, not realizing that Woodrow Wilson had devoted twenty-five years to the study of government, politics and the ways of politicians, found it amazing that this ''amateur in politics'' had achieved such sensational success. He was big news now and his nomination for the Presidency at the Democratic convention in 1912 was at least a possibility.

For a woman with little experience of political life, Ellen was remarkably clear-sighted. Perhaps this was because she always remained in the background, apart from the crowds and the controversies, where events could be seen in perspective. But, whatever the reason, her counsel was as sound now as it had been on other, more familiar matters. She believed that Woodrow's nomination was now much more than a possibility, but she knew that a lost opportunity or even a small mistake in judgment could be fatal. There was, for instance, the problem of William Jennings Bryan, whose support Woodrow must have if he decided to try for the nomination.

Mr. Bryan had written an enthusiastic article in his magazine, *The Commoner,* praising the Governor of New Jersey, but Ellen suspected that he wanted the nomination himself. And, although Woodrow admired him in some respects, he had said publicly that Bryan was ''foolish and dangerous in his theoretical beliefs.'' But the two had never met and Ellen was sure that, if this could be arranged, each would succumb to the other's charm. So, in March, when she heard that the ''Great Commoner'' was coming to Princeton to speak, she acted with speed and dispatch. She sent two telegrams—one to Mr. Bryan inviting him to dinner after his speech, the other to Woodrow urging him to hurry home. It worked. Bryan accepted, Woodrow obeyed, and the dinner was a great success. An understanding was established that evening which eventually became a lasting friendship, for both men were idealists, both were dedicated to the welfare of their country, and each recognized the other's sincerity.

Joseph Tumulty, the Governor's young Irish secretary, was elated when he heard what Ellen had accomplished.

"You've nominated your husband," he told her.

Ellen smiled. "It was nothing," she said. "It was just good manners."

Woodrow, however, refused to become an active candidate until he had found out for himself whether or not the people—or an appreciable number of people—would support him. In May, he went on an extended tour of the country.

Ellen stayed at home—if four rooms at the Princeton Inn could be called home. New Jersey did not provide a house for its governors in Trenton, and Woodrow preferred to travel the twenty miles each day to his office and come back to Princeton at night. But there was a summer "mansion" near the ocean at Sea Girt, where they would have to go in June, and while he was away Ellen began, with only a small sigh, to plan to transform another "great, stately troublesome place" into a home. She also spent hours clipping and pasting in albums every word that was printed about her husband, and, whenever there was a chance for a letter to catch up with him she wrote to tell him how proud she was of him and, when necessary, to advise him.

Princeton, New Jersey
May 11, 1911

My own darling,

You can imagine with what absorbing interest we are following your movements as far as we are able; *How* fine it all is! I am longing for more news though,—more papers. A few, a very few clippings from Denver are all I have had. The "Times" gives but little, of course, and the other papers I see, the speeches, but few other details. I am hungry for all sorts of particulars. There was one fine article in the "Evening Post" on Sat., I think, telling exactly what I wanted to know.... But the speeches do all that is *necessary;* they are *perfection;*—and I am not the only one who thinks so. How very interesting the story about the telephone from Denver! *—the N.Y. reporter asking "what is the news

* On the occasion of the first telephone connection between New York and Denver.

in Denver'' and the answer:—''the town is wild over Woodrow Wilson and is booming him for President.'' Even the ''Times'' had to put *that* in—as news!...

By-the-way, *please* don't say again that you ''are not thinking about the presidency.'' All who know you well know that that is *fundamentally* true, but *superficially* it can't be true; and it gives the cynics an opening which they seize with glee. The ''Sun'' of course had an outrageous little editorial about it.

... On last Saturday Jessie, Nell and I went to Sea Girt. It was a perfect day. The house is really most attractive.... We took a long drive to the shore and back into the woods in the state carriage with the two fine horses....

But I mustn't write more, for you haven't time to even *read* long letters. Ah, how I love, love *love* you, dearest. I am with you in spirit every moment. May God bless you and keep you well and strong to do His work....

Ellen, too, was asked to make speeches, but no power on earth could persuade her to do it. Southern women, she told her friends and her family, knew better than to show off in public. She could not, however, as the Governor's wife, refuse to attend functions where other women spoke.

Princeton, May 15th, 1911

... My amazement at your powers of endurance is more profound than usual to-night because of the exhausting effect upon me of the awful club ''breakfast'' which came off to-day here at the Inn. It lasted four hours, there were a dozen speeches, most of them very poor,—and I was bored almost to extinction. I am perfectly sure that I would rather die than go to as many public dinners as you do. All the other women at the table with me had to make speeches later and of course had no conversation in the meantime. I had to do all of that. It was deadly.

Thank you very much, dear, for the clippings. They were most welcome; and the telegrams more so. The one from Los Angeles was especially satisfactory and reassuring. I am inexpressibly thankful that you are standing it so well and *enjoying* it indeed. And what a wonderful triumph you are having! And no one is in the least surprised for all *knew* beforehand that it would be so. As the ''Press'' said, they are ''so worn to a frazzle praising'' you that they take every sort of demonstration as a mere matter of course.

News comes from Washington that Bryan has now conceded your nomination. Whether true or not I do not know. I enclose today's editorial from the "True American." I think it handles that remark of yours which caused so much comment very well. Another paper defended you well too. It said that your mind was occupied not with an *office* but with *principles,* and that you were equally ready to work for them as a leader or in the ranks. . . .

She wrote from Connecticut, where she had gone for a few weeks to rest and paint:

Old Lyme, Conn., May 22nd, 1911

. . . I feel very much in touch with my darling just now. Some of the cousins,* I suppose, in Denver sent quite a packet of clippings from there which were very much enjoyed. Otherwise I have not seen many from the west. I hope you will come back *loaded!* Isn't it all perfectly splendid and wonderful? It is like a royal progress. Surely you must be a man of destiny.

I made a beginning at the painting to-day but did not accomplish much. Everybody was trying apple-blossom subjects and swearing over them and declaring them impossible. . . .

Ah, darling, how I wish I could tell you how I love you! . . . Oh, for the great heart word! . . .

Woodrow made his last speeches in the South and, on the way home, stopped over in Washington to consult with a group of his supporters. They were elated over the impression he had made on his tour and wanted his permission to organize a Wilson-for-President campaign on a nation-wide basis. But, to their surprise and dismay, he said that he did not want to be "promoted as a candidate." The movement in his favor should, he advised, be allowed to "take care of itself."

There were two letters from Ellen waiting for him at his hotel.

Old Lyme, June 1st, 1911

. . . I wonder how long you will be in Washington and if exciting things will happen there. Did you see the account of the informal poll of Demo-

* Mrs. Harriet Woodrow Welles and family.

cratic representatives in which four-fifths (of those voting) voted for you for nominee?... I am very curious to know how Bryan behaved when you were in Lincoln,—if he invited you to his house, etc....

Old Lyme, June 2, 1911

My own darling,

Just a line to catch the morning mail. There is a persistent rumour that is worrying some of your friends, that another "tour" is being arranged for you,—the inference being that you are *consenting*. Of course I know that you are *not*,—that there is no truth in it, beyond the fact that much pressure is doubtless being brought to bear on you to fall in with such plans. But it is said to be making a bad impression,— in New Jersey particularly, but also in New York—and I was wondering if it could not be publicly contradicted in some way. I enclose an editorial that alludes to it....

What a tremendous ovation you had in Raleigh!...

The first summer at Sea Girt was far from restful. The Governor's house is on the edge of New Jersey's National Guard campground, and in July the annual training period began. The Wilsons and their relatives were awakened very early every morning by reveille, followed by the crackle of target practice. Citizens of New Jersey, by the hundreds, came every weekend to watch the drills, swarm over the wide porches of the summer mansion and peer through windows at its occupants. The Wilson-for-President boom was taking care of itself with a vengeance and reporters came, uninvited, to interview the Governor, his wife, and his daughters. Ellen dreaded these visitations. She had told her children years ago not to talk about their father "to other people" and she, and they, had adhered to that rule consistently. Now she was expected to tell these strangers all about him, as well as about herself. She was very courteous but firm in her refusal to answer personal questions, relenting only once when a society reporter asked:

"Why don't you and your daughters ever wear any jewelry, Mrs. Wilson? Have you some sort of moral prejudice against it?"

"Why no," Ellen said. "We haven't any jewelry."

Margaret, Jessie and Nellie, however, found the new life amusing. For the first time the family had an automobile, a big unwieldy thing driven nervously by an old man who continuously mourned the sale of the "state carriage" in June and the indignity of having to drive "this contraption." The girls had new dresses; there were parties with plenty of young officers standing in line to dance with them. Their only problem was how to fit a dozen engagements into one short day. Ellen was pleased, for she had been afraid that her two elder daughters were too serious. Yet she thought they all overdid it. "If you plan your future lives with half the care you give to your time here," she told them, "you will be brilliantly successful." Woodrow did not object to gaiety, but his manner toward the young men who called more than once on any one of his daughters was peculiar. He greeted them coldly, stalked from the room and, when Ellen joined him, wanted to know why "that young fool kept hanging around?" On one such occasion, Ellen said mildly, "You're not being very complimentary to your daughters when you call every man who finds them attractive a fool." He behaved a little better after that.

In the fall of 1911, the Wilsons rented a small house on Cleveland Lane and moved from the Princeton Inn. Margaret went to New York to study singing, Jessie to Philadelphia to work at a settlement house. Nellie, trying hard to believe, as her sisters did, that there was more to life than just having fun, commuted daily to Philadelphia to study painting at the Pennsylvania Academy of Fine Arts.

That winter Woodrow finally agreed to announce that he was a candidate for the Presidency and to allow his supporters to organize nationally. In the spring he campaigned in various states before the primary elections. None of Ellen's letters during that time have been found, and only one of his:

Augusta, Ga., 19 Nov., 1911

My precious one,

Don't be surprised to see me follow this soon! I am having a good time, full of interest and pleasure,—but with no *rest* at all. I am not left to myself at all. Publicity (my own dear pet, Publicity!) has closed about me like a prison. I am freer at home than anywhere else,—and *you* are there, my darling. I think I will come back and put my vacation into taking you to the theatre.

I am perfectly well,—and strangely enough, do not feel fagged. I am snatching a moment before going to church,—to father's old church. Even there I am to be made a public man of! But what I am most *conscious* of being is

Your own
Woodrow.

Compared to the second summer at Sea Girt in 1912, the first seemed in retrospect to have been as peaceful as the grave. It began quietly. After church on the first Sunday, the Wilson family sat by the fire in an upstairs sitting-room, while outside a cold rain kept visitors away. They talked about everything except politics, until Woodrow said, with a sigh, ''Two weeks from to-day we will either have our sweet Sunday calm again or an all-day reception and an army of reporters camped on the lawn.''

Nellie hoped for the reception, but in the sudden, almost grim silence, she did not dare to admit it.

The Democratic National Convention met in Baltimore on the twenty-fifth of June, but William Jennings Bryan fired the opening gun two days ahead of time. It appeared that Alton B. Parker, who represented the most conservative wing of the party, would be selected as temporary chairman and the Great Commoner was outraged. It ''would be suicidal,'' he declared, and sent identical telegrams to the various candidates asking them to state their position in the matter at once, by wire. At every campaign headquarters, managers and delegates went into a frightened huddle. If their candidates rejected Parker, the conservative wing, which included the powerful Tammany-controlled delegation, would be offended. If they did not, Bryan's large following would be antagonistic. So-called practical politicians, believing that Bryan was maneuvering to get the nomination for himself, advised their candidates to ignore the telegram. Others were for compromise. William F. McCombs, Wilson's campaign manager, was among the latter. He sent a wire to Sea Girt suggesting an evasive reply ''in the interests of harmony.''

Woodrow, as usual, sought Ellen's counsel. He found her in their bedroom, with Nellie, and handed her the telegram without comment.

''There must be no hedging,'' she said promptly, and Woodrow smiled because this was what he had hoped she would say. Sitting beside her on the bed he wrote his reply, stating clearly that he was opposed to Mr. Parker as temporary chairman and would advise his friends at the convention to support Mr. Bryan's position.

There are often times in the affairs of men, especially men in politics, when a decision is made which changes the whole course of their lives, although its significance is not always recognized at the time. Champ Clark of Missouri, the leading candidate, sent Mr. Bryan an answer as evasive as McCombs' suggestion; Oscar Underwood of Alabama and Governor Harmon of Ohio supported Parker; the lesser candidates, with one exception, either opposed Bryan or straddled the issue. Woodrow Wilson's unequivocal stand united the progressives behind him, satisfied Mr. Bryan and, in the final analysis, won him the nomination.

On the twenty-fourth of June tents sprang up like mushrooms on the lawn outside the Governor's house and a horde of newspaper cor-

respondents and telegraphers moved in. All day long Wilson delegates
and supporters, on their way to Baltimore, came and went in a steady
stream. On the twenty-fifth, and for the seemingly endless ten days that
followed, the house was as crowded and as busy as a railroad station.
Reporters, ignoring the doorbell, wandered in to inquire how the Wilsons
felt and what they thought about the chances of victory.

There was, of course, no radio then and news of the convention came
only by telegraph, telephone and the press. A direct wire from Wilson
headquarters in Baltimore had been installed, with one extension in
Woodrow's room, the other in a closet under the stairway. Joseph
Tumulty sat in the closet day and night with his ear glued to the re-
ceiver, leaving it only to give the assembled family, friends and relatives
the latest news, or to wolf a sandwich. His expressive Irish face always
registered the news before he spoke. When Parker was elected temporary
chairman, it was a tragic mask. When he heard that the crowd in the
galleries had walked out in protest while Parker delivered the keynote
speech, it was comically round and pink. And when at two o'clock in the
morning of the twenty-sixth, Woodrow Wilson's name was presented to
the convention and the demonstration that followed lasted an hour and
a quarter, his blue eyes blazed as he popped his head out of the closet,
shouting, "It's *still* going on. It isn't over *yet!*" When he came out he
asked blankly, "Where's the Governor?"

The Governor had gone to bed. Every afternoon while the convention lasted, he played golf: almost every evening he retired with Ellen
to the sitting-room and read aloud to her from John Morley's *Gladstone*. When he went to bed Ellen came down again and stayed until
sleep overcame her. Margaret, Jessie, Nellie and Joe Tumulty seldom
slept at all.

The first ballot, taken at seven o'clock in the morning, was disappointing: Champ Clark, 440½; Wilson, 324; the rest divided among
the other candidates. Under the two-thirds rule then in force, 724 votes
were needed for nomination.

For several days there was little change. Then, on the fourth day
and the tenth ballot, Boss Murphy of Tammany Hall delivered New
York's ninety votes to Champ Clark, giving him a majority. A band-
wagon stampede almost invariably followed a majority vote, and
Tumulty's despair was so profound that Ellen was worried about him.
He must not take things so hard, she told him. Didn't he know that
whatever happened was meant to be?

There was, surprisingly, no stampede. The Wilson lines held firm
and only a few delegates deserted the other candidates. But early the
next morning McCombs telephoned from Baltimore to tell Woodrow
that the battle was lost and to advise him to release his delegates. Woodrow, unaware that McCombs had reached this conclusion without con-

sulting his committee, said that he would send the release by wire and went to tell Ellen. He must have breakfast before he wrote the telegram, she said calmly, but there were tears in her eyes. When their daughters joined them, Woodrow was laughing. He had found an illustrated catalogue from an undertaking firm in his morning mail:

"This is certainly prompt service," he remarked. "Will you help me choose a coffin for a dead duck?" Then looking across the table at Ellen's wan smile, he said gently, "Now we can see Rydal again."

In Baltimore William Gibbs McAdoo, builder of the Hudson tunnel and a member of the Wilson campaign committee, had arrived at headquarters to find McCombs slumped miserably over his desk. What, McAdoo asked, was the matter? McCombs told him about the telephone call to Sea Girt, and the scene that followed became a favorite postconvention tale. When the shouting began, men from nearby rooms gathered in the doorway. McAdoo, very tall, white with rage, towered over the desk, denouncing, threatening, while the small man behind the desk shrieked in his own defense. It was necessary at last to take Mr. McCombs to a safer place. McAdoo grabbed the telephone.

At Sea Girt Tumulty ran to the dining-room. McAdoo was calling. McAdoo said McCombs was crazy! Woodrow went to the telephone, with Ellen, Margaret, Jessie and Nellie in close pursuit. Mr. McAdoo begged him not to release his delegates and swore that they would be able to prevent Clark from getting a two-thirds vote. Woodrow agreed to wait for further developments.

Later that day, during the fourteenth ballot, Bryan announced to a tensely quiet crowd that he was casting his vote for Woodrow Wilson and pandemonium broke out, not only at the convention, but in Tumulty's mercurial soul. But, although the Nebraska delegation followed its leader and Wilson gained a few votes on succeeding ballots, the dogged struggle continued. After the twenty-fifth try, Woodrow remarked, "I've been figuring that, at the present rate of gain, I'll be nominated in one hundred and seventy-five more ballots."

At midnight on Saturday the convention adjourned until Monday.

On Sunday the Wilson family went to church, as usual, returning to find Tumulty's face unexpectedly bright.

"They're hearing from the country," he announced. "Thousands of telegrams are pouring in—every one of them for you, Governor!"

At midday dinner, Woodrow urged his family to stick to the rule he had made years before that there must be no discussion of disturbing matters at meals. Unable to think of anything but the battle of Baltimore, they were silent, so he entertained them with anecdotes, jokes, impersonations, rather like an actor trying to prevent a panic when someone cries "Fire!" Tumulty, however, brought the smell of smoke, at intervals, into the room. His optimism over the telegrams gone, he wandered in to moan that this intervening Sunday would give the political "crooks" time to make nefarious deals. Or to groan about persistent rumors that Bryan would try to cause a deadlock which would eventually make him the nominee. Woodrow ordered him to sit down and eat, but Tumulty only stared at him and fled to collect more rumors.

On Monday morning, when the balloting began again, there was still no important change of votes. But in the afternoon, Ellen, the girls and the relatives, sitting in a weary daze on the porch, saw the press emerge en masse from their tents and run toward the house. Not noticing that the Governor was not there, they shouted, "You've passed him, you've passed him!" Then everybody ran together to the Governor's office to tell him the news. Would he make a statement?, the reporters asked.

Woodrow said, "You might say that Governor Wilson received the news that Champ Clark had dropped to second place in a riot of silence."

On Tuesday, July third, Woodrow Wilson was nominated on the forty-sixth ballot. When the flash came, Joe Tumulty rushed out on the porch waving his arms toward a grove of trees. A brass band, collected and instructed by the Governor's secretary the day before, emerged and marched toward the house, blaring, "Hail to the chief." A reporter, standing near Woodrow and Ellen while a cheering crowd gathered, said, "Governor, you don't seem a bit excited."

The professor in politics said, "I can't effervesce."

The Presidential campaign of 1912, three-sided and therefore unique, has been described too often to need retelling, and no letters have been found to reveal Woodrow's and Ellen's private thoughts and emotions during that time. Optimistic Democrats claimed that, with the Republican party split in two, neither Theodore Roosevelt nor William Howard Taft could win. Woodrow made no predictions, yet all through those strenuous months he seemed to his family to be more buoyant than usual. He was also as unperturbed by the possibility of defeat as he had been before the New Jersey election. The only thing that upset him and sometimes tortured Ellen was the now pitiless blaze of publicity in which they had to live. The little house on Cleveland Lane was always more or less in a state of siege. Ellen in a letter to a friend mourned their "old lost peace" and added, "I dare not even let my mind dwell too much on that." * Woodrow called it "slavery."

On election day Woodrow walked to the polling place—a small fire-engine house—and stood in line awaiting his turn. The other voters greeted him with awed respect which he tried, in vain, to break down.

* To Dr. Edward M. Chapman—1912.

In the afternoon he escaped from the house, filled to bursting with people, and took a long, rather wistful walk with a friend. In the evening after supper, he sat by the fire in Ellen's studio while she read Browning aloud to him. Outside the closed door, Joe Tumulty, surrounded by the candidate's relatives, friends and excited daughters, answered the constantly clamorous telephone. At ten o'clock the front door burst open and newsmen shouted, "He's elected!" In the distance, the bell in the tower of Nassau Hall was tolling wildly. Woodrow and Ellen heard the shouting and the bell, but he stayed in the studio while she came out, heard the news and went back alone to tell him. There was no elation in his face when they appeared in the doorway, and the crowd in the living-room was quiet while his daughters hugged him and others shook his hand. But when the Princeton students arrived with torch lights, singing "Old Nassau," Woodrow was deeply moved. Standing on an old rocking chair which Tumulty had dragged out on the porch, he spoke to them in a voice not as firm as usual. "I have no feeling of triumph to-night, but a feeling of solemn responsibility. I know the very great task that lies ahead of me and the men associated with me. I look almost with pleading to you, the young men of America, to stand behind me, to support me in the new administration. Wrongs have been done but they have not been done malevolently. We must have the quietest temper in what we are going to do. We must not let any man divert us. . . . I know what you want and we will not accomplish it through a single man or a single session of the Houses of Congress, but by long processes running through the next generation. . . ."

Then, very simply, he told them about some of the things he hoped to accomplish.

Ten days after the election Woodrow took his family with him to Bermuda. He needed a rest, time to think quietly, escape from ubiquitous newsmen and office seekers; and by sheer grim determination, he managed to achieve these necessities. It was impossible on the ship, where Secret Service men guarded him day and night, reporters assigned to accompany him sought interviews and passengers followed him with cameras. But the house in Bermuda, lent to the Wilsons by Mrs. Peck, now Mrs. Hulbert, was on a secluded point overlooking the sea and there was a high wall around it. The gate was kept locked and no one, not even the Secret Service, was allowed to come in except by invitation. Bermudians and British residents, with their habitual respect for privacy, were very considerate, even aloof.

Woodrow chose most of his Cabinet while he was in Bermuda. In his usual methodical way he made a series of charts—a page for each man under consideration, listing the details of their careers, their qualifications, their friends, even the sort of wives they had. His daughters were fascinated by the charts, and exasperated because he took a long time to make up his mind.

One day Nellie said, "Well, I don't really care who you choose, as long as you make McAdoo Secretary of the Treasury."

Woodrow laughed. "Imagine!" he said to Ellen, "Nell wants me to appoint a man to the Cabinet just because she likes him."

He liked to tease and did not tell her that he had already decided to appoint McAdoo to the Treasury, Bryan as Secretary of State and Josephus Daniels, newspaper owner from Raleigh, North Carolina, as Secretary of the Navy.

On March the third, 1913, Woodrow and Ellen came out of the house on Cleveland Lane, looked at the newsmen, the Secret Service and a large, loaned automobile, and suddenly rebelled. They would walk, alone, to the station, Woodrow announced, and no one dared to protest.

The President-elect and his wife made a detour. Library Place was not on the way to the station, but they wanted to pass by the house which they had struggled and worked and saved to build. It was not a sad pilgrimage. They had worked for this day too. But they knew what lay ahead and they needed one last glimpse of the place where, for seven happy years, they had lived with peace.

When they finally arrived at the station, most of Princeton's population was there, milling around the special train. Five coaches attached to the train were jammed with undergraduates singing "Old Nassau" at the top of their lungs. They had asked to go along as an escort in place of the customary delegation of officials, soldiers and sailors which Woodrow had refused. It was a fine, noisy, heart warming farewell to the man who had been "kicked upstairs to the White House" by Princeton's Board of Trustees.

Part 4
The Presidency

On the fourth of March, after the inauguration ceremony and the parade and the buffet luncheon were over, Ellen went upstairs to the large, high-ceilinged bedroom she had chosen for Woodrow and herself. Her daughters followed a little later and found her standing by a window. She turned, held out her hand to them and said, "Come and look, children." There was a formal garden below the window with graveled paths and geometrical flower beds and a neat lawn. Ellen said, "I'll change that. It will be our rose garden with a high hedge around it." And after a moment, "Now let's go and look at this house." The girls smiled, for it was clear that she was already planning to make the stateliest and most "troublesome" place of all more homelike.

In April, when a Princeton friend came for a visit and expressed surprise over Ellen's comfortable, informal rearrangement of the second floor, where White House families live, and the ease with which she had adapted herself to her new environment, Ellen said, "It's just a bigger Prospect—Sea Girt with no servant problem."

The number and variety of her duties had appalled her at first, but not for long. She planned each day in advance, hour by hour, except Sundays, which were devoted exclusively, after church, to quiet afternoons and evenings with her family. But her schedule was never so rigidly adhered to that she could not interrupt it instantly when Woodrow needed her for counsel and encouragement, and she included nothing which she did not consider directly, or indirectly, helpful to him.

She realized that the American people had a right to know, even to be curious, about the family of every man they sent to the White House, yet because she believed that they respected a President whose wife remained in the background, she refused to give interviews, to appear on public platforms without her husband, or to pose for newspaper photographers. She no longer resented the blaze of publicity to which her daughters were subjected. They had been trained to behave with dignity and would, she believed, be a credit to their father, but their private lives were their own, and when stories began to be published about the men to whom, according to rumor, Margaret, Jessie or Eleanor, were engaged, she was indignant.

Woodrow was angry. One day at his weekly press conference * he faced the group with fire in his eyes.

"I am a public character for the time being," he said, "but the ladies of my household are not public characters, because they are not servants of the government. I deeply resent the treatment they are receiving at the hands of the newspapers. Take the case of one of my daughters. It is a violation of my own instincts even to speak of these things, but she has been represented as being engaged to this or that and the other man in different parts of the country, in some instances to men she has never even met. It is a constant and intolerable annoyance. These things are printed without any attempt to verify them by communication with the White House. . . . If this continues, I shall deal with you not as President, but man to man." The newsmen were more careful after that.

Woodrow, as well as Ellen, had lost no time before going into action. Three days after his inauguration he had called a special session of Congress for the seventh of April to consider the tariff and currency bills which, along with the rest of his legislative reforms, he had outlined to the voters during his campaign and itemized in his inaugural speech. Now, with only a month in which to prepare the bills in detail he spent long hours in consultation with Cabinet members and Congressmen. At the same time many appointments to executive offices and diplomatic posts had to be made before his administration could function. Finding the right men, while an army of "deserving Democrats" and patronage-minded Congressmen clamorously presented their claims, was a maddening experience. He was faced also with an ominous international crisis.

A month before Woodrow Wilson's inauguration Victoriano Huerta had deposed Francisco Madero, President of Mexico, and taken over the government. A few days later he sanctioned the assassination of Madero and the vice-president. Huerta then demanded recognition by the United States Government, but President Taft had refrained from any action in order not to embarrass the new administration. American oil companies and other interests with investments in Mexico favored recognition, while American citizens, stranded there and afraid that their property would be confiscated, demanded U.S. military intervention to depose Huerta. Woodrow had now to investigate the situation and decide as soon as possible what to do about it.

In the latter part of June when humid heat settled down on Washington and the Congressmen wanted to go home, he urged them to stay in session until the bills were passed, and announced that he would take no vacation either. He had rented the American author Winston

---

* Wilson was the first President to establish the custom of "free for all" press conferences at the White House.

Churchill's house, called "Harlakenden," in Cornish, New Hampshire, where he had hoped to spend part of the summer, and because intense heat often made Ellen ill, he insisted that she and the girls must go there without him. He would, he promised, be with them on the Fourth of July and on weekends whenever it was possible. Ellen rebelled at first. He needed her. How could he send her away? But he told her that he would worry about her if she stayed, and she gave in. On the train, she shut the door of her stateroom and cried.

In Cornish when Woodrow's first letter came she did not cry. She read it proudly to her daughters and Helen Bones, who was now her private secretary:

29 June, 1913

THE WHITE HOUSE

My darling Sweetheart,

I can hardly keep back the tears as I write this morning. It is a bitter, bitter thing that I cannot come to my dear ones; but the duty is clear, and that ought to suffice. I cannot choose as an individual what I shall do; I must choose always as President, ready to guard at every turn and in every possible way the success of what I have to do for the people. Apparently the little things count quite as much as the big in this strange business of leading opinion and securing action; and I must not kick against the pricks. I am feeling physically quite fit again; the weather has freshened and grown comfortable once more; there are many ways in which I can make things easier; and so duty wears a by no means intolerable aspect. The President is a superior kind of slave, and must content himself with the reflection that the *kind* is superior!

It came about in this way. I had declined the invitation to Gettysburg along with all others and very much as a matter of course, and it had practically gone out of my mind, as I think you know. But yesterday Mitchell Palmer * called me up and sought an interview with me about it, saying that at first he had looked upon the matter with a good deal of indifference, as something I could afford to put upon the same footing with other invitations, but that, as the event drew near and he listened to the talk about it, among our friends in the two houses and out of them,

* Democratic Congressman from Pennsylvania. Later Attorney General in Wilson's Cabinet.

he came to see that it was something we had to take very seriously indeed. It is no ordinary celebration. It is the half-century anniversary of the turning battle of the war. Both blue and gray are to be there. It is to celebrate the end of all feeling as well as the end of all strife between the sections. Fifty years ago, almost, also on the fourth of July, Mr. Lincoln was there (in the midst of business of the most serious and pressing kind, and at great personal cost and sacrifice to himself). If the President should refuse to go this time and should, instead, merely take a vacation for his own refreshment and pleasure, it would be hotly resented by a very large part of the public. It would be suggested that he is a Southerner and out of sympathy with the occasion. In short, it would be more than a passing mistake; it would amount to a serious blunder. And so I surrendered—the more readily because all this would have been so serious a misapprehension of my own real attitude. Nothing, while I am President must be suffered to make an impression which will subtract by an iota from the force I need to do the work assigned me. I can do this without any real risk to my health, and shall lose, not what I need but only what I want (ah, how much!)

My glimpse of Harlakenden is only postponed, my sweet one; and I shall study to get a little pleasure and frequent refreshment here. I shall probably go off a couple of days this week, before the fourth, on one of the boats, for a sniff of the sea. I shall play golf more often. I shall curtail as much as I dare the weary interviewing at the office. In brief, I shall thrive, *if only I surrender my will to the inevitable.*

How shall I tell you what my heart is full of? It is literally full to overflowing with yearning love for you, my incomparable darling, and for the sweet daughters whom I love with so deep a passion, and admire as much as I love! I dare not pour it out to-day. I am too lonely. I must think quietly and not with rebellion. The big house is very still: I must copy its stately peace, and try to be worthy of the trust of those whom I try to serve and those who make me happy by their wonderful love!

Your own
Woodrow

Ten days later he spent a week in Cornish, and while he was there Ellen, always concerned about his health, made him promise to save every possible hour on weekdays for rest or recreation and to write to her only on Sundays.

She, however, wrote to him almost every day, after she had been assured that this was what he wanted.

The President's Cottage
Cornish, New Hampshire *

... I am wondering if you would like me to write every day. I would of course be glad to. Somehow I have a feeling that perhaps you are too busy to be bothered with daily letters. ...

20 July, 1913

THE WHITE HOUSE

My precious Sweetheart,

What shall I say to a little girl whom I love with all my heart and yearn for almost more than I can stand who *asks me if I would like a daily letter,* saying that she had hesitated to write every day because she was afraid I was too busy to be "bothered" with a daily letter now! I do not know how to explain things to such a dull person! You dear, dear goose! Why, I have not begged for a letter every day, and do not beg for it now, only because I cannot return the infinite favour in kind. I do not wish to be selfish, and it would be selfish to ask for more than I can give: for I am vain enough to believe that you would like a letter every day from me! What a treat it would be: for the loneliness of being without you is sometimes more than I can bear, it seems to me,—but your days are full, very full, and I want them to be, of painting and driving and seeing interesting people and making friends, and of anything and everything that may make the summer rich with refreshment and of the things that you do not and cannot get here. I am so happy, for your sake, that you are there and not here. I am well, perfectly well. I do not wither under the heat, even when it is hot; and I do not need to be taken care of,—indeed I fancy that I need as little as any man in Washington, outside the things that affect my heart; and my heart is quietest when things are as I would have them for you. So there is the whole matter; write me whenever you *feel* like it and as often as you can without interfering with the things I most want you to have and do!

* Some of Ellen's letters are not dated.

Yes, it was largely through Mrs. Borden Harriman's * initiative, Tumulty † tells me, that the conference was brought about which will lead, I still hope, to a settlement of the difficulty between the railroads and their trainmen and conductors, and I am so glad that she got the credit that was due to her! I say "I still hope" because the railroad authorities have, since the conference, introduced matters of controversy which may again throw matters out of joint, in what seems to me entire disregard of the strict good faith of our understanding of last Monday.

Monday morning! less than a week ago! It seems a month since I left Cornish! The days are so full of matters of consequence and even anxiety that they count for quite four times the hours they contain. And yet they have a certain relish in them too. I would not have you think that it is all burden or that the burden distresses. It is heavy, very heavy, but the strength to carry it seems to go along with it, and there is the satisfaction of the task set forward. Things continue to go on the whole very well indeed. We have a difficult Banking and Currency Committee to deal with in the House; but by constant watchfulness and tact and suggestion we manage to keep things going as they should go; and the tariff matter is at last in a way to approach its conclusion.

Thank dear Helen for her note, enclosing the limericks . . . I was glad to get the limericks, but so much more glad to receive Helen's own sweet note. I hope she will be obliged to write to me frequently! Give her a heart-full of love.

Ah! my sweet, sweet Nelly! how shall I tell you what those eight days at Cornish meant to me! They were like a new honeymoon! All the days were days of contentment, renewal, and delight. I begin to think that I am just learning what a holiday means. Perhaps when we were college people we were a bit spoiled. We had so much liberty that we did not realize how precious it was. Now I know. And it pleases me to learn of the friendships you are making, and the new experiences you are having. Bully for Mr. Vonnoh! ‡ I hope the picture will be a success, even if it must be "impressionistic". Is he up to a really good thing? Give to my dear ones as much love as they can wish for or imagine from

---

* Daughter-in-law of railroad magnate E. H. Harriman, and ardent Wilson supporter.

† Joseph Tumulty was now secretary to the President.

‡ Robert Vonnoh, artist, was painting a group picture of Ellen and the daughters.

their father, and keep for yourself, my adorable darling, whatever is your heart's desire from

> *Your devoted*
> *Woodrow*

Tell Nennie * I have sent the left-hand golf clubs I promised.

The President's Cottage

My own darling,

Your wonderful letter came this morning and you may well believe that my heart has been full to overflowing with the joy of it ever since. How wonderful you are to take time to write such a letter when things are pressing so upon you! I shall keep this special letter among my chief treasures always.

Of course I knew you would like a little love message daily. What I was really thinking, I suppose, was that a longish letter giving the little details of our days here might take up too much of your time and attention. And I am sure you *do not* crave a daily comment on the political situation!

> *27 July, 1913*

THE WHITE HOUSE

My darling,

How incomparably sweet and dear you are! Your letters warm my heart so and give me so constant and vivid a realization of you that even this barren house seems full of you, my heart is serene and strong for every turn of the day, and even loneliness is tempered with a delightful sense of moving in an atmosphere of assured love and comradeship. Bless you for it all!

Something of the way I feel must have stolen into my letter of last week to make you speak of it as you do. It seems to me that I never loved you as I do now! It would be strange if none of the feeling which moves me so deeply and governs me so constantly got into my letters, written with my whole mind and heart intent upon you.

* Another nickname for Eleanor.

Please do not be anxious about me. There is absolutely nothing to cause anxiety. The weather is excellent. Even when it is hottest there is some life in it and I am never overcome by it, but always rest and am revived very easily. The strain is great, very great; eternal watchfulness, incessant shifts of personal sensitiveness and jealousy, incalculable currents to be watched for and offset and controlled, an infinite drift of talk and comment and conjecture about affairs in Mexico and elsewhere, where we cannot control and cannot foresee; but it is not a breaking strain. Discount what you see in the papers. The difficulties in handling the currency question * are not as great as the papers would have the country believe. It happens, by very hard luck, that practically *all* the men likely to oppose and give trouble, whether in the House or in the Senate, are on the committees now handling the matter. When once it is out of their hands, I believe that we shall have comparatively plain sailing. At any rate, everything is well in hand up to date. I will tell you if anything really goes wrong. The Senate is infinitely slow, but even it is feeling the impatience of the country and is likely to act sooner than was expected. . . .

The sum of the whole matter is, therefore, that so long as you and the dear ones with you keep well and are happy, and so long as you continue to feed me with the sweet affection upon which I live, I shall fare excellently,—just as well as a man could who was never intended to be a bachelor for so much as seven days together. Both Tumulty and Dr. Grayson † are living with me, and they wear extremely well. Tumulty is an exceedingly poor bachelor. He *cannot* stand it for seven days together. By Saturday his staying powers are exhausted and he makes straight for Avon where his little flock are. I'm not saying I would not do the same, if mine were so accessible! The Doctor and I played golf three times this week, and are great chums. He went to church with me this morning. Last week I went alone.

But I do not sit down here on Sunday afternoon to think and speak of this dull place or this dull life here, but to think and speak of you: the dearest indulgence I can allow myself. It was so sweet, the other

* A currency reform bill, called eventually The Federal Reserve Act, had been presented to Congress by Wilson on June 23. Passed by the House of Representatives September 18, by the Senate December 19.

† Cary T. Grayson, U.S. Navy doctor, appointed White House personal physician by Wilson.

night, to pick up a New York afternoon paper and see the picture of you I enclose. And the story with it is most attractive, whether true or not. Bless you, how everybody up there will love and admire you before the summer is over. The glimpses you give me of what you are doing enable me to see just how charming and natural and genuine a friend and neighbour you are making of yourself. I like to sit and imagine how pretty and charming you are in it all! I adore you! No President but myself ever had *exactly* the right sort of wife! I am certainly the most fortunate man alive!

I go to the theatre twice a week (this week the plays were delightful and delightfully played), and I take long rides, I play golf as often as possible, I do everything I can to keep elastic and young, but the real source of youth and renewal for me is my love for you, the sweetheart I picked out the moment I laid eyes on her and who has been my fountain of joy and comfort ever since.... We are wedded sweethearts. If there be any sweeter thing in life, I have not found it.

Deepest love to all.

Your own
Woodrow

July 28th

The President's Cottage

My own darling,

Your wonderful, your adorable Sunday letter has just come and has made me fairly drunk with happiness. I would give anything to be able to *express* my love as perfectly as you do, dear heart, for then indeed I might hope to make you as happy as you make me. But then no one else in the world can express anything so perfectly as you,—so there's no help for it, unless when you write those "great heart words" you will say to yourself "her heart is as great as mine and it echoes all I say, though she has not the genius for expression."

Oh, how I adore you! I am perfectly sure that you are the greatest, most wonderful, most lovable man who *ever* lived. I am not expressing an opinion, I am simply stating a self-evident fact.

Certainly such love is the real source of youth and renewal for women—for me—and it is a joy too deep for words to hear you say and feel that it is the same for you.

God bless you my darling, my darling....

July 31st

The President's Cottage

... We are all much concerned about the terrible storm in Washington and the wrecked trees in the White House grounds. Do make someone write to us just what the damage is—how *many* trees suffered.

I am also concerned at the report in the "Times" that Congress is disposed to take a different view from your own as regards Wilson * and the Mexican situation. He is said to have "made a very favourable impression" on it. I don't want *you* to be troubled to write me on these points—make Mr. Tumulty do it!...

With love inexpressible
Your devoted
Eileen

3 August, 1913

THE WHITE HOUSE

My precious darling,

How I look forward to Sunday and to my little chat with my darling! The weeks between are very long. I feel so ungrateful reading your daily letters, which are the tonic that keeps me going, and yet sending nothing in return but this, a weekly letter. How sweet you are in what you say of these letters! I can only explain their satisfying you by the fact that they are indeed the outpouring of my heart to you. All the longing of the week is concentrated in them: all the sweet thoughts I have of you; all the consciousness of what you mean, and have always meant, in my life; all the thoughts both of the past and of the future that are the food of my heart's life. I can think of nothing, I can feel nothing, while I write, but only *you*. My days are not half so full of anxiety and of the sense of deep responsibility as they are of you, my absent darling, who yet plays the leading part in my life every minute of the day. Bless you

* Henry Lane Wilson, U.S. Ambassador to Mexico, appointed by President Taft.

for the letters! They are meat and drink to me. Each day, as one of them is laid before me on my table in the office, as the tide of business swirls about me, a certain brightness comes into everything and the immediate task is made easy.

Do not worry about the storm. It was bad enough. It was terrible, indeed. . . . The whole air grew black as night. Some of the finest trees on these grounds were uprooted entirely and others were twisted to pieces: for it was not a hurricane but a cyclone, which picked and chose which it would torture amongst the trees. . . . There has not been such a storm here since 1897.

And do not worry about the Mexican situation, either. It is bad enough, in all conscience, as the storm was, but the newspapers do not know what they are talking about. The Senate is inclined to form an opinion of its own, but it is not inclined to interfere with me, so far as the Democratic members are concerned; and my policy will soon be too clearly disclosed to be interfered with. Tomorrow or next day ex-gov. Lind, of Minnesota, will start for Mexico City, commissioned to advise the embassy there as my personal representative, and with definite instructions of mediation in his pocket; Henry Lane Wilson's resignation will be asked for and accepted; and foreign governments will presently be informed what we are about in a way which will make it very rude for them to interfere or advise. They have left us a perfectly free hand so far, the papers (that is, the Hearst papers) to the contrary notwithstanding. It looks a little as if the situation were clearing up a bit of itself. It is an anxious business, but not impossible, and my head has never been as muddled about it as the heads of some editors seem to be. There is never an hour that I do not have to be watchful; but so far all is as well as could have been expected. And the situation with regard to the currency seems satisfactory, too.

There is no reason in the world why on Sundays I should not take time to make love to my sweetheart. What an adorable family I have, and how incomparable is the dear little lady who is its crown and glory! I shall never understand how such fortune fell to me: such a wife, such lovely daughters, such sweet cousins as Helen, such friends as Lucy and Mary *: such faith and confidence and unselfish love to sustain me: such a glow of love keeping my own heart fresh and fit for every turn! I am

* Misses Lucy and Mary Smith, New Orleans friends—at Harlakenden for the summer.

more happy and more fortunate than any man whose life I have known. It seems to me that I have been lifted to such things as I have accomplished merely by the inspiration of love and faith and sweet example. I am not good at all. I am only the fruit and reflection of noble loving women and faithful friends....

Sunday, August 3rd

The President's Cottage

... We went again to hear Dr. Fitch and had another delightful sermon. He read the story of the three children in the fiery furnace in a way that made us feel as if we had never heard it before. Of course the world and its troubles is the fiery furnace into which we are all flung, but if the Son of God walks with us we will pass through unhurt. His picture of our human predicament was very touching—of how we were thrown in *bound*. I only thought he failed to bring out the finest touch in the story if he used it as a human allegory, viz. that it was the fire test that loosed their bonds and set them *free*. "Did we not cast three men bound into the midst of the fire?" They answered and said unto the king, "True, oh King." He answered and said, "Lo, I see four men loose walking into the midst of the fire and they have no hurt; and the form of the fourth is like the Son of God."

5th August, 1913

THE WHITE HOUSE

My precious darling,

This being "Cabinet day" and there being no Cabinet here, I am surprised to find myself with a few minutes during which I have no engagement, tho' one is liable to pounce upon me unbeknownst at any moment; and my heart is so full of you that I must send just a few lines to unburden it. I am all right; the heat has lightened considerably; I play golf now almost every day and keep in fine shape; but oh! the difference to me that my darling is not here. Don't beg to come down here to see me, *please*, my darling! How am I to say No? And yet if I were to say Yes and you were to come, I should in fact be unhappy. When I look into the very centre of my thoughts I know that my real peace of mind depends upon your being where you are, engaged as you are. That my heart is set upon. My steadiness here depends in reality upon the programme being seen through to the end....

Be a Spartan wife (whom I can see only by stealth!) and it will make it easy for me to be a Spartan statesman. And yet how am I to get two incompatible things? I give you this advice (or, rather, beg this kind of love of you) and yet want *also* just the opposite.... I *want* you to long for me and to be an insurgent against the circumstances that separate us! In short I am a doting lover, and yet at the same time a man trying to live out his ideals, the ideals he has dreamed of ever since he was a boy, in regard to public life and political duty.... The little cry for me you utter in this letter that came this morning, and so nearly broke me down, is sweet to my ear: I should be unhappy if I did not hear it once and again; but you are for the nonce a soldier's wife. How deeply I love both the soft and the stern aspects of life, the romantic and the harshly real!

This letter is written to pour out my heart to you: the tenderest and deepest things it contains, my loyalty and admiration and love and longing,—to relieve my heart of a strain which words will a little ease. And yet I speak the mere truth when I say that all is well with me. I am strong, confident in my work, and willing to stick at it for the whole summer without a moment of repining or looking back....

Ellen, artist and lover of beauty, would have been completely happy that summer if Woodrow had been always with her. They had chosen Cornish for their summer home for several reasons. It was a beautiful place where the Connecticut River flowed between wooded hills and lovely meadows. And Ellen's favorite kind of people lived there—artists, writers, sculptors and poets—who, she hoped, would not treat her like a celebrity. She was not disappointed. The Wilsons were welcomed with simple hospitality, which Ellen returned in kind. They never questioned her right to privacy, and when the President's wife, with her easel, stool and palette, sat painting happily in the fields and woods no one came near her. The girls were invited to informal parties where no one stared or questioned them. Jessie's engagement to Francis Sayre * had been announced early in July, and when he came to visit at Harlakenden, the colony seemed unaware that his name had been featured in every newspaper in the country. He and Jessie were allowed, like any other engaged couple, all the time alone they wanted.

* Then Assistant District Attorney, New York City.

Among the Wilsons' new friends were Maxfield Parrish, Augustus St. Gaudens, Witter Bynner, Norman Hapgood, the ornithologist Ernest Harold Baynes, and the famous poet Percy MacKaye. Mr. Baynes hoped to establish a sanctuary for birds in a forest grove not far from Cornish, and Mr. MacKaye had written a play called *Bird Masque* which they planned to present in order to raise the necessary funds. MacKaye read the Masque to Ellen and her daughters and asked Margaret to sing the opening verse and Nellie to play the ''Bird Spirit.'' Ellen, not sure that Woodrow would approve, wrote for his permission, and also did some private lobbying for a bill which was troubling her artist friends.

August 5th

The President's Cottage

My own darling,

Many, many thanks from us *all* for your dear letter! It has made us all happy. You assuredly are the most lovable person in the world—not to mention any of your other traits. So naturally you live in an atmosphere of ''love and faith and confidence''. I am glad, darling, that you feel and enjoy the glow of it. You make me happy all the time just by being what you are,—but superlatively so when you show that *you* are happy. I love you until my heart fairly aches with it!...

They are to have here a little ''masque'' written by the playwright Percy MacKaye in the interests of a society for bird conservation. It is to be given in the forest, no one present but invited guests, and to be a very ''high class'' thing altogether. There are to be only some six actors besides a band of children and they came today to ask Nell to be the ''bird spirit''. I do not see the least objection but to make sure I told them I would ask you before committing myself. So please drop me a line about it as soon as you read this. You know, of course, that this colony is rather famous for its high class pageants and such things. But this is quite a simple little affair—not like its elaborate pageants.

I went to the club today and they discussed the duty on pictures and decided to follow the example of many other artist organizations and send a petition to the Senate. It seems to me that this duty is really ridiculous in view of the fact that the very persons to be, supposedly, benefitted by it are to a man opposed to it and that the revenue derived from it is *admitted* to be so small as to be almost negligible. Can't something be done about it? It is actually *worse* than the one it replaces, for that admitted pictures free if they were 20 years old and this requires that they shall be *50 years old*.... You know the regular House bill admitted all art free. This trouble only began in the Senate. I think that the artists in working so hard for free art are really giving the country a wonderful and beautiful example of real patriotism and of unselfish devotion to the ideal. For it would of course be to their personal advantage to have the foreign things kept out....

This was a gorgeous violet and green and gold day with splendid clouds. It fairly took one's breath away. Ah, but the world is a beautiful place in spite of all the drawbacks!

I love you darling

Your own
Eileen.

7 August, 1913

THE WHITE HOUSE

Darling,

I have no objection in the world to Nell's taking the part they want her to take in the little forest play. I only wish I were going to see her in it. I know that she will be fascinating.

I shall of course do what I can to get the duty on art and the objectionable provisions about the birds taken out of the bill when it gets into conference. I have not yet had a chance to take the matter up; and this is not yet the moment.

God bless you all, as your love blesses me!

In desperate haste,
Your own
Woodrow

Ellen had always been interested in the origin and history of her forebears, and one branch of these was born and bred in New England.

August 7th, 1913

The President's Cottage

My own darling,

We are leaving this morning at 9.30. It is a brilliant, beautiful day and cool besides. So we are all in high spirits and sure to have a delightful time.... We choose our stopping place today partly to break the journey and partly because it leads through Bridgewater and Hebron where the Hoyts * lived. They are on the shores of Newfound Lake, a beautiful sheet of water, and also on the shores of the lake is a little grave-yard in which my great-grandfather and mother and their forebears are buried.... So this is a "pious pilgrimage" as well as a pleasure trip. How perfectly enchanting it would all be if our darling were here with us! My eyes fill with tears in spite of myself as I think of it. Is that very bad for a soldier's wife....

God bless you my darling....

10 August, 1913

THE WHITE HOUSE

My own darling,

How sweet is this Sunday afternoon hour! All the turmoil of the week still for a little space; a quieting sleep in the morning, a church service that takes me back to the days when I was a boy in the South, and then an hour all my own when I can sit down and think of nothing *but* the little lady who carries my happiness in her heart, talk only to her, live in the full consciousness of all that she is and of all that she has been to me.... I must (whatever Nature may have indicated to the contrary in my ornery appearance) have been meant for a lover. I am not happy unless I am opening my heart to those I love and look to for my life. I cannot tell you how constantly my thoughts follow you every day! In the midst of the most engrossing business, I am conscious of what you are doing,—at any rate, conscious of *you*, and your image lurks all the while just about me in the dim spaces of my imagination.

How I enjoy your life at Cornish! I could not be happy if I were there, because I would know all the while that it was my duty to be

* Ellen's maternal ancestors.

here, where affairs wait upon me, for some decision or other, every hour of the day. That knowledge would spoil even the sweet content of being with you. But I share your life up there, none the less. My mind is full all day long of happy images of what you are doing, how you are dressed, how you look, how you move among the people who are learning to know and love you, how the dear ones move round about you, how your sweet eyes look when you feel that you must go upstairs and write to your waiting lover. *I* am not bound so long as you are free!... In order to serve me you have only to go through each day with zest, grow more brown in the good air, with that delicious mellow blend of red and brown that is so characteristic of your dear cheeks when you are a great deal in the open in summer time....

I am perfectly well... struggling with difficulties (chiefly the difficulty of dealing with a man,—Huerta,—whose mind and passions I cannot understand and am therefore at a loss to meet) but with no moment of dismay and with a calm and resolute purpose as I feel my way from step to step; and ready to enjoy the game out at the country club or the play at the theatre whenever the hour of momentary release turns up. In short, thanks to the freedom of those I love and my re-assuring thoughts about them, I am in fine fettle. And my game of golf at last shows slight signs of improving. I am *learning* a little from day to day, with numerous disheartening back-slidings, but a movement for the better which can be seen even with the naked eye if the measurement be from week to week and not from day to day.... The doctor goes to church with me and is a very sedate and excellent imitation of a Presbyterian. He is a sterling enough character to make a good Christian of whatever name or sort the label may be! His golf is improving as fast as mine, if it is not improving faster, so that I have stimulation enough; and we try it now about six times a week. There is no personal news. I do not know which paper you read, and therefore cannot tell you which parts of the general news you think you know is false. Believe very little that you read in the Times!...

August 11, 1913

The President's Cottage

...I am getting too many invitations for the evenings—three already for this week. They are all too nice and informal for me to assume the "presidential attitude" and decline. Also I must give two more teas next week;—and the "discussion" club next Tuesday! The subject is "Does Human Nature Change?" What do you think about that!... The papers this morning seem less panicky about Mexico and as if they and the Senate were beginning to have some faint understanding and appreciation of your plan and policy; which, I take it, is to try to give the Mexicans (if they can be induced to take it) a great lesson in self-government; to show them that they could and they would settle their affairs without "shooting each other up". Oh, how I hope and pray, pray, pray that you may succeed! If only John Lind * had your eloquent tongue and great personality—*and* a command of Spanish....

August 12th, 1913

The President's Cottage

... I have your beloved letter and I could almost "wear it in my bosom" like a lovesick girl—it makes me so happy.... Oh, but you are splendid!

August 13th, 1913

The President's Cottage

My own darling,

I have just finished reading the papers and feel distinctly cheered about Mexico.... I have just returned from a little dinner at the Stephen Parrish's. Helen † and I were invited and we had a delightful time. There were just that perfect old dear, Stephen himself, the sweet young cousin who keeps house for him, the adorable Maxfield (Mrs. Max was not well) and Judge and Mrs. Hand. I think I have already written about her and how fine and unusual she is. He is very interesting too. I had not met him before. He is a Bull Moose but seems to be infatuated with you in spite of it; he can talk of nothing else. He says he met you some years ago and you impressed him then as the most powerful personality he had ever seen....

* Sent by W.W. as special commissioner to Mexico.
† Miss Helen Bones—Woodrow's cousin and Ellen's secretary.

12 August, 1913

THE WHITE HOUSE

... I must steal a few minutes to reassure you about Mexico ... Huerta was bluffing, of course, and nothing has come of it but to make him a little more ridiculous. Lind is in no sort of danger, and is just the well balanced sort not to be disquieted by what goes on about him. The demonstration Huerta got up on the night of his arrival fell flat and made no impression on anybody. In brief, the situation is not changed. Huerta may not consent to entertain our proposals, but that is not the end of our peaceful program, so far as action by the United States is concerned. We shall then bring pressure of various kinds from various quarters to bear on him. . . .

So you see you might as well have slept Saturday night as not! You darling, how I love you for your deep concern to see my leadership sustained! ...

August 17th

The President's Cottage

... I have just seen in the papers that the drought is broken in the west and south, but not before the corn crop was reduced by several million dollars worth. Oh, I am so sorry, for anything that goes wrong with the crops will, I suppose, affect the popular view of the tariff—so reasonable are our dear people! But apparently it is not yet a calamity. . . .

There is quite a nice article about us at Harlakenden in the Sunday Magazine of the "World" today. And as it is written by a woman reporter who came up to get an interview from me, and whom I positively refused, I think she has rather heaped coals of fire on my head, for she certainly makes me a lovable person! It is absurdly sentimental, but there is no other objection to it. . . .

We had another fine sermon by Dr. Fitch today. . . . This time it was the translation of Elijah and the succession of Elisha, especially his request for a "double spirit of Elijah". The subject was really "The old order passeth giving place to new and God fulfills Himself in many ways." Elijah represented the old, stern, almost fierce spirit of *our* forbears, largely engaged, like Bunyan's pilgrim, in escaping from the

City of Destruction and denouncing the inhabitants. Elijah really *lived* in the wilderness. Elisha was of the new order in which the brotherhood of man is emphasized—the more "social" religion. At its best it "does not want anything, not even 'salvation' if it can't share it with the rest." And, by the way, if one thinks of it so it might justify Elisha's rather exacting demand for a *double* spirit of Elijah! One would need a double spirit if it is to go *all* around!

But don't you think that after all this "new order" is simply a return to the *oldest* order under Christ. His own religion was of the most modern "social" type. "John the Baptist came neither eating or drinking and ye say 'he hath a devil'. The Son of Man came eating and drinking and ye say 'Behold a gluttonous man and a wine-bibber, a friend of publicans and sinners.' "...

Woodrow Wilson never lost his faith in the American people. If they made a wrong decision it was always, he believed, because they had become confused by lies, or lack of information. He was always confident and relaxed when he spoke to crowds, felt "a sort of transformation," but he had never felt so close to them, individually, as he did that first summer in the White House, and in one of his most moving and revealing letters he told Ellen what had happened, and why.

17 August, 1913

THE WHITE HOUSE

My precious darling,

Henry McAlpin, of Savannah, dropped in to see me the other day, and what do you suppose he brought me? Our original marriage license, with your grandfather's signature and all the other correct endorsements on it! It seems that all this while, though I did not know it, I have been entitled to the possession of this original, it having been copied into the records of the clerk's office immediately upon its return. I wonder if you can imagine how it made me feel? I was as much thrilled as if the paper itself had been a tangible embodiment of all that has made my life bright and blessed. I never held in my hand anything more thoroughly and wholly romantic than that piece of paper....

The reason I do not speak of anything but love in these weekly letters to you, my sweet one, (leaving everything else in my life out of my reckoning) is, not that I am weary of everything that makes my weeks weary and anxious and laborious, but that I am jealous of this brief hour when I seem to be with you to the exclusion of the whole world and need to let the whole pent up passion of my days out into words, in order that my heart may not break. I cannot bear to bring anything in that does not touch directly our intimate selves. It is the single hour when I can be a lover and nothing else.... Love alone keeps my pulses going and makes the world of anxious business endurable.

I seem in my present isolation to feel more than ever my relations of fellowship and innate sympathy with all the unnamed people about me. The little children in the streets and on the roads, the plain people at the cottage doors and in the fields and coming and going in the hot city bring the tears to my eyes. My responsibility to them somehow makes me comprehend them better. I seem to know what they are thinking and what they are longing for. And the lamp that guides my thought in it all is my love for you and for our darling daughters, the sweet, incomparable little ladies who are the fruit and sanction of our love for one another,—or rather, what I know of *your* hearts. Loving you, I have learned how to love, and at last the whole world seems to me a lesson in love.... When you were here it did not mean much to me that my dressing-room was full of pictures of you, for you yourself were there, in your own dear, incomparable person, always ready to give me a sweet kiss or a tender embrace and let me feel the warm, palpitating love that filled you; but now they are to me almost like living images of yourself. It makes me happy to look into their eyes, which seem almost to kindle in response to mine. It relieves me a little of the pain at my heart to kiss them passionately. And they are a sort of history of you, for the enchanting series runs back to the time you were a mere slip of a girl. I keep away from the sitting-room. I live in the dressing-room, the bedroom and the study. I have got used to their stillness; and the dressing-room and bedroom are full of you, to my imagination.... My love! my love! you are all the world to me! I fill my thoughts all day long with your lovely person, the happy little household at Harlakenden, your freedom, your growing realization of what you mean to the people about you, old friends and new. There is no thought about you that is not delightful....

Ellen had never been a "clubwoman," but that summer she accepted an invitation to join a "discussion club" partly because she did not want to seem aloof, and also because the members were delightful women.

August 19th

My own darling,

It is six o'clock and my home meeting of the Club has just ended. ... The subject which I chose was "How can we best promote a fuller and more general appreciation of *American* art?" We had one good laugh over it. Someone said that we must not neglect to talk about the next generation—no discussion was complete without that! Later it was said (of course) that we should have, like the French, a Government bureau of art to purchase works of art, to give prizes, to encourage it in every possible way. Then I said I thought the Congressmen who would take that view were not yet born. So, after all, we *had* to drag in the next generation! ...

Well, all this gossip is very well but it is just whistling to keep my courage up, for I am consumed with anxiety about the Mexican situation. ... Oh, my darling, you are so brave and wise and well-poised ... I love you until it hurts. I think of you every moment. A thousand thanks for that *wonderful* letter.

Your own
Nell

19 August, 1913

THE WHITE HOUSE

My sweet darling,

I realize how unfair it is not to keep you posted about the essential things, at least, of politics. I ought not to be so selfish as to *confine* myself to love-making when I write. It is so much more important to me than anything else in the world, when you are concerned.

Lind was instructed to ask Huerta for assurances that he would not be a candidate at the elections; that the elections should occur at an earlier date than that fixed in October; that there should be an armistice agreed upon meanwhile; and that full guarantees of a free and fair election be given. These proposals have been rejected, and we are told, in effect, that the Huerta people regard us, Democrats, as only a temporary arrangement and without the real support of the country. It was our duty to propose a settlement and to offer our good offices to bring it about; but we have been rebuffed, and must choose another course. The absurd and sensational reports in this morning's papers, that we had been given until midnight of last night to recognize Huerta and that the chargé d'affaires had been given his passports, were of course utterly and maliciously false. It looks today as if some sort of conferences were still going on between Lind and Huerta. Probably we shall now simply take hands off, isolate Huerta, so far as we are concerned, and give them a certain time in which to settle their own affairs. Intervention must be avoided until a time comes when it is inevitable, which God forbid! This is all that is in my private mind at present. Fuller advices from Mexico City may point out another practicable course to pursue.... I am well and keeping my head....

August 20th

The President's Cottage

... To-morrow afternoon I have a tea party from 4.30 to 5.30—and at 6.30 I take the train for *Washington!* Ha! What is my lord to do about it? Nothing! Except perhaps meet me at the train. When he gets this it will be too late to say me nay.

I telegraphed Dr. Grayson this morning to be sure you were not coming here this week.... His answer came tonight. He says he thinks "it will be fine for me to come at this time." I told him, of course, not to tell you.... Oh, I am so glad to be going! Something tight about my heart seems to have loosened with the decision. Honestly I could not have stood it any longer with things apparently going so badly. I got your letter to-night telling about Huerta's attitude. Of course it is a relief that he is not behaving quite as badly as was reported.—Now tonight a fresh shock. "The World" reports that Owen * has "killed the

---

* Senator from Oklahoma.

currency bill.'' Killed the bill that was named for him. Is it false, or
has he gone mad? You may imagine how dazed and heartsick I am about
that.

But anyhow I am going to see my darling, *my darling,* and if he is
troubled share his anxieties. . . . I wonder if you know how tremendously
I love you. I don't know if I can sleep to-night because I **am to see
you!** . . .

When she returned to Cornish, Ellen wrote:

The President's Cottage

. . . I can't express to you what a delight it was to see you so **happy, or**
what a wonderful, warm feeling about my heart that blessed week has
left me. We were so close to each other that I hardly feel even yet as if
we are really separated. I am with you in spirit constantly. I hope you
have some consciousness of that left, in spite of all the burdens.

As ever your little wife
Eileen

7 September, 1913

THE WHITE HOUSE

My precious darling,

I enclose two things: a deposit slip for the salary for August and for
royalty from Houghton, Mifflin & Co., and an extract from a speech
made in the Senate the other day by Senator Morris Sheppard of Texas.
I was so much gratified, and indeed touched, by what he was generous
enough to say about me that I wanted you to see it and read it also. I
know that it will make you a warm friend of Senator Sheppard. He is a
most lovable man, whom I want you to know.

No; there is no new trouble about the currency. I have seen all along
that it is going to be a hard matter to get it through the Senate Committee on Banking and Currency without radical changes because of
Senator O'Gorman * and Senator Hitchcock,† who happen to be members

* Democrat, New York.
† Democrat, Nebraska.

of the committee and almost the only two serious critics of the bill on our side of the house in the Senate; but there are no new snags, so far as I can see, and I feel confident that things can be guided to a successful issue. Please do not let yourself be disturbed by what the newspapers say. They are all the while looking for something out of the usual. Trouble makes news; the ordinary course of business and of human conduct does not. Pay no attention to them,—particularly since those which are controlled are determined that there *shall* be trouble, and will make it themselves if no one else will. They do not determine what is going to happen in Washington, and so far as I can ascertain nothing new has turned up here in regard to the situation, either with regard to the currency or with regard to the tariff.

I took the liberty of breaking another precedent this morning by going to service in a white suit. It was simply too hot to wear a cloth suit, and I took the rules of propriety into my own hands. We (Dr. Grayson and I) had the Lord Provost of Glasgow to lunch with us, a very juicy and interesting and most unusual man he proved to be: a slim, scrawny little gentleman whose outside did not in the least give intimation of what was inside him; and slimmer than usual, he gave us to understand, because the heat of this handsome continent had taken some eight pounds of flesh off his bones since he landed. An American summer is a terrible ordeal for a Scotsman!...

Sundays are hard for me, dearest. I have time then to think—about myself,—and to feel lonely, and it is not profitable. It spoils me to go to Cornish. It softens my power of steadfast addiction to my duty. It fills me with a longing which it is impossible for me to conquer. Indeed, I do not know that I can truthfully say that I try to conquer it. It is sweet, even when it hurts, to dwell upon my love for you,—to sit and dream of you, to realize you, to fill my thoughts of every kind *of you*. It is like drinking my fill at the fountain from which most of my strength and happiness come. I would grow dry and hard, I fear, if I did not. Life would look gray and dun, and I would have no zest in anything. At any rate I can't help it. I must have you one way or another.

How I do daily bless you for your letters!

Every day either Foster * or Pat McKenna † comes in and stands one of them up in front of me about the middle of the morning as I

* White House Executive Secretary.
† Secretary.

work, evidently knowing perfectly well what it means to me and feeling that it will lighten the labour of the day, which both of them, bless them! want to do when they can. *I know* that it gives them real pleasure to put the letter there. As for me, it is meat and drink to me!...

Sept. 9th

The President's Cottage

My own darling,

Your dear, dear letter reached me last night and made me very happy —for a dozen different reasons. Every word of it exactly met and filled some deeply felt need either of my mind or heart. Bless you for it.

All you say about the currency was most reassuring and took a weight off my mind. I am waiting most eagerly now to hear that the Tariff Act has passed....

Nell and Ruth * were of course rehearsing. Everyone is wild over Nell's performance—her grace and her real gift as an actress. But, dear me, I don't know what I will do if this cold, shivery weather lasts until Friday night. It will be too dangerous for them with those thin things on. Nell's costume is charming—a white, shimmering silk slip and fluttering, rainbow-tinted gauze scarves arranged to suggest wings....

Mr. Vonnoh came around this morning to look at my work and gave me a criticism. He was very encouraging.... He said I was "a real artist" and that, if I will go on, my work will be really distinguished....

9 September, 1913

THE WHITE HOUSE

My darling,

Just a line to enclose this additional memorandum of deposit. It represents an unexpected royalty on "The New Freedom" † of which, it seems, some ten thousand copies have been sold.

I am perfectly well. I am not disturbed about the currency. To say

---

* Miss Ruth Hall, Eleanor (Nell) Wilson's friend from Princeton, one of the *Bird Masque* cast.

† Book of Wilson's 1912 campaign speeches, edited by William Bayard Hall. Title taken from Wilson's phrase: "I am seeking a new freedom."

that I have my back against the wall is ridiculous. The Senate is tired, some of the members of its Committee are irritable and will have to be indulged with a few days of rest, but there will be no insuperable difficulty in handling the situation so far as I can see. *Please* pay no attention to what the papers say.

Mexico is *sui generis.* I do not know what to make of it. The apparent situation changes like quicksilver. But the real situation, I fancy, remains the same, and is likely to yield to absent treatment.

I love you with all my heart. I love you all.

> *In tearing haste,*
> *Your own*
> *Woodrow*

Sept. 10th

The President's Cottage

My own darling,

I was so glad—so very happy over the passing of the Tariff bill. 'Twas good in you to send us the telegram, for no matter how sure we are that a thing is *going* to happen, we are always a little more sure when it *has* happened! And the majority was unexpectedly satisfactory. I had just come to bed when the telegram came and the girls rushed up wildly with it. You may imagine the rejoicing and the excitement in the house. ... What a wonderful six months it has been! It is so splendid that everyone knows how great you are! Even when they are opposed to you they feel your power....

The next weekend Woodrow went to Cornish, in time to see the masque, which was a great success. After he left, Ellen wrote to him:

Sept. 15th

The President's Cottage

My own darling,

Didn't we have a good time at the Fitch's and aren't they perfect dears? This was such a happy little visit, dearest. I wish I could tell you how intensely I enjoyed every moment of it....

Please *make* the office collect Sunday papers telling about the Masque. We know that a number of them were going to feature it with pictures and we shall be sadly disappointed if we miss them all. Aren't our daughters wonderful girls and adorable? And how intensely they all love you! It really is a sort of adoration and Helen is just as bad as the rest! If your happiness depends upon being greatly loved, as you say, you surely have every reason to be happy, dear heart. As for me, words fail me as usual—but *you know.*

> *As always*
> *Yours in every heart throb*
> *Eileen*

Sept. 16th

The President's Cottage

... Everyone at the Club to-day was singing the praises of our two girls; it was very delightful. Mrs. St. Gaudens the sculptor says Nell has the dignity of sculpture in her movements. You know she does beautiful figures in low relief on vases. She is going to do one with all the characters of the masque on it. I think it will be charming. Of course she will have to do it from photographs.

Goodnight my dear, *dear* love. I try not to think how much I miss you, much less *tell* you. It is not safe.

> *With love inexpressible*
> *Your own*
> *Eileen*

21 September, 1913

THE WHITE HOUSE

My darling,

Stockton * is here. He turned up last night. The doctor and I found him when we returned from our Saturday afternoon ride, exploring (this time very bad) roads. He is looking his best—radiates good health and vigor. ...

I am expecting now to go up to Princeton on Tuesday to vote at the

* Stockton Axson (Ellen's Brother).

primaries, and probably he will go with me, but I shall try to bring him back with me. It is such a pleasure to have him, and he is better company than ever. We all three went to church together this morning, and he liked Mr. Taylor * very much indeed. He preached one of the most interesting sermons I have heard from him. By the way Stock says that Dr. Fitch † preached at Princeton last winter. He did not hear him but he noted the unprecedented circumstance that the undergraduates discussed him and his sermon with the deepest interest not only throughout Sunday but for several days afterwards. He caught echoes of it all even in his preceptorial conferences. Do you wonder? How he might spiritualize a college!

Yes, that *was* a delightful lunch party at his little home up on the mountain. There was only one thing that disappointed me and made me feel uncomfortable (for with me, as you know, the keenest discomfort comes from self-consciousness). He had the bad taste to remind me again and again that I was President of the United States. I had expected him to have the right intuition about me and to know that I wanted, in such circumstances, to forget that and be his comrade. I did not feel that I was natural or spontaneous for a moment while I was there, as a consequence of my disappointment in that. But this is not criticism; it is just disappointment. How I hate the office when it holds me off from the people I want to get close to! As a barrier it is intolerable to me.

What a delight it is to have Sunday come and bring with it this chance to chat with my darling and take the strain off the longing with which thoughts of her sometimes almost overwhelm me! I can not *really* tell her what is in my heart, but it is such fun, and such a relief, to try! My heart, dearest, in every sense, is the seat of my life. I cannot understand the lives of those men who seem to feed on their minds—on science, speculation, imaginative writing, the absorptions of scholarly research. They seem to me something less than human—men like Herbert Spencer, for instance, and a lot of the Germans. My happiness, my very life, depends on my relations with my fellow beings. And ah! what an unspeakable pleasure it is to me to think of what God has given me, my incomparable little wife and wonderful daughters, compact of every charm of mind and heart and person! It is too wonderful to comprehend.

* James H. Taylor, Pastor of Presbyterian Church in Washington.
† Pastor of Presbyterian Church near Cornish.

And then dear creatures like Helen, for largess, and friends like Lucy and Mary, singular in any place or circle for their charm and interest and sweetness. I never did anything to deserve all this, but I could not have done what I have done without such support and subtle joy, such exhilaration of deep enjoyment as I get from such associations. And how my heart leaps when you tell me how much the girls and Helen and Lucy and Mary love me! That's tonic and joy enough for any man, and when added to your incomparable love and devotion, is almost more than there are terms to reckon.... My love, my love, my sweet, sweet love! How bright you make my way through every test and trial of my life!

Although in the beginning of their married life Ellen did not know how to make out a simple bank check, she became, eventually, Woodrow's "business partner." Her advice was always good, her judgment in money matters sound, and Woodrow relied upon her to keep the family's financial ship on an even keel. In a letter written on the twentieth of September, she mentioned certain investments for which, undoubtedly, she assumed responsibility.

20 Sept., 1913

The President's Cottage

Did you send me a splendid article about you from "The Westminster Gazette" called "President Wilson's First Lap" by Edward Porritt? I simply found it in the mail. If you have not seen it, I want to send it to you, if you think it won't get lost! It is one of the finest things we have had. I do so love to have foreign ones about you, to feel that all the world is beginning to know how great and good you are.

The Mexican affair is worth the trouble it is costing you because of the great opportunity it has offered to set a completely new standard in international morality. I am quite immoderately proud of all you have done and said and refrained from doing. It makes one laugh to think how completely you must mystify the average diplomat....
P.S. I am investing $5,500 ... $1,300 of it being from coupons. We invested $3,000 besides paying $6,000 for our debt....

22 Sept., 1913

The President's Cottage

My own darling,

Your lovely letter reached me just before dinner and made us *all* very happy—for I read to the others the dear things you said about them. Oh, but you are sweet. . . .

Alas, I fear my good times in the studio are almost over, for I shall have no secretary here the rest of the summer. Helen goes to the hospital tomorrow . . . all the more reason for returning to Washington if you can't come here. But oh, I hope you can come once more. It is so perfectly lovely now. And the air is so sweet and fresh and soft now that the drought is over. . . .

I wish I could tell you, my darling, how happy your letter made me! *But I can't.* I think you must know without the telling. . . .

28 Sept., 1913

THE WHITE HOUSE

My precious darling,

The fact that I do not read the newspapers gives your letters to me a curious interest. You do read the newspapers and your mind is occupied with questions and anxieties which seem new to me—and also with interests which I do not share. For example, I did not read the editorial about Mexico in the "Times" to which you refer in the letter received this morning, and I cannot share your elation about it simply because it does not make the least difference to me, or excite even a mild interest, *what* the *Times* thinks or says about anything. As a matter of fact things do seem to have been effected in Mexico by our attitude which I must admit I did not expect. We have good reason to think that Huerta has actually eliminated himself from the field of choice for President chiefly through the influence of the Catholic party, whose candidate Gamboa has now become, and our chief object seems to have been attained. It is by no means clear that Gamboa would be the mere *alter ego* of Huerta, if elected; and, besides, his nomination *may* bring about a genuine contest for the office; the Congress may not accept his candidacy; the liberal

and progressive elements of the country are strongly anti-Catholic in
the field of politics and may run some nominee of their own. We have
sent word indirectly to the revolutionaries in the north that they cannot
afford to stand aloof from a constitutional election, if they wish to retain our sympathy or tolerance. On the whole, therefore, I feel that real
progress has been made, and the moral pressure has, after all, proved
pretty powerful. If it should prove to be all-powerful, as there is reason
to hope now, it will mean the beginning of a new era in the Latin American states. New forces are asserting themselves in Mexico at any rate,
and there can hardly be a dictatorship.

As for my coming again to Cornish, my darling, that depends entirely on the Committee of the Senate on Banking and Currency. As
soon as they report the bill out in a satisfactory form I may be able to
run off for a week's end. Ah how I long to! How deeply happy a glimpse
of my dear ones would make me! How my heart *needs* them! But it is
impossible, as yet, for me to predict what that unusual aggregation of in-
dividuals will do. This, however, seems clear to me. I ought not to urge
you to stay up there longer than the middle of October. The weather
here now is wholly delightful, and you will need quite a month to get
ready for the wedding.* By the way, sweetheart, when you go down to
New York to shop, please take Murphy † along. It will make me feel so
much easier. You will then be safe against any kind of annoyance. Notice
you cannot in any case hope to escape.

My visit to Princeton was very interesting—just how interesting
probably no one outside the family could realize. The only call I made
was on the Ricketts. Unfortunately I ran across Hibben † just before
leaving. Stock says that I behaved pretty well, and did not freeze him. . . .
When we went into the Mann § home I was for a moment taken aback.
The first floor was so fully furnished and the rugs on the floors gave it
such an occupied appearance that I could hardly believe that I was not
walking unbidden into someone's home. How familiar it all looked and
how many memories it stirred up! And how my heart ached for the
sweet lady of whom I was thinking all the while! Dearest, you seem
at each step of my life to be a larger, more intimate, sweeter part of it.

---

* Jessie's wedding in January.
† Secret Service man.
‡ Hibben, estranged since the Princeton controversies, had succeeded W.W. as
president of Princeton.
§ House on Cleveland Lane rented by Wilsons in 1911.

I think more and more in terms of myself *and you!* It is very wonderful how you have loved me. The soul of me is very selfish. I have gone my way after a fashion that made me the centre of the plan. And you, who are so individual, who are so independent in spirit and in judgment, whose soul is also a kingdom, have been so loyal, so forgiving, so self-sacrificing in your willingness to live *my* life. Nothing but love could have accomplished so wonderful a thing. If I have not justified it, I have been deeply grateful. I at least have sense enough to know what treasure I have enjoyed and lived upon, and how pitifully poor I should have been without it . . .

Early in October Ellen went to New York to shop for Jessie's trousseau. On her return to Cornish she wrote to Woodrow, telling him of her pride in his speech on the occasion of the signing of the tariff bill,* and asking him to be sure to have all newspaper editorials saved. Throughout Woodrow's administration, Mr. Tumulty cut out and pasted on large yellow foolscap the most important, interesting or significant news, comments and editorials concerning the administration from the country's newspapers. These were called the "yellow books" by the family. Now Ellen wanted the recent sheets concerning the news and editorials written after the passing of the tariff bill.

The President's Cottage

. . . Mary and I went out just after lunch for a ride. . . . Now I have found a lot of important letters awaiting me and should have gone straight to them, I suppose, but was so excited over the signing of the Tariff bill that I could only devour the papers. Oh, my dear, how I wish I had been there! Your speech was *beautiful.* I am inexpressibly, profoundly happy and thankful. I hope for once you will break your rule and read the papers, for the editorials are all so fine. . . . Also the two or three I have seen from English papers. *Please* get Mr. Tumulty to make me up a "yellow book" of just editorials.

Good-bye, you dear, splendid, wonderful man. How we all *ache* to get at you and make a fuss over you and work off some of our excitement over the bill.

Love, love, love from
Your devoted wife
Ellen

* Underwood-Simmon's Tariff Bill, to replace Payne-Aldrich high protective tariff laws, embodied most of Wilson's ideas.

Oct. 5

The President's Cottage

My own darling,

We are back from one of the most beautiful drives we have had yet and how we did long for you! Just Jessie, Nell and I went. It was to what is called "The Gulch", a deep mountain pass close to Ascutney. It is almost sublime in its noble beauty. I have been hearing about it all summer and am glad to have seen it before we leave. Oh, it's hard that you are never here to enjoy all these things with us! But of course *we* are enjoying with *you* something much more splendid than "all these things". I wish I could express the depth and soul-satisfying quality of the happiness I am deriving from the tariff victory. It is all-pervading, never out of my consciousness for a moment. It is on a *large* stage—one worthy of the splendid combination of qualities with which He endowed you. It would have been tragic if such gifts had been even partially wasted for want of the great opportunity. It has been the most remarkable life history I ever read about—and to think I have *lived* it with you. I wonder if I am dreaming and will wake up and find I am married to a bank clerk, say.

Their letters crossed, and on the fifth of October Woodrow wrote:

5 Oct., 1913

THE WHITE HOUSE

My precious darling,

I suppose you read about the scene at the signing of the Tariff bill! It was really most impressive. I was very much moved and can only hope that the printed words of my little speech had something like the same effect the spoken words had. I am told that there were tears running down the cheeks of even one or two of the reporters before I finished speaking.

Are Hitchcock and O'Gorman listening to reason? No. Hitchcock never will. O'Gorman is showing signs of yielding, but not to reason—to the force of opinion in the country and particularly among his colleagues in the Senate. A little patience, and a little *im*patience, will

work the things out. I shall exercise both to the utmost. I have practically
a unanimous sentiment behind me among the Democrats of the Senate,
outside the Committee. . . .

It is hard work every day to keep things going, constant toil and
trouble, but they go slowly forward. "Westward look, the land is
bright." * A stout heart and infinite staying powers will bring things
to the right issue. . . .

October 8, 1913

The President's Cottage

My own darling,

What exciting reading the paper is today as regards the currency bill. . . .
One thing that was said struck me as having force, viz: that it was a pity
to be forced to make it a party issue; but that was necessary because
the Republicans (those, of course, who put *party* first, before country)
felt that it would never do to let the Democrats win the tremendous prestige of passing those two great bills in one session. And for that reason
would fight it to the last ditch. It sounds like the sort of thing politicians
would do!

I wonder if it is hot again in Washington. It is so warm here that
I sat out of doors sketching all morning in shirt waist and bare-headed.
Delicious weather— it is a luxury to be alive. And the beauty everywhere
is thrilling. I really believe that this is the loveliest country I have ever
seen. It is partly, of course, that thanks to the great, splendid car I have
seen it more completely than any other year. I have done bravely without
you all these weeks, and should in fact have been unhappy had you insisted on staying here; but now I am reaching the limit of my powers in
that matter. I *must* have you soon. How soon? I am well, and my heart
is full to overflowing with love of all of you. . . .

Thirty years had passed since Woodrow had written his first love
letter to Ellen. Now on the Sunday before she came home, loving her
as ardently as he had loved her then—and more completely—he wrote
his last:

---

* Quotation from "Say Not the Struggle Nought Availeth" by Arthur Hugh
Clough. Used memorably by Winston Churchill when the United States joined the
Allies in World War II.

The Priceless Gift

12 *October, 1913*

THE WHITE HOUSE

My precious darling,

How it makes my pulses jump, how it lightens my heart and changes the whole outlook to think that this is the last Sunday without my sweet one, my mate, the incomparable lady who is the centre of my life! It has been a long, long pull. . . . I am free now to admit that I have been desperately lonely. I am just realizing it in its fullness. So long as the thing was an established, accepted fact, made part of the programme by my own choice and insistence, I did not let my thoughts dwell on it one way or the other. I accepted it as part of the life I had devoted myself to, and let the business of the day swallow it up, not letting myself realize even that it took resolution to carry it through. And I was happy, with a deep satisfaction that things were right and that all was well with those I love much more deeply than I love myself. But now I can indulge what would then have been mere weakness and made me ashamed. I can now tell you of the deep longing that has filled the summer, the longing for you and for the dear girls. Now that it is all to end and there is almost immediately to be happy homecoming, I have grown infinitely impatient and find it difficult to wait the five days that separate us!

The long embargo will begin to be lifted tomorrow, when dear Helen comes home . . . then on Thursday morning our precious Nell comes, does she not? Hoover * tells me that was the message sent him— that she would be here in time for breakfast on Thursday. So that my contentment will steadily accumulate through the week, till all my dear ones are here. Ah! there will be a happy man, a grateful husband and father, in this old house next Friday, if you all turn up safe and sound —a fellow with overflowing heart! Do you realize that I have been alone (what I consider alone) in this old mansion for just about half of the time I have been President? No doubt it was best for him, to begin with systematic discipline, but decidedly tough on him, nevertheless. He will require till next summer to recover and be thoroughly spoiled again. Then we shall have to resume the discipline for the good of the nation. It does not do to indulge presidents for twelve months together. These lose tone and fibre, and begin to feel their oats too much. Their house-

* Chief usher at the White House.

holds are too apt to deem them great men and persuade them, by mere iteration, to entertain the same notion. Several months consorting with mere men, who have no such soft delusions, is wholesome for them, and should be administered in small doses. Just at this moment the medicine tastes bitter enough. I am rolling it upon my palate because I want by so much the more to enhance the sweetness of what I am to have at the end of the week. I shall be fairly drunk with the change, and may be unfit for serious business for a whole month to follow. I shall have the time of my life keeping my head! Ah! my darling, my darling! I am beside myself with the joy of it all! My exile is over. I am about to come out of the gray country of duty (fine enough in its way) into the sweet gardens where you are and all that you mean to me. God bless you and keep you and speed you! My heart is too full to go on—full to overflowing with love for you all, but particularly for the sweetest wife in the world.

> *Your own*
> *Woodrow*

That autumn, when his "exile" was over, and during the rest of 1913, Woodrow's family had never seen him so buoyant, self-confident and optimistic. With his first two battles for legislative reform won, his leadership established and his popularity increasing daily throughout the country, there remained only the crisis in Mexico to trouble him —he called it the "thorn in my side." He knew of course that a long struggle lay ahead before the comprehensive reforms he had promised were achieved, and that powerful reactionary groups were marshaling to stop him. But Woodrow Wilson was no longer the over-sensitive man who had been deeply hurt by criticism and opposition at Princeton. He was a seasoned veteran now, well armed and ready for battle.

"This is an office in which a man must put on his warpaint," he told an audience in Staunton, Virginia, after his election, "and there must be some good, hard fighting . . . in order to achieve what we have set out to achieve." *

Ellen, looking rested and refreshed after her summer in Cornish, took on a new task.

To the casual visitor the national capital seemed a beautiful, clean city. But hidden away in almost every part of Washington there were slums as disgraceful as those in the great industrial centers. Most of Washington's 90,000 negroes lived in ancient shacks in narrow, filthy alleys. For years philanthropists had tried in vain to persuade Congress to do some-

* December 28, 1912.

thing about it. When Ellen heard this, she went to work. Quietly, without any fanfare, she visited the worst of the slums, sometimes taking groups of Congressmen with her. She talked to the unhappy people forced to live under such appalling conditions. She consulted with philanthropists and with city planners and architects. Finally she succeeded in getting a bill authorizing slum clearance presented to Congress.

Years before she had said to Florence Hoyt: "I wonder how anyone who reaches middle age can bear it if she cannot feel, on looking back, that whatever mistakes she has made, she has on the whole lived for others and not for herself." This was Ellen's creed, and even Woodrow's anxiety lest she overtax her strength could not make her discard it.

Jessie's marriage in November was the only saddening event of that year. It was the first break in the family circle and wise, deeply religious, beautiful Jessie held a very special place in her parents' and her sisters' hearts. They were happy for her but very forlorn for days after the wedding.

Woodrow wrote to a friend:

"I need not tell you what effect it has had on our spirits to part with her. But Ellen has acted with noble unselfishness in hiding her distress, and I have tried to emulate her example. It is easier, of course, for me than for her. She lives in the house from which the dear one has now gone for good and all, while I am in the office the greater part of the time and busy with a thousand things from which I *cannot* draw my attention. My very burdens are at such juncture my blessings."

The Wilsons and Helen Bones spent the Christmas holidays in a rambling frame house in Pan Christian on the Gulf of Mexico.

Except for missing Jessie it was a happy interlude. Lucy and Mary Smith came from New Orleans with presents for Woodrow on his fifty-seventh birthday. And at twelve o'clock on New Year's Eve they all greeted 1914, as usual, in the Scottish tradition, standing on chairs around a table with their arms entwined, while they sang "Auld Lang Syne."

Back in Washington, Ellen returned to her duties and her slum-clearance crusade with renewed vigor. But a few weeks later she began to lose weight and the lovely color in her cheeks disappeared. One night, after shaking hands with 3,000 people during a White House reception, she fainted. She insisted, afterwards, that it was nothing. "This goose," she said, smiling at Woodrow, "is worrying about me for no reason at all!"

The Secretary of the Treasury was a widower, admired and pursued by various handsome and uninhibited Washington widows. The President's youngest daughter admired him, too, but shyly, with a touch of awe, and Mr. McAdoo, born and raised in the old South, where pursuit was left to the men, found this attractive. After a whirlwind courtship there was another wedding in the White House in May. . . . Three days later, Woodrow wrote:

"Ah! how desperately my heart aches that she has gone. She was simply part of me . . . and I feel the loneliness more than I dare admit even to myself. The wedding was as simple and beautiful as any I ever saw or imagined and she has married a noble man who will make her happy and proud, too. But just now I can realize, in my selfishness, only that I have lost her, for good and all. . . ." *

But this was not painful loneliness—not the desolate sense of being only half alive that he felt whenever he and Ellen were separated. And Margaret's companionship was a constant joy because she was so like him in character and intellect.

Toward the end of May he began to be seriously worried about Ellen's health. She admitted reluctantly that she was very tired, but denied that she was ill. It was not until the end of June that Dr. Grayson finally persuaded her to give up her activities and spend most of each day in bed. In July, two other physicians, called in for consultation, found that she had tuberculosis of the kidneys, so far advanced that it was incurable.

The end came in the first week in August—the end of peace in the world, and the end of his own small, sweet world.

The day after war broke out in Europe he sent for Jessie and Nellie and Stockton Axson and, sitting bent and haggard, like a very old man, outside of Ellen's closed door, told them that she was dying.

Jessie said, "Mother will never die," and he said, "I know." But for the first time in their lives they saw him weep.

When they went in together to sit beside her bed, Ellen smiled at them. "My bill has passed," she told Jessie. "Did you know?" †

She had not been told of the tragedy in Europe. She knew that she was dying and she was not afraid, only desperately anxious about Woodrow, for she knew his weakness as well as his strength. Strong in his Christian faith, he could endure grief, but not loneliness. He could not live without love. The day before she died she made Dr. Grayson promise to tell him—"later, when he will listen"—that she wanted him to marry again.

She was buried beside her father and mother in Rome, Georgia. Every store in the city was closed that day and, while all the church bells tolled, everyone mourned for her, standing silently in the church-yard or the quiet streets.

When the family returned to the White House, Woodrow's grief was so profound that he could not bear to speak of Ellen, even to his

* To Mrs. Hulbert, May 10, 1914.

† The Senate, notified that Ellen's illness was critical, had voted at once for the slum clearance bill. The House took similar action soon afterwards.

daughters. Only his sense of duty seemed to keep him alive. He worked all day and far into the night, grimly, often impatiently, as though nothing mattered very much. Margaret and Helen saw him only at meals, sitting in deep, brooding silence, seemingly unaware of their presence.

One evening, when his youngest daughter came to see him, he could not be found. The household staff searched in vain in every part of the house except the huge, closed East Room where Nellie went at last. There was no light in the room, but she groped in the dark and touched her father's arm. He took her hand, and they walked back and forth together in silence. Finally he said, "I can't bear it. I can't think, I can't work without her."

Nellie wept, finding no words to comfort him. And after another long silence he said, "Don't cry. She was always so brave." It was as if he rebuked himself as well as Ellen's daughter.

He was no longer grim after that, or impatient, or unaware of his daughters' grief. He had found one shred of comfort and, able at last to talk about Ellen, he shared it with them.

"She was so radiant," he said, "so happy! We must be grateful for her sake that she did not see the world crash into ruin. It would have broken her heart."

Index